THE CASE FOR DEMOCRACY

THE CASE FOR
DEMOCRACY

The Power of Freedom
to Overcome Tyranny and Terror

NATAN SHARANSKY

WITH RON DERMER

PublicAffairs
New York

Copyright © 2004 by Natan Sharansky and Ron Dermer.

Published in the United States by PublicAffairs™,
a member of the Perseus Books Group.

Book design and composition by Mark McGarry
Set in Sabon

Library of Congress Cataloging-in-Publication Data
Sharansky, Natan (Anatoly).
The case for democracy: the power of freedom to overcome
tyranny and terror / Natan Sharansky.—1st ed.
p. cm.
Includes bibliographical references and index.
ISBN 1-58648-261-0
1. Democracy. 2. Liberty. 3. Despotism. I. Title.
JC423.S495 2004
321.8—dc22
2004057333

10 9 8 7 6 5

To the memory of Andrei Sakharov
A man who proved that with moral clarity
and courage, we can change the world

CONTENTS

PREFACE

IN FEBRUARY 1986, I became the first political prisoner released by Mikhail Gorbachev. Nine years earlier, I had been arrested on false charges of high treason. My real crimes: fighting for human rights inside the Soviet Union and for the right of Soviet Jews, myself included, to emigrate. The KGB derisively referred to the many people in the West who were working so diligently to free Soviet Jewry as "a bunch of students and housewives." But the power of this volunteer army to help us win our freedom was greatly underestimated by the Soviet leadership.

Credit for the final push that led to my release goes to President Ronald Reagan. As my wife, Avital, was demonstrating outside a superpower summit in Geneva at the end of 1985, President Reagan, pointing at her, turned to Gorbachev and said: "You can keep saying that Sharansky is an American spy, but my people trust that woman. And as long as you keep him and other political prisoners locked up, we will not be able to establish a relationship of trust."

Very soon after that conversation, I was moved from my cell in a prison camp in the Urals to a hospital. Those in charge of the Soviet penal system had developed a series of eighteen diets for "reeducation" purposes. When I checked into the hospital, my diet was immediately upgraded from the lowest level to the highest one. Over the course of the next seven weeks, the Soviets worked to rehabilitate my weakened body with plenty of food, medicines, and vitamins, as well as two hours of fresh air every day. They treated me like a cow being fattened for sale.

At that time, Gorbachev was still not ready to admit, as he would a few months later, that there were political prisoners in the USSR. That is why he tried to make my release part of a larger "spy exchange" between East and West. Fortunately, the Americans were not willing to give credence to this lie. They insisted I be set free thirty minutes before the official exchange of arrested spies.

On Glinecke Bridge, I crossed from East Berlin to West Berlin, from East Germany to West Germany, from the world of slavery to the world of freedom. In the morning I was a prisoner of the KGB. In the afternoon, I was reunited with Avital, after a twelve-year separation. In the evening, I was swept off my feet and swimming on a sea of shoulders at the Western Wall in Jerusalem. In a few hours, I had ascended from hell to paradise, from the grim reality of evil to the fantasy world of my imagination.

Despite the transcendent feeling of being transported to a different dimension, I could not forget for one moment the friends I had left behind in prison or behind the Iron Curtain. The struggle for my freedom had ended. The struggle for their freedom would continue. Though I knew there were many difficult challenges ahead, from the heights to which I had ascended, these challenges appeared insignificant. My greatest fear was that I would release Avital's hand and suddenly find myself back in a cold, dark punishment cell. I was in the world of my dreams, and I did not want to wake.

But from the heavens, there is only one way to go: down. I realized the descent would inevitably bring disappointment, both to myself and to the many whose expectations of me could not be any higher. Yet I was ready to return to the real world and lead a normal life. I was also confident that I would be able to meet the challenges ahead. In large part, this confidence was rooted in a belief that my experiences had left me not simply memories of the past but also a perspective that could serve me well in the future. During my long journey through the world of evil, I had discovered three sources of power: the power of an individual's inner freedom, the power of a free society, and the power of the solidarity of the free world.

The Soviet Union did its best to turn individuals into what Stalin called "the cogs" of a totalitarian machine, transforming them from *Homo Sapiens* into *Homo Sovieti-*

cus. They did this by depriving individuals not merely of their property but also of their connections to their own history, religion, nationality, and culture. In my experience, rebuilding these connections was the key to confronting tyranny. Going back to my roots, reestablishing a link with my people—both ancient and modern—had given me the strength to shed the loyal Soviet citizen's life of doublethink. It had given me the strength to fight for my own rights as well as the rights of others.

But in addition to drawing upon inner freedom, I found the idea of living in a free society a powerful source of strength. As a schoolboy, I would supplement my English lessons by buying and reading *The Morning Star*, a foreign English-language newspaper that was available in the USSR. The Soviets permitted us to read this Communist daily published in London because, in being very critical of the democratic and capitalist world, the paper parroted the ideological line of the party. For me, however, its effect would prove highly subversive. What left a lasting impression was not the content of the criticism but the very fact that people outside the Soviet Union were free to criticize their own government without going to prison. The stronger the criticism, the more impressed I was by the degree of freedom enjoyed elsewhere. Years later, I would discover that the belief that the right to dissent was more important than the content of dissent was the glue that united all dissidents in the Soviet Union. For us, the profound moral difference between our society and a free society was that people in free societies could publicly express their own ideas and persuade others to accept those ideas as well. We all understood, therefore, that free societies had a basic respect for human rights.

Finally, in fighting with the Soviet regime, we dissidents came to appreciate the power of the solidarity of the free world. We believed that a state's respect for the rights of its own citizens should be the criterion by which to measure that state's intentions. In the readiness of democratic leaders to link their relations with other states to the extent those states respected human rights, we saw great potential for the development and expansion of freedom across the globe.

While I brought this perspective on freedom with me to my new life in Israel, I soon realized that there were few who shared it. For many years, I have been asking myself why so many of those who have always lived in liberty do not appreciate the enormous power of freedom. With time, I have come to understand that my exposure to the black-and-white world of the Soviet Union provided me with a unique laboratory to discover the line between good and evil. In the free world, with its varying shades of gray, isolating the black and white, finding moral clarity, becomes far more difficult.

"The Prisoner of Zion's struggle for freedom is only now beginning."[1] One of Israel's most prominent journalists used these words three days after my arrival in Israel to warn me about the indigenous forces of "darkness" I would soon be confronting. From the rough translation I received at the time, I surmised that "darkness" for this writer meant religion and nationalism, especially the combination of the two.

No sooner had I set foot in the country, he noted cynically, than my wife, Avital, having become religious during our long separation, was changing my name from Anatoly to Natan and slapping a kippah on my head.

I was shocked. For nine years in a KGB prison, I had been struggling and praying to be reunited with my wife and my people and to start a new life in a Jewish and democratic state. How could anyone possibly believe that my real struggle for freedom was only *now* beginning? As somebody whose inner freedom stemmed from my reconnection to the history and religion of my people, this argument made no sense at all. How could anyone in Israel have a problem with a Jewish-sounding name?

My grandfather hoped I would be named after his father, Natan, the patriarchal figure of the family who had passed away during the first decade of the twentieth century. Since I was born in 1948 during a new wave of persecutions against Jews, my parents were afraid to subject their son to any more anti-Semitism than could otherwise be expected. So they told my grandfather that "Anatoly" was an appropriate equivalent. Grandpa called me Natanchik anyway. The moment I broke free of the world of doublethink and began my work as a Zionist and dissident, I asked friends to call me Natan. My grandfather, no longer alive, would surely have been proud to know that his grandson, no longer afraid, finally bore the name intended for him.

Similarly, I could not understand how covering one's head could be so politicized. For many secularists in Israel, it would be as treasonable for me to decide to wear a kippah as it would be to submit to the KGB. On the other hand, for religious groups, a kippah would be a clear signal that I was firmly ensconced in their camp, adopting their friends as well as their enemies.

In prison, I thought one wore a kippah whenever one felt close to God. During my confinement, there were many such moments, but I did not have a kippah to commemorate them. That is, until my non-Jewish Ukranian cellmate, knowing how much it would mean to me, used the fabric that protected his feet from frostbite to sew one. To this day, I wear that kippah at every Passover Seder, the holiday when Jews celebrate their people's journey from slavery to freedom.

It is difficult to imagine a moment in which I would feel closer to God than when I arrived in Israel for the first time. Putting on a kippah in the airport was such a natural response. I could not understand how anyone could see the symbol of my inner freedom in the Soviet Union as a symbol of slavery in Israel.

If anyone would have asked me in prison if I felt more solidarity with Labor or Likud, religious or secular, Orthodox or Reform, I would have considered the question ridiculous. Having served as an activist and spokesman for Soviet Jewish groups, I was certainly aware of internecine rivalries and conflicts—and experienced quite a few firsthand—but in prison, in the struggle against the KGB, against evil itself, these differences were meaningless. It was the connection I felt with all the people of Israel, with our mutual history and destiny, that was the source of my strength.

But on arriving in Israel, I was immediately besieged by all sorts of groups demanding support for their causes. Left-wing groups called on me to fight for Palestinian rights in Israel as vigorously as I fought for human rights in the Soviet Union. Right-wing groups, insisting that only they were the keepers of the Zionist flame, called on me, as a "symbol" of Zionism, to support their struggle for a Greater Land of Israel. Some demanded that I fight against the theocratization of Israeli society, while others wanted me to join their struggle against undermining the Jewish character of the state.

That I felt like a human wishbone being pulled in different directions was bad enough. But it also quickly became clear that identifying with one group was tantamount to rejecting all the rest. To support one cause was to deny another. To endorse one aspect of a struggle was to its opponents to champion it wholesale. From my perspective, forged in the Soviet Union, these groups shared vast common ground and an underlying unity. But from the perspective of most Israelis, they were worlds apart, incapable of being reconciled.

The extent to which this attitude prevailed within Israel could be seen in the debate surrounding my marriage. In terms of practical observance, Avital, having become Orthodox during our long separation, was clearly more "religious" than I was. Now that we were reunited, people wondered whether she would become more secular or whether I would become more religious. The common assumption was that if neither of us changed, the marriage would not last or could not be real because Jews of different levels of observance could not build a home together. In prison, I had learned that people with completely separate backgrounds and ideologies could live together quite happily in one cell if they felt that their mutual struggle was far more important than their differences. But in Israel, my deep connection with Avital, which had survived twelve years of separation, was seen as incapable of withstanding minor differences between us.

Shortly after I arrived in Israel, I was invited to the Knesset, Israel's parliament. Shlomo Hillel, then speaker of the Knesset, greeted me warmly, pledging that the fight to free Soviet Jewry would continue. What I thought was a perfectly innocent statement triggered a heated confrontation. "Why don't we work to free non-Jews as well?" shouted one Knesset member. To which another shouted back: "Why are you always interested in non-Jews? Are Jews not interesting enough?" I was thoroughly confused. I did not realize then that these politicians were not speaking to me, nor even to each other, but to their electorates. They were seizing upon the one point that would rally their constituencies and differentiate themselves from their political opponents.

Among those who have always lived in a democracy, this story will raise few eyebrows. After all, in the free world, the competition of ideas and of parties flourishes, and allegiances are often based on a single common principle or purpose that struggles against a competing point of view.

Though generally healthy for a society, this competition can be quite dangerous if we lose sight of the fact that there is a far greater divide between the world of freedom and the world of fear than there is between the competing factions within a free society. If we fail to recognize this, we lose moral clarity. The legitimate differences among us, the shades of gray in a free society, will be wrongly perceived as black and white. Then, the real black-and-white line that divides free societies from fear societies, the real line that divides good from evil, will no longer be distinguishable.

A lack of moral clarity is why an Israeli journalist compared a kippah to a prison. It is why people living in free societies cannot distinguish between religious fundamentalists in democratic states and religious terrorists in fundamentalist states. It is why people living in free societies can come to see their fellow citizens as their enemies, and foreign dictators as their friends.

Those who seek to move the earth must first, as Archimedes explained, have a place to stand. Moral clarity provides us with a place to stand, a reference point from where to leverage our talents, ideas, and energies to create a better world. Without moral clarity, without a reference point, those same talents, ideas, and energies are just as likely to do harm as good.

This is the tragedy that has befallen the contemporary struggle for human rights. The great dividing line in that struggle is the line that separates free societies that thrive on dissent from fear societies that ban it. Societies that do not allow dissent will *never* protect human rights.

But today, detached from the concept of a free society, human rights have no reference point. The concept of human rights has come to mean sympathy for the poor, the weak, and the suffering. To be sure, this sympathy is essential if we want to live in moral societies and should be encouraged and cultivated by families, faiths, schools, and governments. Yet without moral clarity, sympathy can also be placed in the service of evil.

A world without moral clarity, is a world in which dictators speak about human rights even as they kill thousands, tens of thousands, hundreds of thousands, millions, and even tens of millions of people. It is a world in which the only democracy in the Middle East is perceived as the greatest violator of human rights in the world. It is a world in which a human rights conference against racism, such as the one that took place in Durban, South Africa a few years ago, can be turned into a carnival of hate.

A lack of moral clarity is also the tragedy that has befallen efforts to advance peace and security in the world. Promoting peace and security is fundamentally connected to promoting freedom and democracy. As I learned from my teacher Andrei Sakharov, the world cannot depend on leaders who do not depend on their own people.

But today, the struggle for peace and security in the world is not linked to promoting democracy. The road to peace is seen as paved with good intentions, goodwill, and faith in the brotherhood of man. Likewise, security is believed to be a function of strong leaders and powerful armies. All of these, of course, can help advance peace and security, but detached from the idea of a free society, they can just as easily be placed in the service of evil.

A world without moral clarity, is a world in which, in

the name of peace, pacifists in the West marched alongside emissaries of the KGB who, posing as peace activists, sought to undermine the efforts of a free world to defend itself against Soviet aggression. It is a world in which a strong dictator can be seen as a reliable partner for peace. It is a world in which those who dream of peace are willing to place a wolf and lamb in the same cage and hope for the best—again and again.

A couple of years after my release from prison, I met former President Jimmy Carter during his visit to Israel. I felt an obligation to express my gratitude. When I was arrested, he took the unprecedented step of declaring that I was not an American spy. After thanking him, we began talking about the situation in the Middle East. I told him I thought the reason why Palestinians were suffering and why states in the region were not at peace was the lack of democracy in this part of the world. Furthermore, I explained why Israel must link its concessions in the future to the development of democracy among it neighbors. Carter replied: "You know, you are right, but don't try to be too rational about these things. The moment you see people suffering, you should feel solidarity with them and try to help them without thinking too much about the reasons."

As far as peace depending on democracy, Carter said Israel should not wait. "It's true," he said, "Assad is a dictator. But you can rely on him. He never lied to me. If you sign an agreement, he'll keep it. When I was president, I visited Syria. Our intelligence knew that Assad had violated one of his obligations on a security-related issue. When I raised the question with Assad, he emphatically denied it. Before leaving for the airport, I told people in our delegation how disappointed I was because Assad never lied to me before and now he clearly was. But on the way to the airport, Assad called to apologize. He told me he had checked the point I raised and that he had been mistaken. He promised to correct the problem."

"So you see," Carter told me, "he never lies. If he signs an agreement with Israel, he'll keep it."

I have no doubt that the causes of peace and human rights are both very dear to Carter's heart. For his indefatigable efforts to bring parties together all over the world, he was awarded the Nobel Peace Prize. As for human rights, he turned them into a banner during his first presidential campaign, and in doing so, upgraded the struggle of all dissidents around the world. While it was true that we dissidents were later disappointed when Carter's rhetoric was not backed by forceful action, I always believed that Carter at least understood the meaning of human rights. But here he was speaking about blind sympathy for the suffering and about trust for dictators. He only had to read the testimonies of those who once placed great faith in Stalin's "workers' paradise" to understand how misplaced sympathy for the weak can be manipulated by tyrants, or the stories of how Stalin toyed with his foreign guests by bugging their rooms and surrounding them with informers.

This exchange with Carter is only one episode of many that has convinced me how easy it is for those living in a free society to lose moral clarity. In our television age, when pictures without context immediately influence our emotions, when cause and effect are deemed irrelevant, when only suffering is important, human sympathy and a deep desire for peace can turn into a weapon of tyranny. Sadly, I have watched many of those who yearn for peace and who champion human rights turn their backs on the freedom that makes both possible.

Over the years, I have come to understand a critical difference between the world of fear and the world of freedom. In the former, the primary challenge is finding the inner strength to confront evil. In the latter, the primary challenge is finding the moral clarity to see evil.

After my release from prison, I dedicated myself to the struggle to free Soviet Jewry. I wrote about my experiences in prison, lectured around the world, met with democratic leaders, and worked on numerous campaigns and petitions. I even moved to the United States for three months to help organize and promote a 1987 rally in Washington on behalf of Soviet Jewry, which became one of the largest rallies in the history of the capital.

In 1988, sensing that Soviet Jews would soon be free and would be arriving in droves in Israel, I and other Jewish activists from the USSR founded the Soviet Jewry Zionist Forum to ease the absorption of new immigrants into Israeli society. In 1989, the Iron Curtain fell and the flood of Soviet Jews began. Over the next decade, one million Jews moved to Israel, a proportional equivalent of 50 million immigrants moving to America over a similar time period.

Despite a number of overtures to join Israeli politics over the years, I refused. I was afraid that by joining one faction, or one party, in Israel's highly politicized society, I would lose the powerful feeling of interconnection with all the people of Israel—a feeling that had given me so much strength and inspiration through the years.

But in 1995, I finally entered political life when I realized that my ability to help Soviet Jews integrate into Israeli society from outside the political system has long been limited. Even though Israel is a country whose lifeblood has long been immigration, it was conventional wisdom that the first generation of immigrants would be a "generation of the desert," and that only their children would fully integrate into Israeli life. I disagreed with this approach. Like many other immigrant activists, I believed that it was vital for both Israel and for the new immigrants that the tremendous potential of these highly educated and ambitious Soviet Jews be harnessed by immediately opening the doors of Israeli society to them. I discovered that the only way this was going to happen was to establish a political force that could push open those doors. As the slogan of our party, Yisrael Ba'aliyah, made clear, there could be "no integration without representation." Since another leader of our party, Yuli Edelstein, was a Soviet dissident who had served three years in prison, we also thought we had a powerful selling point in noting that we were a different kind of party: Our leaders first go to prison and only then go into politics.

In the years ahead, our party focused on issues relating to the absorption of new immigrants and was responsible for a number of important achievements. The paradox was that as a party dedicated to integrating new immigrants into Israeli life, the more we succeeded, the less justification there would be for our existence. I always understood that our party was an inherently temporary project, designed for a particular historical moment and task. And so it proved to be. In 1996, the party received seven seats in the Israeli Knesset, and three years later, it won six seats. By 2003, our Knesset faction had shrunk to two. Despite this dwindling support, I felt a deep satisfaction that our party had achieved its aims and one more chapter in Jewish history had closed. The Jews of the Soviet Union, an assimilated and almost lost tribe behind the Iron Curtain, had escaped tyranny, returned to their ancestral homeland, and quickly become an integral and important part of the modern State of Israel.

But as I look back on my political journey, along with this sense of satisfaction, I also feel a profound disappointment. Whatever the reasons one enters Israeli politics, there is no avoiding the existential issues that have confronted the country since the day it was born. The question of how Israel can achieve peace and security is one no Israeli leader can ignore. This was especially true during the last decade when the peace process became the central issue of our public discourse, and during the last four years, when the fight against terror was the primary concern of our people and our government.

Like most people, Israelis immediately classify public figures according to familiar labels: Are you in the "peace camp" or the "national camp"? Are you on the Left or the Right? But perhaps because of the gravity of the issues at stake, Israel's debate is particularly divisive. In grappling with these life-and-death questions, many attack not only your positions but your motives as well. In this contentious climate, persuading others to accept your view is a unique challenge. It has been no less challenging for me to get people to *understand* my views. Ironically the same principles that allowed nearly all the people of Israel to feel some connection with me when I was a dissident have left me almost alone as a politician.

But the principles that guided me as a dissident in the struggle against tyranny continue to guide me today. I believe that all people are capable of building a free society. I believe that all free societies will guarantee security and peace. And I believe that by linking international policy to building free societies, the free world can once again secure a better future for hundreds of millions of people around the world.

Serving in both Right-wing and Left-wing governments, in both narrow and broad coalitions, under both Likud and Labor prime ministers, I have argued for these principles. When hopes for peace were at their highest and when despair over Palestinian terror was at its deepest, I have argued for these principles. For me, it was never about Left and Right, but about right and wrong.

Now that we are entering what some have called World War IV, we must restore the moral clarity that helped win the last world war without firing a shot. We must understand the difference between fear societies and free societies, between dictators and democrats. We must understand the link between democracy and peace and between human rights and security. Above all, we must bring back moral clarity so that we may draw on the power of free individuals, free nations, and the free world for the enormous challenges ahead. I have written this book in the hope that it may help us meet those challenges.

Introduction

"Hear ye, hear ye, the case of the peoples of the Soviet Union vs. Henry Kissinger is now in session."

"Mr. Kissinger, you are accused of betraying the cause of liberty and trying to appease tyranny. How do you plead?"

"Not Guilty," replied the defendant's co-counsel Mr. Nixon and Mr. Brezhnev.

"Very well, then. Prosecutors Jackson and Sakharov, you may proceed with your case against the accused."

IN 1975 I was teaching English to a group of dissidents in an apartment in Moscow. Our KGB tails were waiting downstairs. In those days, dissidents fired from their jobs had to find other ways to make a living. Sometimes, we could earn a bit of money by giving each other lessons in various subjects. I taught English.

I tried to compensate for my limited 1,000-word vocabulary by being as entertaining as possible. On this particular afternoon, I employed my favorite pedagogical device: the mock trial. Henry Kissinger, who was then the American Secretary of State, was in the dock. His crime: support of détente. Détente, a French word meaning "relaxation," was used during the Cold War to describe a policy approach that was supposed to "ease tensions" between the superpowers. Its detractors—including Soviet dissidents—saw it as a euphemism for appeasement.

One of my students played Kissinger. Since I had four other pupils, two defended Kissinger and two prosecuted him. To spice things up a bit, I decided to have these students also assume the identities of famous figures. Who better to defend Kissinger, I thought, than Richard Nixon and Leonid Brezhnev? While the American president and Soviet Premier might have seemed like natural opponents, when it came to détente, each propped up the other. Both believed an "easing of tensions" served their interests. Nixon, like Kissinger, saw détente as a means to forge a "structure of peace" in which global security and stability could be most effectively advanced. Brezhnev, on the other hand, saw it as a means to preserve the Soviet regime's grip over its subject populations, weaken the West's resolve to firmly challenge Soviet expansionism, and prevent an economic, technological and scientific competition for which the Soviets were ill prepared.

The prosecutors would be Henry "Scoop" Jackson and Andrei Sakharov, two courageous figures who had rejected détente. A Democratic senator from the state of Washington, Jackson had co-authored the Jackson-Vanik amendment, a historic piece of legislation that linked most favored nation (MFN) status, under which countries received preferential terms of trade with America, to a foreign government's protection of its citizens' right to emigrate. The Soviets had slammed the doors shut on millions who wanted to leave the USSR, including hundreds of thousands of Jews like myself. Jackson's amendment was designed to force them to open those doors. But Kissinger saw Jackson's amendment as an attempt to undermine plans to smoothly carve up the geopolitical pie between the superpowers. It was. Jackson believed that the Soviets had to be confronted, not appeased.

Andrei Sakharov was another vociferous opponent of détente. He thought it swept the Soviet's human rights record under the rug in the name of improved superpower relations. Sakharov was the father of the Soviet hydrogen bomb, which was tested in 1953. Years later, he unleashed an even more powerful weapon against his own totalitarian rulers by openly calling on them to respect human rights. My relative proficiency in English as well as my eagerness to contribute to the human rights struggle had earned me the privilege of helping Sakharov in his contacts with the international press and visitors from abroad. One message he would consistently convey to these foreigners was that human rights must never be considered a humanitarian issue alone. For him, it was also a matter of international security. As he succinctly put it: "A country that does not respect the rights of its own people will not respect the rights of its neighbors."

I assigned myself the most enviable part of all in our trial, judge. In the spirit of all Soviet mock trials, I made up my mind ahead of time: Kissinger would be stripped of his American citizenship, sentenced to exile in the Soviet Union, and forced to try to emigrate without the benefit of the Jackson Amendment!

I imagine that our mock trial of Henry Kissinger, whose sharp analyses of world affairs are rightfully admired around the world and with whom I would develop a friendly relationship after my release from prison, appears as absurd today as it would have back then to anyone who was not a dissident. The important borders during the Cold War were seen as those that separated capitalists from communists, Americans from Soviets, East from West. But not to dissidents. Of course, more than anyone else, we were painfully aware of these fault lines because we often paid the price for crossing them. Merely talking to a foreign diplomat or entering a foreign journalist's home could land us in an interrogation room or prison cell. Still, while the fault lines framed the larger geopolitical and ideological contours of the superpower face-off, they failed to capture what for many of us was an even more important threshold—a border that did not separate the world as it was, but rather as it might be. On one side stood those who were prepared to confront evil. On the other stood those who were prepared to appease it.

The evil was a totalitarian regime that had killed tens of millions of its own subjects, and ruled an empire of fear by repressing all dissent for over half a century. Those in the West who were willing to reconcile themselves to this tyranny came in all stripes—European and American, Left and Right, Democrat and Republican. Some were well-intentioned, some were naïve, others were venal. Many were simply afraid. But all had one thing in common: They did not believe in the power of freedom to transform the USSR.

More than any other factor, the presence or absence of this belief determined on which side of the border one stood.

There were many skeptics. During the Cold War they included almost every American president and secretary of state and almost every Western European government (with the notable exception of Thatcher's government in the UK) and most of the mainstream media. While the reasons for their skepticism varied, the effect was the same: Actively or passively they supported policies that helped deprive the hundreds of millions of people living in the Soviet Union of their freedom.

For Soviet leaders, whether a bloodthirsty tyrant like Stalin was at the helm or men of a more moderate disposition like Kruschev and Brezhnev, accommodation with the West was invariably viewed as a means to consolidate the regime's control and expand Soviet power. In contrast, support in the West for détente stemmed from less malevolent motives. There were those who questioned whether the peoples behind the Iron Curtain really wanted democracy. The Russians, after all, had lived under autocratic czars for nearly a millennium. Worse, their brief experiment with democracy in early 1917 led to the rise of an even greater tyranny a few months later. Given that the Russian people and their culture were intrinsically inclined toward despotism, the argument went, pressing for democratic changes within the USSR, though a noble undertaking, was simply a waste of time.

Another argument offered in favor of détente was that a democratic Soviet Union would not necessarily serve the interests of the West. The Soviet regime was brutal, but predictable. Democratic reforms, on the other hand, could unleash chaos and instability. During the fragmentation of the Soviet Union, this argument was particularly prominent. A single nuclear power was seen as safer and more controllable than a proliferation of small states, each with their own decaying facilities. Additionally, despite the external dangers it posed and its own internal shortcomings, the Soviet Union was seen as helping to put a lid on many smaller conflicts around the world. A decade after the collapse of the USSR, many are still making these same arguments.

The idea that certain peoples are incapable of democratic self-rule or have no desire for it has a long pedigree in Western diplomatic thinking. So too does the notion that the spread of democracy is not always in the democratic world's interest. Still, for most of the Cold War few people bothered to re-examine these old prejudices because almost no one believed that a democratic revolution in the USSR was possible. Efforts by the West to "impose" its values on the Soviets were considered completely unrealistic. The Soviets may not have been the ideal partner, but they were seen as strong and going nowhere. Confrontation, it was believed, would only make things worse—for America, for the Soviets, for everybody. Better to work out a compromise that would bring order and stability to world affairs than to engage in a reckless brinkmanship that had no chance of success. Put simply, most people believed there was little point in fighting a war that could not be won.

Our world has changed so much over the last fifteen years that it may be difficult for today's reader to get a sense of the degree of skepticism there once was in the West over the possibility of a democratic transformation inside the Soviet Union. In the early 1980s, when some were actually arguing that the Soviet Union could be challenged, confronted, and broken, the possibility was dismissed out of hand. The distinguished historian Arthur Schlesinger Jr., expressing the sentiments of nearly all of the Sovietologists, intellectuals, and opinion makers of the time, said that "those in the United States who think the Soviet Union is on the verge of economic and social collapse, ready with one small push to go over the brink are wishful thinkers who are only kidding themselves."[1]

An even better measure of the skepticism of the era was the absolute shock that greeted the collapse of the USSR. The most prescient politicians, the most learned academics, the most perceptive journalists did not foresee that hundreds of millions of people could be liberated from decades of totalitarian rule in just a few months. In April 1989, just seven months before the fall of the Berlin Wall, Senator J. William Fulbright, who had served for 15 years as chairman of the Senate's Foreign Relations Committee, co-authored an article dismissing the views of those in the "evil empire school" who believed that Gorbachev's reforms were "no more than the final, feeble, foredoomed effort to hold off the historically inevitable collapse of a wicked system based on an evil philosophy."[2] Instead, Fulbright offered insight into how the "détente school," in which he included himself, understood the changes that were then taking place behind the Iron Curtain:

> We suspect that the reforms being carried out in the Soviet Union and Hungary may be evidence not of the terminal enfeeblement of Marxism but of a hitherto unsuspected resiliency and adaptability, of something akin to Roosevelt's New Deal, which revived and rejuvenated an apparently moribund capitalism in the years of Great Depression.[3]

If scholars and leaders in the West could be so blind to what was happening only months before the fall of the Berlin Wall, imagine what the thinking was in 1975. Back then, the suggestion that the Soviet Union's collapse was inevitable, much less imminent, would have been regarded as absurd by everyone.

Well, almost everyone.

In 1969, a Soviet dissident named Andrei Amalrik wrote *Will the Soviet Union Survive until 1984?*, in which he predicted the collapse of the USSR. Amalrik, to whom I would later have the privilege to teach English, explained that any state forced to devote so much of its energies to physically and psychologically controlling millions of its own subjects could not survive indefinitely. The unforgettable image he left the reader with was that of a soldier who must always point a gun at his enemy. His arms begin to tire until their weight becomes unbearable. Exhausted, he lowers his weapon and his prisoner escapes.

While many in the West hailed Amalrik's courage—he was imprisoned for years and exiled for his observations—almost no one outside the Soviet Union took his ideas seriously. When he wrote his book, short-sighted democratic leaders were convinced the USSR would last forever, and according to many economic indicators, the Soviet Union appeared to be closing the gap on the U.S. Amalrik must have seemed downright delusional.

But inside the USSR, Amalrik's book was not dismissed as the ranting of a lunatic. The leadership knew that Amalrik had exposed the Soviet regime's soft underbelly. They understood their vulnerability to dissident ideas: Even the smallest spark of freedom could set their entire totalitarian world ablaze. That's why dissidents were held in isolation, dissident books were confiscated, and every typewriter had to be registered with the authorities. The regime knew the volatile potential of free thought and speech, so they spared no effort at extinguishing the spark.

I was arrested in 1977 on charges of high treason as well as for "anti-Soviet" activities. After my own mock trial a year later, I was sentenced to thirteen years in prison. In 1984, my KGB jailers, swelling with pride, reminded me of Amalrik's prediction: "You see, Amalrik is dead"—he had died in a car accident in France in 1980—"and the USSR is still standing!"

But Almarik's prediction had not missed by much. Within a few months of that encounter in the Gulag, Mikhail Gorbachev came to power. Faced with an American administration ready to confront him and realizing that the Soviet regime no longer had the strength both to maintain control of its subjects and compete with the West, Gorbachev reluctantly implemented his "glasnost" reforms. This limited attempt at "openness" would usher in changes far beyond what Gorbachev intended. Just as Amalrik had predicted, the second the regime lowered its arms, the people it had terrorized for decades overwhelmed it.

How was one Soviet dissident able to see what legions of analysts and policymakers in the West were blind to? Did Amalrik have access to more information than they did? Was he smarter than all the Sovietologists put together? Of course not. Amalrik was neither better informed nor more intelligent than those who had failed to predict the demise of the USSR. But unlike them, he understood the awesome power of freedom.

Dissidents understood the power of freedom because it had already transformed our own lives. It liberated us the day we stopped living in a world where "truth" and "falsehood" were, like everything else, the property of the State. And for the most part, this liberation did not stop when we were sentenced to prison. Having already removed the shackles that imprisoned our minds, our physical confinement could not dull the sense of freedom that coursed through our veins.

We perceived the Soviet Union as a wooden house riddled with termites. From the outside, it might appear strong and sturdy. But inside it was rotting. The Soviets had enough nuclear missiles to destroy the world ten times over. Over 30 percent of the earth's surface was under communist rule and the Soviets possessed enormous natural resources.

Its people were highly educated, and its children second to none in mathematic and scientific achievement. But forced to devote an increasing share of its energies to controlling its own people, the USSR was decaying from within. The peoples behind the Iron Curtain yearned to be free, to speak their minds, to publish their thoughts, and most of all, to think for themselves. While a few dissidents had the courage to express those yearnings openly, most were simply afraid. We dissidents were certain, however, that freedom would be seized by the masses at the first opportunity because we understood that fear and a deep desire for liberty are not mutually exclusive.

Fortunately there were a few leaders in the West who could look beyond the facade of Soviet power to see the fundamental weakness of a state that denied its citizens freedom. Western policies of accommodation, regardless of their intent, were effectively propping up the Soviet's tiring arms. Had that accommodation continued, the USSR might have survived for decades longer. By adopting a policy of confrontation instead, an enervated Soviet regime was further burdened. Amalrik's analysis of Soviet weakness was correct because he understood the inherent instability of totalitarian rule. But the timing of his prediction proved accurate only because people both inside and outside the Soviet Union who understood the power of freedom were determined to harness that power.

For me, and for many other dissidents, the two men leading the forces of confrontation in America were Senator Henry Jackson and President Ronald Reagan. One a Democrat, the other a Republican, their shared conviction that the individual's desire for freedom was an unstoppable force convinced them of the possibility of a democratic transformation inside the Soviet Union. Crucially, they also believed that the free world had a critical role to play in accelerating this transformation. Their efforts to press for democratic reform did not stem solely from humanitarian considerations. Like Sakharov, these men understood that the spread of human rights and democracy among their enemies was essential to their own nation's security.

Had Reagan and Jackson listened to their critics, who called them dangerous warmongers, I am convinced that hundreds of millions of people would still be living under totalitarian rule. Instead, they ignored the critics and doggedly pursued an activist policy that linked the Soviet Union's international standing to the regime's treatment of its own people.

The logic of linkage was simple. The Soviets needed things from the West—legitimacy, economic benefits, technology, etc. To get them, leaders like Reagan and Jackson demanded that the Soviets change their behavior toward their own people. For all it simplicity, this was nothing less than a revolution in diplomatic thinking. Whereas statesmen before them had tried to link their countries' foreign policies to a rival regime's *international* conduct, Jackson and Reagan would link America's policies to the Soviet's *domestic* conduct.[4]

In pursing this linkage, Jackson, Reagan, and those who supported them found the Achilles heel of their enemies. Beset on the inside by dissidents demanding the regime live up to its international commitments and pressed on the outside by leaders willing to link their diplomacy to internal Soviet changes, Soviet leaders were forced to lower their arms. The spark of freedom that was unleashed spread like a brushfire to burn down an empire. As a dumbfounded West watched in awe, the people of the East taught them a lesson in the power of freedom.

Dazzled by success, policymakers in the West quickly forgot what had provided the basis for it. Astonishingly, the lessons of the West's spectacular victory in which an empire crumbled without a shot fired or a missile launched were neglected. More than fifteen years after the fall of the Berlin Wall, the free world continues to underestimate the universal appeal of its own ideas. Rather than place its faith in the power of freedom to rapidly transform authoritarian states, it is eager once again to achieve "peaceful coexistence" and "détente" with dictatorial regimes.

Less than two years after the collapse of the Berlin Wall and immediately after the first Gulf War ended, I met with the editorial board of one of America's most influential newspapers. I suggested that the United States, which had just saved Saudi Arabia and Kuwait from extinction, had an historic opportunity. Now was the time to use America's primacy in the Middle East to start bringing freedom to a region of the world where hundreds of millions are still denied it. I argued that just as the United States had effectively used "linkage" to accelerate changes within the Soviet Union, America should link its policies towards the Arab states to those regimes' respect for the human rights of their subjects. As a first step, I suggested that America's new-found leverage in the region might be used to insist that Saudi Arabia accept an opposition newspaper or remove some of its severe restrictions on emigration.

The eyes of my hosts quickly glazed over. Their reaction was expressed in terms that Kissinger easily could have used in 1975 in discussing the Soviet Union: "You must understand," they replied politely, "the Saudis control the world's largest oil reserves. They are our allies. It is of no concern to America how the Saudis rule their own country. Saudi Arabia is not about democracy. It is about the stability of the West."

On September 11, 2001, we saw the consequences of that stability. Nineteen terrorists, spawned in a region awash with tyranny, massacred three thousand Americans. I would like to believe that horrific day has dispelled the free world of its illusions and that democratic policymakers recognize that the price for "stability" inside a nondemocratic regime is terror outside of it. I would like to believe that the leaders of the free world are now unequivocally committed to advancing freedom throughout the region not merely for the sake of the hundreds of millions who have never tasted it, but also for the sake of their own countries' security. Most of all, I would like to believe that those who are confident of the power of freedom to change the world will once again see their ideas prevail.

But I have serious doubts. There are, to be sure, important signs of hope. I am heartened by the American-led effort currently underway in the region to build democratic societies in Afghanistan and Iraq as well as by President Bush's determination to see this effort succeed. Moreover, as was true a generation ago, the belief in the power of freedom is not confined to one side of the political and ideological divide. Across the Atlantic, a left of center British prime minister, Tony Blair, appears no less committed than President Bush to a democratic transformation of the Middle East. And to his credit, Mr. Blair has had to make the case for democracy against the views of many in his own Labour Party and the overwhelming doubt of the British public.

But those who believe that a democratic Middle East is possible are few in number. Within certain parts of America, and nearly everywhere outside of it, the voices of skepticism appear ascendant. Many have questioned whether the democratic world has a right to impose its values on a region that is said to reject them. Most argue that military intervention in the Middle East is causing more harm than good. Even within the Bush administration, the president's words, expressing a profound faith in freedom, are not always translated into policies that reflect that faith.

Freedom's skeptics have returned. They may couch their disbelief in different terms than they did a generation ago. Then, with Soviet's nuclear-tipped missiles pointed at Western capitals, the focus was on the inability of the free world to win the war. Now, it is on the inability to win the peace. Nevertheless, the arguments peddled by the skeptics sound all too familiar.

They insist that there are certain cultures and civilizations that are not compatible with democracy and certain peoples who do not desire it. They argue that the Arabs need and want iron-fisted rulers, that they have never had democracy and never will, and that their "values are not our values."

Once again, it is asserted that democracy in certain parts of the world is not in the best interests of the "West." While it will be readily admitted that the current regimes in the Middle East suppress freedom, those regimes are believed to also suppress a far worse alternative: the radicals and fundamentalists who might win democratic elections. The message is clear: It is better to deal with a Middle Eastern dictatorship that is our friend than a democratic regime that is our enemy.

Finally, it is said that even if the free world might be made more secure by the region's democratization, there is little the democracies can do to help. We are told that freedom cannot be imposed from the outside and that any attempt to do so will only backfire, further fanning the flames of hatred. Since democratic reform can only come from within, the prudent role for leaders of the free world, it is argued, is to make the best of a bad situation. Rather than recklessly trying to create a new Middle East that is beyond reach and which will provoke greater hostility toward the "West," democratic leaders are advised to work with the "moderate" non-democratic regimes in the region to promote peace and stability.

One thing unites all of these arguments: They deny the power of freedom to transform the Middle East. In this book, I hope to explain why the skeptics are as wrong today as they were a generation ago and why the West must not betray the freedoms on which it was built.

I am convinced that *all* peoples desire to be free. I am convinced that freedom *anywhere* will make the world safer *everywhere*. And I am convinced that democratic nations, led by the United States, have a critical role to play in expanding freedom around the globe. By pursuing clear and consistent policies that link its relations with nondemocratic regimes to the degree of freedom enjoyed by the subjects of those regimes, the free world can transform any society on earth, including those that dominate the current landscape of the Middle East. In so doing, tyranny can become, like slavery, an evil without a future.

The great debate of my youth has returned. Once again, the world is divided between those who are prepared to confront evil and those who are willing to appease it. And once again, the question that ultimately separates members of the two camps remains this: Do you believe in the power of freedom to change the world? I hope that those who read this book will count themselves, like me, among the believers. Here, then, is the case for democracy.

CHAPTER I

Is Freedom for Everyone?

There is a myth that though we love freedom, others don't; that our attachment to freedom is a product of culture; that freedom, democracy, human rights, the rule of law are American values, or Western values.... Ours are not western values, they are the universal values of the human spirit. And anywhere, any time ordinary people are given the chance to choose, the choice is the same: freedom, not tyranny; democracy, not dictatorship; the rule of law, not the rule of the secret police.[1]

THESE ARE THE WORDS of British Prime Minister Tony Blair, spoken to a joint session of the United States Congress in the summer of 2003. Over the last few years, similar sentiments have been expressed by U.S. President George W. Bush, who has reiterated on numerous occasions his fervent belief that "freedom is not America's gift to the world, it is God's gift to humanity."

The conviction that freedom is a universal desire is not the property of any political camp. Its proponents cannot be neatly divided into Left and Right, Democrat and Republican, or even American and European. Its detractors are equally diverse, coming from all sides of the political spectrum. Because this conviction transcends party and ideology, it can potentially gain an enormous following. Yet those who hold it remain a precious few, outnumbered many times over by the skeptics who don't.

For many years, the question of whether freedom is for everyone was relegated to the sidelines of the debate in the democratic world. It might have made for a fascinating academic thesis or an interesting topic of conversation, but its answer was not thought to affect our lives or our futures.

Then came September 11.

Suddenly, the nature of nondemocratic societies halfway across the globe, from what their state-controlled media were broadcasting to what their schools were teaching to what their religious figures were preaching, was on everyone's agenda. For some world leaders, the Twin Towers were not the only things that collapsed on 9/11. So too did the conception that what took place inside foreign countries was not relevant to international security and peace.

Before that horrific September day, the question of a democratic Middle East was on few radar screens. Policymakers across the world saw the Middle East as a huge swathe of despotism that could not, should not, and would not be changed any time soon. What was important in this rough and brutal region, the conventional wisdom went, was to maintain "stability." That could be achieved, it was widely believed, by seeking accommodations with "moderate" nondemocratic regimes.

But the attacks on Washington and New York and the global War on Terror that was launched in their wake changed all that. The stability of the pre–9/11 world was not a stability with which America could live. That something had to be done was clear. Still, had the American government responded to the attacks on its homeland differently, perhaps the question of whether a democratic Middle East is possible would have remained consigned to the ivory towers of universities and the lecture halls of a handful of think tanks. But within days of 9/11, President Bush declared a global War on Terror whose *strategy* was based on the assumption that freedom is for everyone.

The War on Terror was not billed as a war only against Al Qaeda. True, Al Qaeda, an international terrorist organization led by Osama bin Laden, was behind the attacks in Washington and New York and had also been responsible for the bombings of two U.S. embassies in East Africa in 1998 and the strike on the USS *Cole* in 2000. But the declared objective of the war was far broader: to neutralize the threat posed by terrorism—mainly Islamic fundamentalist terrorism—to the safety and security of the free world. The war would end, President Bush declared, only when "every terrorist group of global reach has been found, stopped and defeated."[2]

Does achieving this objective, in which there is wide agreement across the political spectrum, require building free societies in the Middle East? For President Bush, Prime Minister Blair, and many (though by no means all) of those prosecuting the War on Terror, it does. To them, building free societies has in fact become a key element in what appears to be a two-part strategy to win the War on Terror.

The first part of that strategy is to end *state support* for terrorism. In his initial speech to the American people after the 9/11 attacks, President Bush said that his government would "make no distinction between the terrorists who committed these acts and those who harbor them."[3] In other words, instead of focusing only on bringing individual terrorists to justice and using all available means to dismantle the terror organizations, now the *regimes* sponsoring terror would also be targeted. These regimes would not be allowed to provide money, weapons, training grounds, diplomatic cover, ideological backing, and other support to terror groups. By severing the link between the terror network and their state sponsors, it was thought that the terror organizations could no longer indoctrinate their recruits, hatch their plots, and wage their murderous campaigns with impunity.

The second part of the strategy, even more controversial than the first, was to replace terror-sponsoring regimes with democratic governments. Why this strategy would be so controversial is easy to understand. It is one thing to topple the Taliban and Sadaam and install new strongmen in their place. That has been tried many times before. It is quite another to replace those brutal tyrannies with free societies. For this, there are fewer precedents.

This strategy is a radical departure from traditional foreign-policy approaches that are essentially unconcerned with the internal affairs of other countries. Whether a non-democratic regime respected the human rights of its own subjects was almost always less important to democratic policymakers than whether that regime's ruler was "for us or against us," or, as a less-than-subtle President Lyndon Johnson once put it, whether the ruler was "*our* son-of-a-bitch." Rather than turn a blind eye to the internal polices of others, this new strategy is based on the assumption that the breeding ground for terror is tyranny and that building an open society is the best way to drain the swamp. As President Bush himself argued, "freedom and democracy are critical to defeating terror" because "free nations that respect human rights will help overcome hatred, resentment and the ideologies of murder."[4]

Many have argued that one or both aspects of this strategy for fighting the war are unnecessary and, ultimately, counterproductive. Some maintain that the free world, led by the United States, can use its power to target the terrorist organizations, dry up their financing, and punish their leaders, without having to topple regimes. And if regimes must be toppled, they should only be toppled when they are directly responsible for an attack. Such a policy, it is argued, is a prudent method to fight terrorism and to restore deterrence against threats from rogue regimes. Anything beyond that is seen as either immoral or dangerous or both.

Many other critics of the strategy do not accept the premise that terrorism is primarily a function of the absence of democracy. Some think the root cause of terror is poverty or that it is the product of a desperate effort to redress political, economic, or social grievances. Naturally, those who think that terror is largely unrelated to nondemocratic rule will not be convinced that the War on Terror can be won with the advance of liberal democratic values. They might argue instead for waging war on poverty or redressing the grievances that ostensibly drive terrorists to commit their savagery.

Still, it is hard to imagine many who would contend that if the region's tyrannies were transformed into *genuinely* free societies, the world would not be more secure. Surely, few would argue that the successful transformation of the nondemocratic regimes of the Middle East into governments that respect the rule of law, protect individual rights, cherish human life, and dedicate themselves to improving the well-being of their citizens would not be better for everyone.

But proving what would be good in theory is not the same as proving what can be achieved in practice. As George Will, the influential and erudite columnist for the *Washington Post,* warned, "the premise—that terrorism thrives where democracy does not—may seem to generate a duty to universalize democracy. But it is axiomatic that one cannot have a duty to do something that cannot be done."[5] No doubt, we would all agree that a democratic Middle East that provides its population with freedom and opportunity would be preferable to a despotic Middle East that oppresses its subjects at home and exports terrorism abroad. But is Will right that it cannot be done? Do all peoples really desire freedom? Are some societies simply unfit for democracy?

A HOPEFUL HISTORY

The idea that there are certain peoples and societies unsuited to democratic life is certainly not new. In 1934, the renowned historian Arnold Toynbee saw the rise of fascism in Italy as clear proof that democracy was a "special local growth which could not be guaranteed to acclimatize itself in alien soil." [6]

> [N]o parliamentarian can close his eyes to the significance of the portent of Fascism in post-war Italy; for Italy lies near the heart of our western world; she has made one of the greatest single contributions made by any country to our common western civilization; and in the nineteenth century her adoption of Anglo-French parliamentarism seemed to be the essence of her national resurrection. In these circumstances, her repudiation of "democracy" (in our conventional use of the term) has made it an open question whether this political plant can really strike permanent root anywhere except its native soil.[7]

Similarly, sixty years ago, most people would have considered the claim that Germany could become a thriving liberal democracy absolutely preposterous. Germany had spawned the most fanatical regime in history, which in little more than a decade in power murdered millions of its subjects, terrorized tens of millions more, and waged war against the democratic world, indeed, against the very idea of democracy. Writing in 1943 and expressing the conventional wisdom of the age, one expert scoffed at the notion that democracy could succeed in Germany.

To go back and create a liberal Germany, as most emigrants from Germany want to do, is likewise impossible. It did not succeed the first time. How can anyone think that after these new outbursts the Germans can become democrats overnight? Is there a democratic serum which one can inject and thus immunize a people against militarism, against desire for world domination, or passion for submission to superiors in uniform? Such a serum has not been invented.[8]

In fact, during the darkest days of World War II when anti-democratic forces had cast a shadow over much of the civilized world, some scholars questioned whether democracy could survive *anywhere* in the West.

In Western Europe, where the religion of democracy was nurtured through its hazardous childhood, it is today engaged in a great struggle for survival. In Germany, Italy, Fascized Spain—in fact, on the whole Continent—its very existence is threatened. And the threat will outlast Hitler, since Fascism itself is a mere end-product of deep-grained anti-democratic forces within the very texture of modern European thought, and of the whole industrialized West: forces which have penetrated into the altars of democracy, Great Britain, France and the United States: forces which unconciously corrupt in large measure the liberal and radical thought that complacently leads the fight against Fascism.[9]

With a half a century of hindsight, what seems absurd is that anyone ever believed that democracy could *not* take hold in Germany, Italy, or elsewhere in Europe. Today, Germany and Italy are liberal democracies with governments that protect the rights of their citizens and peoples who live at peace with their neighbors. Hundreds of millions of Europeans have no memory of life without democracy, and would surely pooh-pooh the claim that there is something inherent in European thought and life that makes the Continent unsuitable for democratic life.

Still, some people may believe that the success of democracy in Europe tells us little about the chances of democracy succeeding elsewhere. After all, the democracies based in Rome, Berlin, and the other capitals of Europe are said to rest on the strongest of foundations: broad middle classes, thriving civil societies, and highly educated populations. Others will correctly point out that these democracies were not built on entirely unfertile ground. The Germans had a brief, albeit unsuccessful, experiment with democracy before the rise of Hitler. Republics flourished on Italian soil for two thousand years, and in the nineteenth century, Italians fought for four decades for their liberty.

These arguments cannot be ignored, and had democracy only taken root in the Anglo-Saxon world and on the European Continent, they might be hard to refute. But democracy has spread elsewhere, both to cultures that have almost no experience with democratic life and to places that do not possess what are thought to be the natural building blocks of democracy.

Take Russia for example. For hundreds of years, the Russians were believed to be "different" from their European cousins. When the French political theorist Jean Bodin visited Russia in the sixteenth century, he observed that the czarist regime's absolute power stood in sharp contrast to the more limited rule of European kings and emperors.[10] Unlike the Russians, who were thought to prefer subservience to freedom, the people of Europe would never tolerate such absolutism, Bodin wrote. When the Marquis de Custine traveled extensively in Russia in 1839, he wrote that whereas other nations tolerated the oppression of their rulers, the Russians "loved it."[11] Not surprisingly, when the czar's absolutism was replaced by Soviet totalitarianism, it only confirmed for many that Russians were not cut out for democracy. As Richard Pipes, a leading expert on Russia, put it, "[I]t's no coincidence that Marxist ideas developed into a reformist social democracy in many places around the world but evolved into the most extreme forms of repression in Russia."[12]

To be sure, there were many substantive reasons to believe that Russia was not cut out for democracy. As scholars like Pipes pointed out, Russia has no tradition of limited government, no institution of private property, and a history that shows little regard for the rule of law.[13] Moreover, Russia's civil society was weak, its middle class nonexistent, and, unlike some European nations, the subjects of the Russian empire did not share a common faith, culture, or language. Simply put, judging by its culture and traditions, there was little reason to believe that democracy could take hold in Russia.

In fact, despite the collapse of the Soviet Union, the setbacks on the road to democracy in Russia today—some of which are very troubling—leave many doubtful that democracy there will stand the test of time. The skeptics are more likely to see the current climate in Russia as evidence that the country is consigned to a future in which "long stretches of absolutism are briefly interrupted by fleeting periods of reform."[14]

But we should keep things in perspective. Compared to a Soviet Union in which millions worked for the KGB, millions were in prison, tens of millions lost their lives, and hundreds of millions lived in fear, present day Russia is a bastion of freedom. We must also remember that Russian democracy is in its infancy. Comparing it to mature democracies that are centuries in the making is misleading. Twelve years after a revolution occurred in France in the name of liberty, equality, and fraternity, its people lived under a dictatorship. Did that mean that French society could not abide democracy? More than eighty years after the American Revolution, African-Americans were still slaves. Did the practice of slavery in the nineteenth century mean that Americans were incapable of building a democratic society? Surely, the fact that democratic societies are not built overnight is not evidence that they cannot be built at all.

The breathtaking collapse of the Soviet Union should have been proof enough of the Russian people's powerful thirst for freedom. Up until the very last moment of Soviet totalitarian rule, various experts on Russia were predicting it would continue. But like the Poles, Hungarians, Czechs,

Lithuanians, Romanians, and the rest of the peoples of Eastern Europe, the Russian people replaced tyranny with a democratic government. Nonetheless, little more than a decade later, some still question whether Russians really want to live in a free society. For them, the bumps on Russia's road to democracy are evidence of a deep longing by its people to return to an authoritarian past. Here is how one journalist, writing for the *New Statesmen*, put it:

> What conjures up the Gulag for many of us is for many Russians a present comfort. KGB members were an elite successfully promoted in the post-Stalin years as protectors of the fatherland rather than as terrorists of the population. Now, the memory of a time in which the KGB was the backbone of order is precious.[15]

Only those who have no understanding of tyranny could take such nonsense seriously. Russians do not want to return to totalitarianism. To believe that the Russians long for a return to a totalitarian past because of the difficulties they have encountered in the present is like believing that African-Americans who suffer from unemployment and poverty long for a return to slavery. Even those Russians who claim to want to go back to the "Russia of old" do not want to return to a world where people are arbitrarily killed, where family members can be suddenly arrested or imprisoned, or where the government controls nearly every aspect of life.

If the example of Russia leaves readers unconvinced,

then Japan's transition to democracy should quell any doubts that democracy cannot "acclimatize itself in alien soil." When World War II came to an end, there was little to suggest that Japanese democracy would work. Japan had been isolated from Western influence for centuries, and its hierarchical society, authoritarian political system, and conformist culture should have made it impervious to a democratic transformation. Joshua Muravchik, a scholar at the American Enterprise Institute, points out just how strange the idea of democracy was to the Japanese: "When the concept of rights was imported into Japanese politics in the late nineteenth century, it was so foreign that it was not easily translated into Japanese: It required a compound word consisting of four characters to express it."[16]

In 1938, Japan's ambassador to Rome proudly noted that it makes Japanese hearts "warm" to see totalitarian ideas that have influenced the Japanese for centuries embodied in the systems of the modern states of Europe.[17] Not surprisingly, few people in those years believed a democratic transformation of Japan was possible. Employing arguments that will sound familiar to those who follow the contemporary debate about whether democracy can spread to the Middle East, many experts at the time were certain that Japanese civilization would prove inimical to democratic life. Here is what one of those experts wrote in *Foreign Affairs* in 1941:

> We should be deceiving ourselves if we thought that the present day Japanese are fundamentally opposed to autocratic forms of government and are awaiting the

day when they can reverse the current political trend and set up democratic institutions.... The truth seems to be that what we in our country call a democratic outlook is organically related to Christianity; and perhaps it is not seriously falsifying the picture to say crudely that the essential difference between Japan and Western democracies is that Japan is not a Christian country.[18]

In May 1945, State Department official Joseph Grew explained to President Harry Truman that "the best we can hope for in Japan is the development of a constitutional monarchy, experience having shown that democracy in Japan would never work."[19] Even in 1952, when the seven-and-a-half year occupation of Japan was coming to an end and after democratic rule had gained a solid foothold there, another expert observed, in an article entitled "Why Asians Hate the West," that democracy in Asia was in inevitable retreat. Western liberals, the author cautioned, should take a "more realistic view of the short-term prospects of democracy outside the relatively small part of the world where it is well rooted."[20] Of course, history has proven these predictions wrong. Japan has maintained its unique tradition and culture, but has at the same time built a strong democracy that has stood the test of time.

Yet even Japan's remarkable transformation will not silence all the skeptics. For one *National Review* writer, a half century of democratic rule is still not enough proof of the long-term viability of democracy outside the Anglo-Saxon world.

Other cultures can fake it for a few decades, as France, Germany and Japan are currently doing, but their hearts are not really in it and they will swoon gratefully into the arms of a fascist dictator when one comes along.[21]

"BUT THE ARABS ARE DIFFERENT"

I suspect that the above argument will only go so far with those who believe that freedom has no future in the Middle East. True, democracy has been established in a wide range of cultures, and many different peoples have shown that they possess a deep desire for liberty. But leafing through history's pages, we will not find incontrovertible proof that freedom is for everyone. The skeptics were wrong about whether democracy could take hold in Italy, Germany, Japan, Spain, Latin America, Russia, and many other places, but who's to say they are wrong about whether it can take hold in the Middle East? When President Bush says that "the hundreds of millions of people in the Middle East are not condemned by history to live in despotism"[22] or that Islam, the faith of one-fifth of humanity, "is consistent with democracy"[23] why should we believe him? Perhaps the people in the Middle East are condemned to live in tyranny. Perhaps democracy cannot find a home there. It would certainly be comforting to think that the freedom cherished by the democratic world is cherished by everyone. It allows us all to imagine a world where all nations can live together in peace based on shared values. But is it true?

On September 11, 2001, nearly 3,000 Americans were

massacred by nineteen fanatical Muslims. A few hours later, when mourners were holding vigils in the streets of London, Tel Aviv, and Seoul, Muslims were dancing in the streets of Ramallah and Baghdad. Overnight, a mass murderer like Osama bin Laden became a hero to tens of millions of Muslims. How then can we honestly say that freedom, democracy, and human rights are the "universal values of the human spirit?"

At first glance, the case against democracy taking hold in the Middle East is a powerful one. It is not without reason that *The Economist*, a magazine not known for its anti-Muslim prejudices, asked whether there was something "hard-wired" into Islam that made it "incompatible with democracy."[24] In democracies, *The Economist* tells us, men make laws. But Islam contains in the Koran a set of God-given laws dictated to Mohammed that are not open to revision, leading many to conclude that Islam is not compatible with democratic rule.[25] While this can be said of all orthodox faiths that have "God-given" laws, it appears especially true of Islam because of its unique history. As the eminent scholar Bernard Lewis has pointed out, there is no separation of church and state in Islam, as there is in Christianity. Christians were told to render unto Caesar the things which are Caesar's and unto God the things which are God's. By having this public-private distinction as part of its theology, Lewis explains, Christianity paved the way for the separation of church and state that is generally considered a central pillar of modern, democratic life. But Mohammed, unlike Jesus, was a soldier and statesman who founded an empire as well as a faith. Therefore, Lewis notes, for Muslims, religion and power are so inextricably linked that the very idea of a separation of church and state is meaningless, since there are no two entities to separate.[26]

The Islamic faith is not seen as the only strike against democracy emerging in the Middle East. Many also see the treatment of women in the Muslim world in general, and in the Middle East in particular, as a force militating against democracy. While the West still has a long way to go before full equality between the sexes is realized, most people would consider it light years ahead of the Muslim world. Pointing to what they believe is the systematic discrimination against women in the Muslim world in every sphere of life, two scholars write that "the real fault line that divides the West and the Muslim world is attitudes toward women."[27] If, as many believe, a basic notion of equality is a precursor of modern democracy, many find it hard to imagine how Islamic society can fit the bill.

Moreover, the cultural gap is about much more than women. Many Muslim societies that revolve around "shame and honor" appear incomprehensible to those living in the democratic world. When an Egyptian man murders his own daughter for shaming the family with her sexual "promiscuity" or an adulterous Palestinian woman becomes a suicide bomber to restore her family's lost honor, many people conclude that democratic life in those societies doesn't stand a chance.

As for the features that are believed to be critical to sustaining a liberal, democratic order, here too, the countries of the Middle East are seen as ill equipped for democracy. They have little in the way of civil societies, small middle classes, widespread poverty, and rampant illiteracy.

Of course, all of these obstacles can be countered by pointing out that freedom has spread in the Muslim world. Freedom House, an organization that monitors the extent of freedom in countries around the world, did precisely that in one of its recent reports.

> Recent history shows that Islam is not inherently incompatible with democratic values. Indeed, if we take into account the large Muslim populations of such countries as India, Bangladesh, Indonesia, Nigeria, Turkey and the Islamic population of North America and Western Europe, the majority of the world's Muslims live under democratically constituted governments.[28]

But these reports will not erase the doubts. It will be pointed out that the Muslim populations of Western Europe and North America are small minorities who are forced to live in democratic societies and that, though there are over one hundred million Muslims in India, they too are a minority living among nearly a billion Hindus. Others will surely argue that the democracies in Nigeria, Bangladesh, and Indonesia are merely passing episodes in a history full of military coups, authoritarianism, and despotism, or that in Turkey, the military effectively rules the country and has shown that it is prepared to oust any democratically elected government that threatens the secular nature of the state.

An even stronger point could be made as well. While it may be conceded that it is possible for Muslims to govern a democratic society, one could still say that Arabs cannot. It could be plausibly claimed that in the broader Muslim world, in countries that were once exposed to Western values, democracy might have a chance, but that in the Middle East, antidemocratic features tempered elsewhere are far more resilient.

The absence of freedom in the Arab world is so acute today that even Arab scholars, who are not generally known for their willingness to confront the failings of their own societies, prepared a document under the auspices of the United Nations that was critical of the "freedom deficit" in the Arab world. With uncommon candor, the Arab Human Development report concluded:

> The wave of democracy that transformed governance in most of Latin America and East Asia in the 1980s and Eastern Europe and much of Central Asia in the late 1980s and early 1990s has barely reached the Arab States. This freedom deficit undermines human development and is one of the most painful manifestations of lagging political development. While de jure acceptance of democracy and human rights is enshrined in constitutions, legal codes, and government pronouncements, de facto implementation is often neglected and, in some cases, deliberately disregarded.[29]

The release of this report, which noted the critical link between human freedom and human development, might be seen as a welcome sign that there is already increasing awareness inside the Arab world about the need to build free societies. Moreover, within that world, the demands for freedom are growing. Syrians, Egyptians, and even Saudi Arabians have witnessed pro-democracy protests in the last few years.

Still, the protests of a few hundred Arabs in the Middle East out of a population of a few hundred million is not likely to sway the skeptics. The case against democracy in the Middle East appears compelling. While democracy has spread across the globe, the Middle East remains a sea of tyranny. There are twenty-two Arab states and not one of them is democratic, even by the weakest of definitions. Moreover, there has *never* been an Arab democracy, and with the exception of a handful of tyrannies around the world, the world's most repressive regimes are in the Middle East. So while President Bush may "know" that freedom is the "future of every nation,"[30] many others can be forgiven for disagreeing.

The arguments offered by the skeptics, then, are not entirely unpersuasive. The doubts they express and the difficulties they raise frame the extent of the challenge each country will face in making the transition to democracy—a transition that will be easier for some than for others. But though the journey may vary in every society, I am certain that democracy is not beyond any nation's reach.

The source of my confidence that freedom truly is for everyone is not only that democracy has spread around the world, allowing so many different cultures and peoples to enjoy its bounty, my confidence also comes from living in a world of fear, studying it, and fighting it. By dissecting this world, exploring the mechanics of tyranny that operate within it and analyzing how individuals there cope with it, one can understand why modern history has witnessed a remarkable expansion of freedom. There is a universal desire among all peoples not to live in fear. Indeed, given a choice, the *vast majority* of people will always prefer a *free* society to a *fear* society.

CHAPTER 2

A Free Society and a Fear Society

WE GENERALLY associate free societies with the preservation of basic liberties. Yet in no society are those liberties absolute. In America, for instance, freedom of speech and religion are considered sacrosanct. Nevertheless, one is not free to shout fire in a crowded theater, nor is bigamy permitted in the name of religious belief. While discussions on the appropriate boundaries of various freedoms may make for interesting policy debates within democratic societies, they fail to make a crucial distinction between societies that are based on freedom and those that are based on fear.

This distinction was identified by people who ought to know a thing or two about the subject: Soviet dissidents. In the Gulag, there were all kinds of political prisoners: Russian monarchists eager to restore the czarist rule that was wiped out during the Bolshevik revolution; Ukrainian nationalists struggling to win independence for their nation after 300 years of Russian dominance; Pentecostals who sought to practice their faith freely; Crimean Tatars who wanted to return from exile and reestablish autonomy from Moscow; Eurocommunists who wished to put a "human face" on Soviet communism; Jewish Refuseniks, like myself, who wished to emigrate to Israel; and many others.

Although an enormous diversity of opinion was behind bars in the Gulag, dissidents shared one belief in common: We all wanted to live in a free society. And despite our sometimes contradictory visions of the future, the dissident experience enabled all of us to agree on what freedom meant: *A society is free if people have a right to express their views without fear of arrest, imprisonment, or physical harm.* Each dissident envisaged a future in which his concerns were paramount, but no matter how fervent our individual desires, all the dissidents understood that a society that does not protect the right of dissent, even if the society perfectly conforms to their own unique values and ideas, will inevitably turn into a fear society that endangers *everybody.* While we dissidents vehemently disagreed about what type of free society we wanted to live in, we recognized that as long as dissent is possible we would always be safe to fight for our ideas.

A simple way to determine whether the right to dissent in a particular society is being upheld is to apply the town square test: Can a person walk into the middle of the town square and express his or her views without fear of arrest, imprisonment, or physical harm? If he can, then that person is living in a free society. If not, it's a fear society.

Some people who live in free societies may consider this test too expansive since, in addition to the liberal democracies, it includes many countries not always considered free. According to the town square test, societies where women are not allowed to vote, where discrimination is rampant, or where the economy is rigidly controlled can still be free. This valid criticism demonstrates that every society that meets the definition of "free" is not necessarily *just*. Rather, this test shows only that every society that passes it has crossed the threshold of freedom. In contrast, fear societies *never* cross this threshold and are *always* unjust.

THE MECHANICS OF TYRANNY

The formula I have proposed divides the world into two categories, free and fear societies, with nothing in between. I believe there are only two kinds of societies because a society that does not protect dissent will *inevitably* be based on fear. Indeed, the mechanics of tyranny make this inescapable.

Imagine a monolithic society in which every person shares the same values, beliefs, and lifestyle. This hypothetical society is "free" because there are no laws that prevent people from expressing their views and there is no danger in doing so. Since everyone agrees with the prevailing ideology, however, there is also no dissent.

Human diversity suggests that change within any society

is inevitable. No two people, much less all the members of a community, have the exact same background, tastes, interests, priorities, curiosity, intelligence, and experiences. These natural differences will invariably lead people to respond to new situations in different ways. No matter how homogeneous a society may seem, eventually differences will emerge and grow. The speed with which this process occurs will depend on many factors, from how large and complex the society is to the degree of its exposure to outside influences, but differences in opinion are certain.

The question then becomes how the hypothetical society will respond to these inevitable differences in opinion. Will it allow them to be expressed publicly? Will it allow those who want to change the prevailing order to try to do so through democratic means? If the answer is yes, then the society will remain free, but it will also change.

The early kibbutzim, the farming settlements that were established in Israel and became a model of socialist living throughout the world, are a case in point. The kibbutzim were marked by an intense ideological commitment to collectivist values. In contrast to the collectivism of the Soviet Union, which the state imposed by force, the kibbutz way of life was voluntary. There were no laws preventing people from expressing their views and everything was decided by majority rule. The system appeared remarkably stable.

The test for the kibbutzim came when its ideological values, embraced so completely at the beginning, were challenged. Differences began to emerge. Successive generations did not always share their parents' ideological fervor. Though the glue binding the kibbutz together continued to be those values and ideals that were once shared by everyone, factions pressing for change began to emerge. Wanting a different lifestyle for themselves, they abandoned the kibbutz or attempted to change it from within. Today, the kibbutzim are very different than they were two generations ago, looking more like private businesses than the models of collective living they once were.

But what if the majority in a society does not want any changes now, and wants to prevent change in the future? Laws banning dissent will have to be enacted by the majority or imposed by the regime. Whether these laws will be an effective deterrent will depend, among other things, on how committed the dissenters are to their ideas and on the severity of the punishment. But one thing is clear: This will no longer be a free society.

DOUBLETHINK

In any place where dissent is banned, society fractures into three groups. One group is composed of those who remain committed to the prevailing order because they agree with it—the true believers. Another group is made up of those who are willing to defy the prevailing order despite the risk of punishment—the dissidents. For members of these two groups, there will be little or no gap between their private thoughts and public statements. Unlike true believers and dissidents, members of the third group do not say what they think. This group is comprised of people who no longer believe in the prevailing ideology, but who are *afraid* to accept the risks associated with dissent. They are the "doublethinkers."

I was five years old when Stalin died. On the day of his funeral, as solemn music blared from the loudspeakers of our town and enormous portraits of Comrade Stalin lined the streets, my father called my seven-year-old brother and me over to him, making sure we were out of the earshot of the two families with whom we shared an apartment. "Today is a great day that you should always remember," he told us. He explained that the man everyone referred to as "Our Leader and Teacher" had massacred millions of people and was planning a new wave of persecutions against Jews. We were fortunate, he told us, that this "butcher" was dead. He followed these shocking revelations with stern warnings never to repeat what he said to anyone and to behave exactly like all the other children. So, at the tender age of five, singing paeans to Stalin and shedding crocodile tears with my kindergarten classmates over the death of a butcher, I had been initiated into the world of Soviet doublethink.

In *Out of Iran: One Woman's Escape from the Ayatollahs*, Sousan Azadi tells a similar story about the world of doublethink in her former country:

I always warned my son not to tell the teachers anything about what was going on in our home and that if they asked if I had a certain something or other in the house, he was always to say no. One day he came home from school and reported proudly, "Mom, I did something good today. The teacher showed me a Koran and asked me if we had one at home and I said NO." He was just beaming, and it broke my heart to take my little child and show him where my marriage Koran was kept and to admonish him sternly never to say that we did not have the holy book in the house. "You have to tell people that we pray every day even if we don't," I told him, hating myself for teaching him at such an early age to lie for survival.[1]

In a letter smuggled out of North Korea in the 1970s, one North Korean explained how he had learned the art of doublethink. "I learned that if you speak out loud what's on your mind, you die! I learned that if you have something to say, it is much easier to say it with your eyes. I learned to see with my lips and speak with my eyes."[2]

Doublethinkers live in constant tension from the gap between their thoughts and words. They always avoid saying what is not permitted but also try to avoid saying what they do not believe. But fear societies generally do not leave their doublethinkers such a luxury. They demand from their "cogs" constant expressions of loyalty. In kindergartens, schools, universities, workplaces, religious institutions, public meetings, and elsewhere, doublethinkers must parrot the ideology of the regime and hide their true beliefs. This constant self-censorship can be such an inseparable part of a doublethinker's existence that it becomes so habitual that the tension between thoughts and words is almost no longer felt. Indeed, only when doublethinkers are free are they fully aware of the extent of their previous self-imposed intellectual servitude.

Political anecdotes and jokes, which can expose the hypocrisy of a fear society, are used to decrease the tension of the life of doublethink. The way in which these anecdotes and jokes can be conveyed—whether expressed for example, in small circles or in larger ones, orally or in written form—depends on the level of fear in a society. Moreover, the extent to which these anecdotes and jokes permeate a society is a measure of the extent of doublethink in that society.

In books, poetry, plays, art, and music, the cultural elite is constantly testing the borders between doublethink and dissent, competing to be the first to react to changes in the policies of the regime and to discover the new borders of acceptable expression.

Though certain "specialists" can interpret these subtle signals and understand the internal processes taking place within a fear society, to an outside observer, a fear society's doublethinkers are indistinguishable from its true believers: Both groups will *appear* to assent to the prevailing order, though only one actually does. Therefore, to an outsider, a fear society will consist of only two groups, true believers and dissidents. And if the punishment for dissent is high enough, the fear society will have no dissidents either.

In the 1930s, there were no dissidents in the Soviet Union, at least none that were known to the West. Were the more than 150 million people who lived under Stalin's boot in the 1940s all true believers? Or, more plausibly, was the lack of dissent due to the fact that in Stalin's time, dissidents would be summarily executed? Is it not logical that the number of dissidents in a fear society would largely be a measure of the risk of dissent? The USSR of the 1970s, for example, was a relatively less oppressive society than it had been in the 1930s and so a few hundred dissidents appeared. Had Mahatma Gandhi been facing the regime of a Stalin or a Hitler, his struggle against foreign rule would have ended before it began. Fortunately for him, he confronted a British society that, while imperialist, was also liberal and democratic.

If a fear society is repressive enough, it will appear to an outside observer to consist of *only* true believers when in reality it may have thousands, tens of thousands, hundreds of thousands, millions, tens of millions, or even hundreds of millions of doublethinkers living in terror. Moreover, while it is impossible to know how many doublethinkers there are in a fear society, one thing is certain: With every passing day, the number of double thinkers in a fear society almost always increases. It happens because the restrictions of a fear society provide many reasons for true believers to become alienated from the regime. Once alienated, these new doublethinkers are highly unlikely to become loyal supporters of the regime again (although, as we will see later, the regime constantly tries to recruit them).[3]

DECEIVING OURSELVES

In Saudi Arabia, one can definitely be arrested or imprisoned for expressing one's views. While many people who grew up in liberal democratic societies would regard life in Saudi Arabia as oppressive, can it be said that the people of Saudi Arabia, who appear to agree with the prevailing ideology, live in fear? Aren't the Saudi Arabians simply living according to their age-old traditions? Though no one could claim that Saudi Arabia is a free society, does that necessarily make it a fear society?

This question assumes that the people of Saudi Arabia agree with the policies of their regime. But how do we know that? Because of what the Saudis say publicly? Can we assume that what people living in a fear society are willing to say publicly is a true expression of their beliefs? The books of dissidents describing how Saudis flying to Europe hurry to change into their Western clothes while still on the airplane and adopt different modes of behavior when they are abroad are enough to convince me that Saudi Arabia is steeped in doublethink. Even if these stories only refer to the Saudi elite, the process of internal decay, when more and more people are conforming to a world they no longer believe in, is clearly under way. We must always keep in mind that the public statements of those who live in fear societies are motivated by fear. If we fail to recognize this, we will only be deceiving ourselves.

In the 1930s, when Stalin was killing millions of his subjects and starving millions more, Western intellectuals such as George Bernard Shaw, H. G. Wells, Romain Rolland, and Leon Feuchtwanger waxed poetic about the contented Soviet masses. Feuchtwanger, a famous German writer of the era who specialized in historical fiction, visited the Soviet Union in 1937. In a book describing that trip, Feuchtwanger contrasted the "unhappiness in capitalist countries" with the "satisfaction of people in the Soviet Union."[4] At the height of Stalin's repressions, when nearly the entire Soviet population was living in utter terror, Feuchtwanger offered readers in the West his impression of the public mood:

> Though from time to time they criticize a minor short-coming, all the people whom I met, even those whom I met by chance, who could not have been prepared for a discussion with me, all agreed with the existing [Stalinist] system. All the vast city of Moscow was brimming with satisfaction and consent, and even more than this, happiness.[5]

Stalin admired the propaganda value of Feuchtwanger's work so much he granted the writer the rare privilege of attending a public trial. These trials provided Stalin with the means to consolidate his power and liquidate his opponents. They would generally feature prominent Communist Party officials whom he wanted to oust for one reason or another. The officials would be arrested and tortured into confessing their "crimes against the people," and if torture would not suffice, they would be warned that their families would be killed if they refused to comply. By the time they entered the courtroom, the accused were well prepared to deliver carefully scripted public statements that served Stalin's propaganda needs.

In his account of one trial, Feuchtwanger hailed the proceedings as a remarkable display of justice and mutual respect. Feuchtwanger observed that despite the serious charges facing the accused (of the seventeen people on trial, twelve received the death penalty and five long prison sentences—sentences which in Stalin's time usually meant death as well), they were all united in their "love for the machine" of communism. Describing a mutual affection that "encourages the judges and the accused to cooperate so closely with each other," Feuchtwanger compared it to a "feeling similar to the one that connects the government and the opposition in England so closely that the government pays the leader of the opposition 2,000 pounds a year"[6] and noted the solemn approval with which the people greeted the verdicts.

Those who report today on the "Arab street" or on the contented masses in Beijing, Havana, or elsewhere around the world should be wary of falling into the same trap as Feuchtwanger. Almost daily during the wars in Afghanistan and Iraq, democratic audiences watching the news were reminded that though the Taliban and Saddam may not be their cup of tea, they did nonetheless represent the will of large portions of the Afghan and Iraqi people. And how did these reporters know this? Because "the people" told them so.

In one memorable CNN broadcast devoted to finding out what the people of Afghanistan thought, a journalist noted that the Taliban "were controlling where you can go, but not necessarily what you can say while you are there."[7] The journalist did not seem to realize that in a fear society, finding out what people truly believe is not a function of whether the press is given the freedom to ask questions, but rather whether the people feel free to answer them.

In the same broadcast, the journalist whom a member of the Taliban was escorting on a "tour" around Afghanistan, informed his viewers that the Afghans he had spoken with "appear quite passionately, at this stage, behind the Taliban." When the CNN studio host asked whether statements made in the presence of Taliban chaperones were part of a "good propaganda show," the reporter replied,

> No, again, that's a question we have asked, I've asked several Taliban that question. They say, "no." They say that [what people] read of the Taliban and the Afghan mindset is completely erroneous and wrong. That is one of the reasons, also, they want to bring us into these areas. It's not just to show us the civilian casualties, but also to show us the mindset.[8]

Similarly, in an article entitled "Waiting to Kill Americans," a *Time* magazine journalist used the words of a forty-year-old Iraqi war widow to convince readers that the Iraqi "people" were firmly behind Saddam.

> The Americans should be warned that Iraqi women know how to fight and die as well as our men. . . . We will give up our lives for our beloved country, our beloved Baghdad and our beloved Saddam.[9]

Admitting that the woman's words "borrow heavily from official pamphlets and presidential speeches," the journalist nevertheless assured his readers that "the emotion they convey is her own."

These journalists apparently never questioned the authenticity of public statements that were made defending a regime that put its opponents through plastic shredders and tortured children in front of their parents. Perhaps he would have served his readers better by quoting the words of one North Korean defector who explained that "it is the understanding of every average person in [North] Korea that if you say something against the party line, you will be taken to a controlled area."[10]

After the war, journalists heard a very different tune from the Iraqi people from the one they heard only a few weeks earlier. One journalist, noting how many people had told him that their terrible fear of Saddam had prevented them from speaking out, was honest enough to set the record straight.

The painter Rassim described to me how the mere act of talking with foreigners at an art exhibition could result in being hauled away for hours of questioning by the dread Mukhabarat secret police. . . . Mushtak recalled how his teenage son had once blurted, "I hate Sadaam Hussein!" to a group of close friends, only to find himself arrested a few hours later. The police demanded a million Iraqi dinars to free him and then 200,000 more. "My wife and I never discussed politics in front of our children," he told me. "We never knew when one might accidentally reveal something to an informer."[11]

The public statements of those who live in fear are never a reliable indication of people's true opinions. Had a poll been conducted in the Soviet Union in 1985 asking whether respondents supported the policies of the communist regime, 99 percent would have answered yes—incidentally, the same percentage who would have answered yes in 1935, 1945, 1955, 1965, 1975, and every year in between. The opinion of "the people" apparently underwent a dramatic change a few years later when communism collapsed in the face of a popular uprising. Had the people suddenly changed their minds? Had their long love affair with totalitarian communism come to an end overnight? Of course not. The only thing that changed was that the masses of doublethinkers were no longer afraid to express their true beliefs.

In 2001, in one of the first meetings of Prime Minister Ariel Sharon's national unity government, I argued, as I had for many years, that Yasser Arafat was a corrupt dictator whom Israel should stop supporting. A senior minister in the government who was very supportive of continuing negotiations with Arafat and the Palestinian Authority told me that regardless of what Israel thought about Arafat, he was "beloved by his people," as we could see from the "massive public support" he enjoyed. I assured my colleague that Arafat was beloved by his people in the same way Stalin had been beloved by his. Just as there were times in the Soviet Union when one couldn't survive without expressing loyalty to the regime, so too the Palestinians must often express their loyalty to the regime that rules them.

WILLING DUPES?

Doublethinkers, who must play a role their entire lives in order to survive, will have little problem hiding their true beliefs and still convincing an outsider of their sincerity. Their role playing is made easier by the fact that many outside observers have an idealogical bias that allows them to willingly suspend their disbelief and not see the effects of tyranny.

The intellectuals fooled by Stalin in the 1930s shared a sincere belief that communism's egalitarian ideals promised a more just order than the one offered by their own capitalist countries. Convinced that the Soviet attempt to build a "new world" and a "new man" was a noble one, they refused to believe that those championing such ostensibly lofty goals could employ such reprehensible means to obtain them, and they filtered their observations accordingly.

This ideological predilection is so strong in some people that even after the truth is revealed, they cannot acknowledge it. At the end of the 1980s, small unofficial delegations of Soviet cultural and public figures started coming to Israel. It was part of re-establishing relations between the Soviet Union and the "Zionist Enemy," which the Soviets had broken off after the Six Day War in 1967. After decades in which the superpower had served as the main supplier of arms to Israel's enemies and had spearheaded attempts to isolate the Jewish state in international forums, these first contacts were understandably a cause for much excitement in Israel. I had been released from prison some years before, and as a sign of the "thawing" of tensions between the two countries, I was sometimes invited to attend these meetings. I remember that at one of the meetings, Shimon Peres, the leader of Israel's Labor Party made some opening remarks. Searching for common ground with his guests and obviously trying to say something pleasant, Peres reminded the delegation of the two nations' common roots: "We have the kibbutzim, and you have the *kolkhoz.*"

Our Soviet guests were shocked. The *kolkhoz* were the collective farms established by Stalin in 1929 that robbed peasants of their land and stripped them of their rights. Peres did not realize that he was comparing Israel's kibbutzim to what had become a symbol of Soviet slavery, in which millions were killed, millions exiled, and millions starved. Even sixty years later, the *kolkhoz* were an embarrassing reminder of the Communist regime's horrible past. Like Feuchtwanger, Peres was simply unable to take off his ideological blinders. To Peres, the ideal of communal living remained a glorious vision that people in both countries could admire. Peres couldn't appreciate that a collective enterprise in a fear society is utterly different from a collective enterprise in a free society, notwithstanding that they share the same label.

A close friend of mine encountered the same phenomenon in a discussion group that had been formed between Israeli and Palestinian women. When one of the Palestinians mentioned the horrible honor killings that plague her society, an Israeli participant, with a clear anti-religious bias, told her that Israel had a similar problem. In the ultra-orthodox community, she explained, women who cheated on their husbands were also the victims of a shame-and-honor mentality. My friend, not believing what she was hearing, vehemently protested the comparison. The ultra-orthodox, she explained, may ostracize a member of the community, but they would never kill her. Second, the penalty of being ostracized was not limited to sexual indiscretions, but applied to many other facets of ultra-orthodox life, from failing to obey the Sabbath laws to violating dietary restrictions. Therefore, being ostracized has nothing to do with gender issues. Third, in the ultra-orthodox world, unlike the situation in many Muslim countries, this penalty is applied to both men and women. There is no moral equivalence between honor killings in a fear society and ostracization in a free society. But this Israeli woman, because of her anti-religious bias, compared two completely different phenomena.

TRUE BELIEVERS

The power of a fear society is never based solely on an army and a secret police. As important is a regime's ability to control what is read, said, heard, and above all, thought. This is how a regime based on fear attempts to maintain a constant pool of true believers.

The Soviets went to great lengths to shape the minds of their citizens, subjecting the nation's old to a mixture of overt and subtle reprogramming and forcing its youth to imbibe the official wisdom of the Soviet government. The voluminous State Encyclopedia in my father's house was a constant reminder of the malleability of Soviet history. Every few years, after a high-profile death or trial, our family received official pages of revision. We were advised by the authorities to put those pages in the appropriate place and burn the ones earmarked for removal.

For those living in a free society, the idea that a state would try to thoroughly brainwash its subjects is particularly difficult to grasp. On my first trip to America I met with the publisher of Random House, a vociferous critic of the Soviet's human rights record. He asked me whether people in the Soviet Union could freely enter bookstores and buy books. At first, I couldn't believe he was serious. Then I understood that he simply had no idea how a fear society worked. I explained to him that *we* were free to go in, but that the *books* were not.

All fear societies are based on a certain degree of brainwashing. State-controlled television, radio, and newspapers glorify the actions of the regime's leaders and incite their populations against those it deems to be enemies. Recently, an officer in the North Korean army who had defected described how he oversaw experiments at a prison camp in which parents were placed in gas chambers together with their children. Asked how he could take part in such barbarism, the officer replied:

> At the time I felt that they thoroughly deserved such a death. Because all of us were led to believe that all the bad things that were happening to North Korea were their fault; that we were poor, divided and not making

progress as a country.... It would be a total lie for me to say I felt sympathetic about the children dying such a painful death. Under the society and the regime I was in at the time, I only felt that they were the enemies. So I felt no sympathy or pity for them at all.[12]

North Korea's regime has an easier time brainwashing its subjects than do regimes that preside over less insular societies. The Palestinian Authority, however, has shown that it is possible to poison minds in much more open societies as well.

For twenty-five years, the Palestinians lived under Israeli military control. Palestinian laborers worked in Israel and Palestinian society was thoroughly exposed to Israel's democratic way of life. But after Israel transferred control over Palestinian-populated cities to Arafat's Palestinian Authority (PA) under the Oslo accords, the PA used every tool at its disposal to incite Palestinians to hate Israel and hate Jews. Textbooks that did not include Israel on a map of "Palestine" taught Palestinians that the Jewish state had no right to exist; summer camps trained kindergarten children to become suicide bombers; PA-controlled media hailed terrorists who had murdered Israeli civilians as martyrs whose heroic actions were a source of pride to their people.

By the time the campaign of Palestinian terrorism began in September 2000, the level of indoctrination among the Palestinians had reached fever pitch. On PA-run television, five-year-olds donning suicide belts beckoned viewers to join them in the struggle to liberate all of Palestine, and schools were let out so that children could participate in the fighting.

In one chilling interview broadcast on PA television, an eleven-year-old Palestinian girl said becoming a *shahid* (martyr) was more important than achieving a "just peace."[13] From morning to night, martyrdom was portrayed as the highest calling of all Palestinians. To be sure, many of those who took part in this festival of hate were doublethinkers, simply conforming with the prevailing ideology in order to survive. After all, Arafat and the PA controlled the distribution system of food aid, a monopoly over many basic goods, the hundreds of millions of dollars of international aid that were supposed to go to improving conditions for Palestinians, tens of thousands of permits that allowed Palestinians to work in Israel, and much more. Many Palestinians had to express loyalty to Arafat and the PA if they hoped to feed their families. Still, systematic brainwashing is bound to have ill effects, particularly on the young. Not everyone will be lucky enough to have a father who will inform them that their "Great Leader and Teacher" is a butcher.

But the lasting effect of such indoctrination should also not be exaggerated. The day-to-day life of a fear society cannot be made palatable forever. Eventually, bitter experience belies the propaganda so that not even some of the people can be fooled all of the time.

The 1979 revolution against the shah of Iran had broad support in the population. It would quickly become clear, however, that the revolution had imposed a totalitarian religious order that was no less corrupt and even more repressive. In less than a generation, popular support has turned completely against the regime. Though elections in Iran are strictly controlled, with candidates vetted by the ayatollahs and with the media fully controlled by the state, Iranians have increasingly shown their opposition to the mullahs by electing those candidates that are seen as the most hostile to the ideology of the regime. After twenty-five years of failure, oppression, and economic stagnation, few Iranians can be brainwashed into supporting the ayatollahs. The true believers have become doublethinkers, and the doublethinkers, sensing that the regime is weakened, are turning more and more toward open dissent.

Another example of the limits of indoctrination can be found in the common observation that the most anti-American regimes in the Middle East have the most pro-American populations. This is not *despite* those regimes' anti-American propaganda but because of it: The attitude of those living in fear societies toward America is a reflection of their attitudes toward their own regime. If America is seen as supporting that regime, as in Saudi Arabia and Egypt, the people hate America. If America is seen as opposing the regime, as in Iran, the people admire it. A few months ago, a leader of a former Soviet Republic told me about his recent visit to Iran: "It reminded me of the Soviet Union. All the officials criticize and condemn America and all the people love America."

Even those who genuinely do hate America do not necessarily hate free societies. Rather, part of their hatred is due to the perception that by supporting the nondemocratic regimes that are oppressing them, America is betraying the democratic values it claims to uphold.

Even the "truest" of true believers will not indefinitely support a fear society. For decades, Stalin terrorized not only the Soviet people but also the entire Communist Party leadership: A member of the ruling Politburo might be a rising star in the party one day; the next, he could find himself on a train bound to Siberia or facing the death penalty. After Stalin died in 1953, no one in the Communist leadership was willing to grant the same level of absolute authority to his successor. The next leader's power was restricted not because the Communist leadership wanted to bring an end to totalitarian rule but rather because *they themselves* no longer wanted to live in fear.

THE EXHILARATION OF FREEDOM

There is no way of knowing for sure what the precise distribution of doublethinkers and true believers is within a fear society at any point in time. But the experience of living in such a society and my understanding of how individuals cope with such societies has convinced me that the number of true believers is always far smaller, and the number of doublethinkers much larger, than outsiders assume. Moreover, if a majority of those who live in a fear society do not already prefer freedom to fear, they will soon after their fear society collapses.

The deeper the level of control that a society tries to exercise over its subjects, the faster the change will occur. In 1989, a North Korean student who defected a short time after he began his medical studies in Czechoslovakia noted that "most North Koreans, raised almost from birth to regard the two Kims as all-providing deities, accept the propaganda, as I did until I saw the relative freedom of Czechoslovakia."[14] Once the systematic brainwashing stops, once the truth begins to come to light, once the double-thinkers are no longer afraid, in every society a majority who will not be willing to live in fear again quickly emerges.

More than any other reason, this is why Germans, Japanese, Italians, Spaniards, Russians, and so many others made the transition from fear to freedom during the twentieth century. They have very different cultures, beliefs, religions, ideals, values, and lifestyles, but in one respect they are all the same: None of those peoples wanted to live in fear again.

The determination of men and women who are free never to return to a life of fear should never be underestimated. Indeed, the sense of freedom that comes from leaving the world of brainwashing and doublethink is a liberation that is not soon forgotten. My own liberation from the world of fear began when I was still a student at the Moscow Institute of Physics and Technology, a school that liked to compare itself to MIT. Figuring that in this school of "wunderkind," the conventional methods of brainwashing would have little impact, the authorities used other methods. The more sophisticated propaganda we were subjected to appealed to the importance of the work we were doing. All talk of rights, freedom, and justice, we were told, was just that, only talk. What do mere words mean compared with the immutable laws of Newton,

Galileo, and Einstein? Political values will come and go, while science offers universal, eternal truths.

Ironically, I was inspired to leave a life of doublethink by a man perched at the very apex of the world of "eternal truths." In 1968, in an essay directed at the Soviet leadership, Andrei Sakharov, the most prominent scientist in the Soviet Union, wrote that scientific progress could not be disconnected from human freedom. The stifling intellectual environment inside the USSR was retarding its people's capacity for invention and crippling the nation's ability to be a world leader, Sakharov wrote. The ideals of socialism would never be reached, he explained, if the Soviet Union did not embrace intellectual freedom. In one courageous statement, Sakharov had dealt a severe blow to Soviet power. The chief scientist of a superpower that prided itself on its scientific achievement was arguing that the nature of Soviet society was making it impossible for the USSR to keep pace with the free world.

For a young scientist contemplating his future, the message was loud and clear. A man we all revered was warning that the world of falsehood led not to a better future for all mankind, but to intellectual paralysis and scientific regression. Sakharov, who would later risk everything by challenging the regime to respect human rights, became an inspiration for me, and I quickly gravitated to his side. When I later worked as his liaison to foreign journalists, diplomats, and politicians, I saw that there was never a gap between this remarkably humble man's inner thoughts and public statements. In my case, the convergence of my thoughts and words—which happened when I first became a Jewish activist—would bring an end to my own inner discomfort. As self-censorship and doublethink gave way, I was overcome by a powerful sense of liberation. It was as if an enormous weight I had borne for years and whose burden I had become habituated to had finally been lifted. All of a sudden, I was free to think what I liked and say what I thought. Even when I was on a prolonged hunger strike in my punishment cell, the sense of freedom never left me.

For most of those who have lived their entire lives in fear, this feeling will be experienced only when their society is free, when they feel it is safe to go to the town square and express their views without fear. But it will be no less exhilarating. I am certain that this feeling of exhilaration transcends race, religion, creed, and culture, and that the drug of freedom is universally potent. I am equally certain that once a people live in freedom, the vast majority of them will never want to live in fear again. To suggest, as the skeptics do, that the majority of a people would freely choose to live in a fear society is to suggest that most of those who have tasted freedom would freely choose to return to slavery.

CHAPTER 3

Dognat Y Peregnat

FREEDOM from tyranny is not only universally desired, it is also universally desirable. Unfortunately, policymakers often see things differently.

STABILITY TRUMPS DEMOCRACY

In 1990, the Soviet Union was on the brink of collapse. The small hole Gorbachev had grudgingly poked in the dam of Soviet rule a few years earlier had unleashed a flood of freedom. In rapid succession, the Berlin Wall was torn down, Eastern Europe was free, and the USSR was disintegrating. For the peoples within the Soviet Union, it was a time of optimism and hope. After seventy years of Bolshevik totalitarianism and centuries of czarist repression, fear societies behind the Iron Curtain were becoming free societies. Yet at this moment of triumph, there was a growing sense of concern within the White House. True, the end of the USSR's stranglehold over Eastern Europe was certainly welcome news: Freedom for East Germans, Poles, and Hungarians was a longstanding policy objective. But the collapse of the Soviet Union was quite another matter.

In January 1990, I met the first President Bush at the White House. Though he does not have a reputation as a strong friend of Israel, when it came to assisting the efforts to bring Soviet Jewry and Ethiopian Jewry to Israel, I always found President Bush extremely supportive. On this particular occasion, I had requested a meeting to ask for his help in persuading the Soviet government to allow direct flights from the USSR to Israel. When the gates of the USSR opened in 1989, hordes of Soviet Jews, long denied the right to emigrate, took the opportunity to move to Israel. Approximately 15,000 Soviet Jews were arriving in Israel every month, the proportional equivalent of 750,000 immigrants settling in America every month. Despite this immense flood of people, there were no direct flights from the Soviet Union to Israel. Jewish immigrants were forced to travel via other Eastern European countries, making their passage more difficult and subjecting those countries to all sorts of political pressures from those who wanted to curb immigration to the Jewish state.

Bush immediately promised to help. Our conversation

then turned to the larger events taking place at that time in the USSR. The president told me he intended to support Gorbachev's efforts to keep the Soviet Union together and wanted to hear my opinion on how best to help him. When I asked him why America wanted to prevent the breakup of the USSR, he explained that Gorbachev was a man with whom the United States "could do business." Bush argued that it was better to have the Soviet's nuclear arsenal in the hands of a leader America could rely on than under the control of unproven heads of state, even ones who were democratically elected. President Bush also made it clear that he believed dealing with an unelected Soviet leader who could be counted on to help preserve stability around the globe was better than taking a chance on a Pandora's box of international chaos opening up in the wake of the USSR's collapse.

I respectfully told the president that in my view nothing could or should be done to convince Lithuanians, Latvians, and Ukrainians to reject the independence they had craved for so long and which was now finally within their reach. Rather than attempt to thwart the democratic will of these peoples, I suggested that America focus its efforts on helping all parties manage the difficult transition to democracy. By facilitating this process, I argued, America would earn the lasting appreciation of those peoples and also be in a better position to address its own concerns about what might happen in a post-Soviet order.

But President Bush chose a different course. In August 1991, he traveled to the Ukraine where he delivered his notorious "Chicken Kiev" speech, in which he urged Ukrainians not to support a "suicidal nationalism." The speech was an unmitigated disaster. A people who were only months away from realizing their 300-year-old dream of independence were being told by the American president to forget about it. In the end, it made little difference to Ukrainians what President Bush thought. A few months after his visit, the overwhelming majority of them voted to have a country of their own. America had missed a golden opportunity. Instead of playing a leading role in the country's historic transition to democracy and at the same time securing many of America's own interests, the leader of the free world had instead chosen a course that left his nation watching from the sidelines.

The Bush administration was not the first nor will it be the last to try to stifle democracy for the sake of "stability." Stability is perhaps the most important word in the diplomat's dictionary. In its name, autocrats are embraced, dictators are coddled, and tyrants are courted. Even in the free world, the champions of stability outnumber the champions of democracy many times over. Democratic governments across the globe, on the Left and the Right, almost always prefer the nondemocratic regime they know to the democracy they don't. While these governments usually recognize that fear societies are fundamentally at odds with democratic principles, they nevertheless tend to see them as pillars of stability and security. Fear societies may be cruel to their own people, the thinking goes, but they are often invaluable for maintaining a stable and peaceful international order that is critical to the security of all nations. This was the free world's assessment of Stalin's Soviet Union before and during World War II, of Brezhnev's Soviet Union before it invaded Afghanistan, of Saddam Hussein's regime before it invaded Kuwait, and of Saudi Arabia before September 11.

According to the same logic, the prospect of democracy spreading throughout the world, while nice in the abstract, is often viewed with great suspicion, if not outright alarm. To most policymakers, the advance of democracy in some countries would only make the world more dangerous today. For example, many fear that replacing the nondemocratic regimes in Egypt or Pakistan with democratic ones would turn over control of Egypt's formidable army and strategically important Suez Canal to Islamic fundamentalists or allow Pakistan's nuclear arsenal to fall into the hands of sympathizers of Osama bin Laden. If it were true that stability could be guaranteed by nondemocratic regimes, then the case for democracy across the world would be dealt a fatal blow. For when given the choice between promoting morals and promoting interests, democratic nations will almost always choose the latter.

INTERESTS AND MORALS

Those who believe that moral principles have *no* place in diplomacy ascribe to a philosophy that has long dominated international relations and been associated with America's leading diplomats from Hans Morgenthau to George Kennan to Henry Kissinger. Commonly referred to as realism, this approach analyzes and formulates policy based on strategic interests alone and rejects any attempt to infuse moral considerations into the equation.

To the realist, a foreign policy that actively promotes democracy around the world would be at best naïve and at worst dangerous; naïve, because a state's foreign policy is a function not of its internal political arrangements but of largely immutable strategic interests; dangerous, because countries that base their foreign policy on idealism can often damage their own interests. For example, a realist would regard as nonsense the notion that transforming China from a fear society to a free society would seriously change Chinese foreign policy and would warn any nation that would press for democratic change in China that it will end up harming its own interests.

According to the realist, the role of prudent statesmen is to help promote an international order that advances their nation's interests, even if promoting that order abroad requires setting aside principles one would never abandon at home. Though realists may place a high value on democracy and human rights, when it comes to foreign affairs they are likely to follow the advice of U.S. President John Quincy Adams, who admonished his nation in 1821 not to go abroad "in search of monsters to destroy." America, Adams maintained, should be a "well-wisher to the freedom and independence of all," but "champion and vindicator only of her own."[1]

Of course, not all diplomats are realists. Some believe that in addition to the pursuit of national interests, moral principles should also play an important role in a state's foreign policy. Woodrow Wilson, for example, said that America was entering World War I to make the world "safe for democracy." Six decades later, Jimmy Carter said that the advance of human rights around the world would be a priority of his administration.

The advocacy of a more values-based foreign policy has often subjected these "idealists" to the criticism that they back foreign interventions that have nothing to do with their nation's vital interests. Recently, idealists have been vilified not only for risking blood and treasure in strategically insignificant operations that satisfy moral impulses alone—a proclivity one writer memorably labeled "foreign policy as social work"[2]—but also for refusing to contemplate the use of force when vital interests are really at stake. Charles Krauthammer, the brilliant and incisive columnist for the *Washington Post,* made this point when he offered the following explanation for how Cold War and Gulf War doves could turn into Haiti and Balkan hawks:

> The crucial and obvious difference is this: Haiti, Bosnia and Kosovo were humanitarian ventures—fights for right and good, devoid of national interest. And only humanitarian intervention ... is morally pristine enough to justify the use of force.[3]

However true Krauthammer's criticism is, one thing is clear: Idealists almost never couch their support for a values-based foreign policy in terms of their nation's vital interests. Thus, even though realists and idealists view the world through fundamentally different lenses and even though they tend to offer divergent policy prescriptions, they do share one thing in common: They both regard the advance of democracy and human rights as purely "moral" goals. To the idealist, these goals may sometimes justify the use of force. To the realist, they never do. Still, both largely divorce these goals from vital national interests.

Yet when it comes to promoting democracy and human rights across the globe, the values and interests of the free world are one and the same. Indeed, democracy is inextricably linked to national and international security because of the mechanics of democratic societies. But before explaining why democracy supports national security, it is essential that we confront a few truths and myths about what a democracy is.

No Democracy Without Freedom

Though there are a number of features commonly associated with modern democratic society—the rule of law, constitutions, independent courts, political parties, a meaningful opposition, freedom of religion, freedom of the press, and so on—above all, democracies are closely linked in most people's minds with elections. Surely, no one would consider a country democratic if its government were not elected.

But elections are not a true test of a democracy. They are an instrument, one that can be applied well or badly. The same is true of a constitution: The Soviet Union had an impeccable constitution on paper, but it was not applied to the benefit of Soviet citizens in practice. It became a meaningless symbol. Elections can be just as meaningless in the hands of tyrants. Seeking the legitimacy conferred by democracy, they steal its most familiar set of clothes. But they never fit. Under Saddam's rule, for example, Iraqis were presented every few years with a ballot that gave them the option of voting "yes" or "no" to Saddam. Heads of state in Egypt, Syria, and elsewhere are "elected" from time to time in similar fashion. In Iran, candidates for election to its legislature, the Majlis, must first be approved by a religious authority, and in China, prospective representatives to the National People's Congress are first vetted by the Communist Party leadership.

Elections that do not unfairly restrict the choice of candidates are not necessarily any more democratic. Suppose that many names appear on the ballot but that voters are warned that unless they vote for a particular candidate, they will be killed or their land will be taken from them. Clearly, the fact that there are many candidates to choose from does not necessarily mean that people are free to choose.

Given this muddle, can elections ever be used to meaningfully differentiate democratic from nondemocratic societies? They can, provided we remember that for elections to be free, the voting booth must satisfy the same test as the town square: *Free elections are held in an environment where people are free to express their views without fear of arrest, imprisonment, or physical harm.* Put simply, free elections are elections in a free society.

That is why elections are never the beginning of the democratic process. Only when the basic institutions that protect a free society are firmly in place—such as a free press, the rule of law, independent courts, political parties—can free elections be held.

After defeating Hitler, the United States and other allied occupation forces wisely decided not to hold federal elections in Germany for four years. Had elections been held in 1945 or 1946, the results probably would have undermined efforts to build German democracy, something those who hope to help build democratic societies in Afghanistan and Iraq would be wise to keep in mind.

When the Taliban and Saddam were toppled, the fear societies they ruled did not change overnight. While there are undoubtedly fewer Afghans and Iraqis today who are afraid to voice their opinions than there were a couple of years ago, there are still significant portions of these populations afraid to express their views. Until the overwhelming majority of Iraqis and Afghans live without fear of speaking their minds, elections are just as likely to weaken efforts to build democracy as they are to strengthen them. Thus, the goal of those who genuinely want to advance democracy in these countries would be better served by worrying less about how quickly elections are held and more about making the atmosphere in which they will eventually take place as free as possible.

A society that is not free but in which elections are held

should never be considered democratic. Those who would use the potentially dangerous repercussions of elections in fear societies as "proof" of the dangers of democracy are presenting a phony argument—no less phony than if someone would have argued in 1945 that because elections in Germany might have left the Nazis in power, democracy in Germany was dangerous. The dangers that the skeptics have in mind have nothing to do with democracy per se. At most, they deal with the dangers involved in the *transition* to democracy. Clearly, this transition can be long and arduous: The transformation of a fear society to a free society, where the basic right of dissent is protected, to a fully democratic society, where the institutions that protect dissent and sustain freedom are well established, can take many years, even decades. But skeptics should not be able to twist a legitimate debate over *how* democracy can best be established in a particular place into an erroneous assertion that democracy should never be established there at all.

Of course, free elections can bring nondemocrats to power, as was the case in Germany in 1933. But what followed the Nazi ascension to power does not prove that democracy is dangerous. It proves that democracy must *always* be protected. For it was not a democratic election that made Germany a threat to the world but rather the destruction of Germany's free society and the eventual suspension of its democracy. Those who claim that democracy is dangerous for the free world must show that free societies with freely elected governments are dangerous to the world. This, I am quite sure, will prove considerably more difficult.

THE MECHANICS OF DEMOCRACY

Democracies, it is often observed, do not go to war with one another. That scholars have taken to combing the annals of diplomatic history in search of notable exceptions only proves the rule. But though this familiar axiom is often stated as if it needs no further explanation, the logic behind it is crucial for any understanding of the link between democracy and security.

Why don't democracies go to war with one another? Many think the answer lies in the shared values of peoples living in democratic states, such as respect for human life, a love of peace, tolerance of difference, and the desire to improve one's standard of living. These values are believed to make democratic peoples reluctant to fight wars, in which lives are lost and property is destroyed, unless the citizens of the democracies believe there are no alternatives. A measure of the depth of this reluctance is that no matter how large the dispute between modern democracies, the prospect of wars breaking out between them is almost inconceivable. For instance, the idea that tensions between the U.S. and France over intervention in Iraq could precipitate a war between the two countries is laughable. Similarly, the visits by Japanese prime ministers to the shrine honoring Japanese soldiers killed in World War II is deeply offensive to South Koreans, but such visits will not trigger a war between the two Asian democracies. Even an issue as divisive and seemingly intractable as Northern Ireland will never be resolved by war between a democratic Great

Britain and a democratic Ireland. The majority of Americans, Frenchmen, Japanese, Koreans, Britons, and Irishmen, like all democratic peoples, will always try to resolve their differences through nonviolent means.

Still, it is not clear that the preference for the nonviolent resolution of differences is not also shared by people subject to nondemocratic regimes. After all, how many people would want to bear the risks, economic deprivations, and uncertainties of war if other options are available? Do Iranians not want peace and security for their families? Do North Koreans not want to give their children a better future? There may be individuals in every society who do prefer war to peace. They may stand to profit from war or their bellicosity may be the product of a fanatical ideology that rejects peace or of systematic brainwashing. But it is highly doubtful that one would find a *majority* of any people on the planet who would choose death over life.

Some might ask how I, as an Israeli, can believe this when there are so many Palestinians who appear willing to martyr themselves and their children for the Palestinian cause. The answer is that we should not assume that all or even most of the Palestinians who hate Israel are willing to die fighting wars or waging a terror campaign against the Jewish state. There is no question that many Palestinians harbor a deep hatred for Israel. The combination of genuine misery among the Palestinian population coupled with an Arab leadership in general, and a Palestinian leadership in particular, that has blamed Israel for all that suffering fuels such animosity. But this acute hatred does not necessarily translate into a willingness to die. As for the public rhetoric of the "Palestinian masses," we must not be deceived into believing Palestinian doublethink. In a Palestinian society, where dissent against the regime is not tolerated, where the livelihood of hundreds of thousands is tied to the regime, expressing a willingness to die in the struggle against the Jewish state has unfortunately become widespread.

As is the case in any fear society, the true believers among the Palestinians are far fewer in number than we assume. We should remember that those who represent the true believers—from the Nazi regime that ruled Germany between 1933 and 1945 to the mullocracy that has controlled Iran for the last quarter century to the Communist party that has governed China for over five decades—all seized their power through nondemocratic means or suspended democracy once they came to power. Never confident that they represented the majority, they were never willing to subject themselves to a free election despite the enormous legitimacy such an election would provide. Those who advocate "one man, one vote, one time" may mask their hostility to democratic rule behind an ideological facade, but the real reason they don't want free elections is that they realize they cannot stay in power if people are free to reject their ideas.

So if the majority of people in all societies are inherently peace-loving, then what is so unique about democracies that keeps them from waging war with one another? The answer can be found in the political mechanics of every democratic society. Democratic leaders depend on their people. Therefore they have an enormous incentive to satisfy the demands of their constituencies if they want to stay in power. In democracies, the personal interests of the political leadership, even the most venal among them, is effectively tied to improving the lives of those they govern. Those leaders who are perceived to be delivering peace and prosperity tend to be reelected, while those who are not tend to be removed from office.

As the United States learned during Vietnam, and the government of Spain learned during the recent war in Iraq, no democratic government will be able to fight a protracted war that the majority of its citizens does not support. This is especially true when the costs of war are felt close to home. If democratic peoples believe there is an alternative to war— whether that alternative is real or imagined is immaterial— they will demand that their government pursue it. And a democratic government that does not heed the will of the people will sooner or later be replaced by one that does.

Thus, the critical factor that prevents democratic nations from fighting against each other is not values that are particular to democratic peoples but rather the fact that *the power of a democratic government is ultimately dependent on the popular will.* When two democratic states are faced with an issue that can potentially lead to conflict, their leaders, whose own power depends on citizens who see war as a last resort, will do everything possible to avoid war and reach a compromise.

For this reason, democratic leaders also have a propensity towards appeasement. Their first instinct is to seek a peaceful solution first, and they are slow to relinquish this approach. War is almost always seen as an expensive, disruptive last resort, and few democratic leaders embrace the prospect with anything other than extreme caution. Indeed, so strong is the popular antipathy to war that democratic societies are at a disadvantage when confronting threats that require preemptive military action. In response to their voters, most democratic leaders will be inhibited by a pacific reflex, be slow to act, and be overly cautious. This propensity for appeasement can be extremely dangerous if potential threats that could have been nipped in the bud are instead allowed to grow more dangerous.

The cynic who points out that democratic leaders are no better than nondemocratic rulers, since both are only concerned with staying in power, is missing the point. Even if the *motives* of both leaders are identical, the different systems in which they operate will ensure that their *actions* remain worlds apart. Democratic presidents and prime ministers may want to stay in power forever, but the nature of democratic politics makes that practically impossible. In democracies, even the most popular leaders are forced to contend with a host of factors that can eventually lead to their defeat at the polls: a free press that exposes their failures at every turn, an opposition that keeps those failures in the public eye, internal opponents eager to climb the rungs of power, the often mutually exclusive demands of constituents, the vicissitudes of economic and political life, and much more. Some democratic countries, such as U.S. and

France, place limits on the number of terms their heads of government can serve. In those that do not, even the finest leaders are bound to lose an election, as Winston Churchill's electoral defeat in 1945 only weeks after the German surrender attests. Try as they might to avoid defeat, no democratically elected president or prime minister will be able to stay in power indefinitely.

Nondemocratic leaders, on the other hand, have far more tools at their disposal to ensure they never relinquish power. The dynamics that force their democratic counterparts from office are systematically controlled or thwarted. If they subject themselves to a vote, it is a carefully orchestrated fraud. If they allow their actions to be reported, the press serves as a mouthpiece of the regime. If they face a challenge from within, they suppress it. If they face meaningful opposition, they ban it. If they face popular dissent, they crush it. In other words, to stay in power, nondemocratic leaders invariably build and maintain fear societies.

In a fear society, the mechanism that makes the interests of the ruler and the ruled converge breaks down. *Dictators do not depend on their people; their people depend on them.* One does not have to be an expert in political science to understand that what is good for dictators is rarely what is good for their subjects. Cuba's Fidel Castro and North Korea's ruling family have remained in power for decades despite impoverishing their respective countries. To these dictators, what is important is not improving the lives of their subjects, but controlling them.

THE CREATION OF EXTERNAL ENEMIES

A fear society controls its subjects first and foremost through physical force, whether in the form of a special security guard that protects the leader or a secret police that stifles dissent. Control over a society's economic affairs is another important tool of regimes that are based on fear. But while guns and butter may keep rebellion at bay, they will not win the hearts and minds of the cadre of loyal supporters that is critical if a fear society is to function. If fear societies rely on physical power alone to repress dissent, the number of true believers will shrink very rapidly and the number of doublethinkers will grow just as fast, widening the circle of potential opponents of the regime. Maintaining the convictions of true believers and trying to recruit new ones becomes the primary preoccupation of all regimes that are based on fear.

But as we have seen, propaganda, state control of the media, personality cults, and so on will only go so far. The harsh reality of repression cannot be glossed over forever by creating a virtual world where heads of states are infallible, godlike leaders whose actions are applauded unreservedly. In time, the truth will emerge and the forces of disaffection will gather strength.

Accordingly, fear regimes look to other methods to stay in power. One of the oldest and most effective is the creation of external enemies. These external enemies are used by nondemocratic leaders to slow down the natural process of alienation within fear societies and even at times reverse it: The pool of true believers is maintained and double-thinkers are occasionally transformed back into loyalists.

In times of war, even in free societies, people are prepared to accept both economic hardships and curtailments of their freedoms. During World War II, few Americans protested when food was rationed and liberties were restricted. Similarly, after 9/11, large majorities in the Congress passed the Patriot Act, a bill that even its strongest supporters admit curbs certain freedoms. In both cases, the majority of Americans believed that war justified, even demanded, sacrifice.

The people who live in fear societies are no different. They too will make sacrifices if they are convinced that their safety demands it. That is why nondemocratic rulers find the threat of war a particularly attractive device for justifying the repression that is necessary to control their subjects and remain in power. By tapping into the strong national, religious, ethnic, or other sentiments that an "enemy" arouses, regimes in fear societies rally their people to their side and divert attention away from their subject's miserable living conditions and the regime's failure to improve them. The author of a 1997 book on the nature of dictatorship described the multiple benefits of an external enemy this way:

> The stability-enhancing effect of a regime's public defiance of external foes arises from the additional loyalty this defiance elicits from both society and the regime's personnel, notably the upper ranks of the party, military and security organs. In particular, the need to display

unity and stability in the face of the enemy is likely to discourage not only expressions of mass discontent but also moves within the regime to displace the present leadership.[4]

Because external enemies are an effective means of maintaining internal stability, governments in countries as diverse as Cuba, North Korea, and Iran all regard inculcating hatred towards outsiders as critical to their rule. By carefully indoctrinating their subjects, fear societies can keep them mobilized against an enemy and transform potential adversaries within their societies into supporters.

By waging an ideological war against the West, the Soviet regime was able to find an enemy that would help stabilize its rule for nearly seventy years. The military campaign of the Bolsheviks to win control of an empire that encompassed more than a hundred nations and religions was a relatively short one, finishing less than three years after it began in 1917. Yet even during that brief civil war, the means by which the regime would help prop itself up for generations to come were being carefully constructed. Lenin's self-proclaimed "Red Terror," directed against "class enemies" and "the agents of international capitalism and reaction," placed tens of thousands of people in what were the first "concentration camps" (Hitler borrowed the phrase from the Soviets before leaving his own indelible mark on it).

Lenin's successor, Stalin, appreciated the power of "class enemies" to stabilize a rule in which he murdered, exiled, and starved to death tens of millions of people. But he also understood that for the "class struggle" to become the central component of Soviet life, any obstacle that might militate against complete solidarity in fighting the enemy would have to be removed, including solidarity within the family. That was why every Soviet schoolboy came to know the story of Pavlik Marozov, the twelve-year-old boy who became a revolutionary "hero" when he turned his own parents in to the authorities for withholding grain.

Stalin also knew that the fear of amorphous enemies would not be sufficient to mobilize a hundred million people to take part in this historic class war. That is why he turned the economic race with the West into the main arena of the struggle. Stalin insisted that the need to "catch and overcome" the West—*Dognat y Peregnat* in Russian—was a question of life and death for the whole country. He posed a clear challenge to the Soviet people: "We are fifty or one hundred years behind the leading capitalist countries," Stalin proclaimed, and "we have to close the gap in ten."

Stalin unveiled a series of five-year economic plans for the country and meticulously turned the need to produce the ambitious quantities of goods they called for into the main focus of Soviet national life. Naturally, the "battle for coal" and the "battle for steel" would also need its heroes, men like Alexei Stachanov, the coalminer who was said to be able to produce fourteen times the amount of coal as the average worker, a feat everyone else was supposed to emulate.

The regime also manufactured anti-heroes, the "saboteurs" who on orders of Western countries were trying to destroy the Soviet economy, decrease its productivity, hide its coal, destroy its equipment, and do anything that might prevent the Soviets from reaching their economic goals. Show trials brought together a mix of political and economic leaders who were accused of being American, German, or French spies in order to reinforce the class struggle that everyone was engaged in. A typical trial would feature a local party official, a local factory manager, and the factory's engineer in a conspiracy to undermine the fulfillment of the five-year plan. The head of a factory might "confess" to making sure the new equipment he received would break down, and his engineer, would confess to rigging the equipment so that no one could repair it.

The extent to which Stalin's sophisticated propaganda efforts had penetrated the public's consciousness became clear to my father, a journalist, the day he was sent by his newspaper to report on the work being done at a local coal mine. The head of the coal mine, whipped up in the frenzy of the era and no doubt eager to prove his complete loyalty to the regime, decided to name his first child Dognat y Peregnat.

This vast effort to mobilize the Soviet people against an external enemy clearly affected the regime's foreign policies, especially its ability to lead the country to war. Like all populations, Soviet citizens preferred peace to war, but because the regime was constantly mobilizing the masses in class struggle, it found it relatively easy to mobilize them against a particular country that was cast as an agent of Western imperialism and aggression. Military campaigns, whether in

Finland in 1940, Hungary in 1956, Czechoslovakia in 1968, or Afghanistan in 1979, were always justified by the need to defend communism from its capitalist enemies. The external policies of the regime became an extension of the regime's constant effort to maintain internal stability.

During its seventy years, the Soviet regime used many enemies, external and internal, to stabilize its authority, but in its last four decades, none more so than the Jews. From the infamous Doctor's Plot, in which Stalin planned to blame Jews for trying to poison the Soviet leadership, to allegations that Soviet refuseniks like myself were Western spies, thwarting the "Zionist agents" was one of the regime's constant refrains. Though Hitler borrowed the concentration camp from Stalin, Stalin and his successors would learn from the German dictator that hatred for Jews could be the perfect glue to keep a fear society together, providing an "enemy" that was both internal and external, both old and new.

The former Soviet regime is certainly not unique in thinking that external enemies are the key to internal stability. For decades, the Assad family's Alawite dictatorship in Syria has used emergency laws to control the Syrian people, justifying these restrictive measures on the grounds that Israel threatens the security of the Syrian state. A half century after the Korean War, North Korea still demands from its people "iron-clad unity under leader-party-nation" to keep the country safe from "external predators." And the Saudi family, by giving more and more power to the Wahhabi religious authorities within its kingdom and more and more money to spreading their virulent form of Islam around the world, has used external enemies to whitewash its own decadent lifestyle and justify its repressive rule. While it was posturing in the West as a close ally of the United States and a force for stability in the Middle East, the policies of the Saudi regime were actually destabilizing the entire region by mobilizing millions for war against the West, Christians, Jews, and even fellow Muslims. Thus, the global spread of a fanaticism that now threatens our entire civilization is partly rooted in a nondemocratic Saudi regime's need for internal stability.

No Peace with Dictators

Now we can see why nondemocratic regimes imperil the security of the world. They stay in power by controlling their populations. This control invariably requires an increasing amount of repression. To justify this repression and maintain internal stability, external enemies must be manufactured. *The result is that while the mechanics of democracy make democracies inherently peaceful, the mechanics of tyranny make nondemocracies inherently belligerent.* Indeed, in order to avoid collapsing from within, fear societies must maintain a perpetual state of conflict.

Nondemocratic societies have always been powder kegs ready to explode, but today the force of that explosion can be far more lethal than it was in the past. In an age of weapons of mass destruction and global terrorism, the dangers of ignoring the absence of democracy in any part of the world have increased dramatically.

For a half century, the totalitarian regime in Pyongyang has threatened the security of South Korea. Once it developed long-range missiles, it threatened the security of neighboring Japan and endangered other countries with the proliferation of ballistic missile technology. Now that Pyongyang has reportedly developed nuclear weapons—weapons that can be provided to international terrorist organizations—it endangers the security of the entire world.

The threat posed by North Korea is not a function of the increase of the destructive capacity of its weapons. Rather, it is the enhanced capacity of its weapons *coupled* with the nature of its regime that is the source of the problem. Just as nuclear weapons in the hands of a democratizing Russia do not pose the same threat as they did in the hands of the Soviet Union, the weapons of a democratic North Korea would pose no greater danger to the world than if they would be in the hands of a democratic South Korea. In the hands of leaders whose power is dependent on people who see war as a last resort, weapons of mass destruction will be a weapon of last resort. But in the hands of leaders whose survival depends on maintaining a constant state of tension, the danger of these weapons being used directly, or via terrorist proxies, increases enormously.

That is not to say that nondemocratic regimes will never sign peace agreements. From time to time, if it suits their interests, they will. But we must remember that for these regimes, the decision to wage war or make peace is not based upon its impact on the public welfare but on whether it strengthens the regime's control. To democratic governments, whose power is ultimately dependent on the popular will, peace is always an interest. To nondemocratic regimes, peace and war are merely interchangeable methods of subjugation. One day staying in power will necessitate making peace. The next, it will necessitate waging war. That is why a genuine and lasting peace can only be made with democracies.

My fellow Israelis point to the 1979 peace treaty with Egypt and to the twenty-five years of quiet that has prevailed on Israel's southern border as proof that I am wrong. I remind them that our border with Syria, with whom we do not have a peace treaty, has been just as quiet, and suggest that Israeli deterrence is responsible for both. I ask them to consider why, if Israel and Egypt are truly at peace, a future war between the two countries is far from inconceivable? And I inform them of something of which they are generally unaware: Since signing its peace treaty with Israel, Egypt has become one of the most anti-Semitic countries in the entire Arab world.

In fact, the virulent hatred that emanates from Egypt today is a perfect illustration of a dictatorship's use of an external enemy for internal stability. In return for signing a peace treaty with Israel, Egypt received the Sinai Peninsula that Israel captured during the 1967 Six Day War as well as tens of billions of dollars in aid from the United States—aid that helped Egypt upgrade the quality of its antiquated weapons systems. But in making peace with Israel, Egypt was also in danger of losing the "Zionist enemy" that had long helped the regime justify its repressive policies and excuse its immense failure to improve the lives of most Egyptians.

It is not surprising that in the twenty-five years since the Israeli-Egyptian peace accord was signed, the Egyptian government has tried to take all the benefits of the peace agreement—that is, territory, money, legitimacy—without paying the price. Genuine normalization would have required the government to stop fueling hatred toward Israel and start educating Egyptians for a life of peaceful coexistence. But that was something Egypt's inherently unstable nondemocratic regime, which has ruled Egypt under emergency decree for over two decades, can ill afford. Instead, the regime's continuing need for external enemies has resulted in the indoctrination of yet another generation of Egyptians to hate Israel.

The Egyptian government's incitement of its population against Israel, despite the formal peace treaty between the two countries, should remind us of the strong relationship that exists between the level of internal freedom in a society and the degree of its external belligerency. This relationship also becomes obvious when looking at how the various Arab states treat Israel and Jews. Ask an Israeli to rank the governments of the following countries—Syria, Egypt, Morocco, Jordan, and Turkey—according to the nature of their attitude toward Israel and Jews, and you are most likely to get the following answer: Turkey will be seen as the friendliest, followed by Morocco, Jordan, Egypt, and lastly, Syria.

The same order, however, is also observed by simply

opening the latest Freedom House report. Freedom House, a nonprofit organization devoted to spreading democracy and freedom around the world, ranks the degree of political freedom and civil liberties in every country. Countries are given a score of 1 to 7, with 1 being the most free and 7 the most unfree. Dozens of parameters are used to derive a country's score, but none have anything to do with a state's foreign policy. Yet the countries mentioned above would end up in the exact same order, with Turkey (a 3–4 freedom ranking) first, followed by Morroco (5), Jordan (5–6), Egypt (6), and Syria (7). The report only confirms that the more free a society is, the less belligerent it is likely to be toward its neighbors.

MORE WESTERN ILLUSIONS

The failure to appreciate the inherent belligerency of all nondemocratic regimes results in the dangerous illusion that they can serve as reliable allies in preserving international peace and stability. Their shortcomings are overlooked and their support is often seen as critical to fighting greater evils, such as Islamic fundamentalism. Tolerating their illiberal excesses is considered an acceptable price to pay for achieving a far more important objective.

I am certain that the faith many have that today's nondemocratic states will serve as a bulwark against greater evils is as misguided as the World War II Allies' faith that Stalin would not sign a treaty with Hitler's Germany. (He did, in August 1939, and was drawn into the war on the side of

America and the Allies only when the Soviet Union was attacked by Hitler.) Saddam's secular regime, once seen by the free world as a check against a fundamentalist Iranian threat, proved to be no less dangerous to international peace and security than the regime in Tehran. Similarly, many hoped that Yasser Arafat's Palestinian Authority would fight against fundamentalist terrorist organizations like Hamas and Islamic Jihad and make peace with Israel, only to be proven wrong time and again.

Unfortunately, even when the folly of the assumption that a nondemocratic regime will help preserve stability is exposed, fingers are far more likely to be pointed at the bad faith of a particular leader rather than at the inherent belligerency of the regimes in which those leaders operate. After his "election" in 1997, Iran's new president, Moummad Khatami, was hailed as a moderate reformer. Seeing the external threat posed by Iran as largely the product of individual personalities, many believed that the more "open-minded" Iranian president would help usher in a new relationship between Iran and the West. Even after it became apparent that the West's faith in Khatami was misplaced, the failure was attributed to betting on the wrong leader rather than on the belligerent nature of Iran's nondemocratic regime.

The dangerous notion that it is the individual leader who defines a regime, rather than the relationship between the leader and his or her people, is deeply seated in today's political reality. Former U.S. Senator George Mitchell, a highly intelligent man who has played important roles in international peace negotiations, was asked in a public lecture to what extent Yasser Arafat's personality is essential for progress in solving the Middle East conflict. His answer was that, in international relations, personality is everything.

To support his statement, he pointed to Czechoslovakia and Yugoslavia. In Czechoslovakia, the president was Václav Havel; in Yugoslavia, it was Slobodan Milosevic. Czechoslovakia, he said, was split into two countries without any violence, and Yugoslavia was overrun by a horrendous war. Mitchell asked the audience to consider what would have been the case if Havel had been in Yugoslavia and Milosevic in Czechoslovakia. Everything would have been different, Mitchell said, both with Czechoslovakia and with Yugoslavia.

But Mitchell has the argument back to front: Havel emerged in Czechoslovakia precisely because the traditions of a free society existed there. Even under communist control, the Czechs elected Alexander Dubcek in 1968, and democratic structures, in a virtually underground form, always were present. So, when the Eastern Bloc collapsed, Czechoslovakia quickly became a free society and was able to hold free elections in short order. In contrast there was no "Sarajevo Spring" under Tito. In fact, a Stalin-like cult of personality continued in Yugoslavia for decades. Yugoslavia had never been a free society, and a despot like Milosevic could emerge under those conditions. He was not the product of free elections. He was the product of a nondemocratic regime.

Once the mechanics of democracy and the mechanics of

tyranny are properly understood, the notion that peace and security in our world can be better served by supporting friendly dictators than by building belligerent democracies is exposed as nonsense. Since all democratic societies strive for peace, there is no such thing as a belligerent democracy. The advance of democracy does not pose a threat to international peace and security. In fact, the more free a society becomes, the less dangerous it will be. When the voice of the people can be heard, the chances of war are greatly diminished, and when a free people governs itself, the chances of a war being fought against other free peoples is removed almost entirely.

Freedom's skeptics must understand that the democracy that hates you is less dangerous than the dictator who loves you. Indeed, it is the absence of democracy that represents the real threat to peace. The concept of the friendly dictator is a figment of our imagination because the internal dynamics of nondemocratic rule will always require external enemies. Today, the dictator's enemy may be your enemy. But tomorrow, his enemy may be you.

CHAPTER 4

Mission Possible

THE WAR ON TERROR in general, and the war in Iraq in particular, have raised two central questions: Can the free world help transform fear societies into free societies? If so, how? To some, the options for exporting democracy are fairly limited. Democracy, the skeptics warn, cannot be "imposed" from the outside. The transformation of a fear society into a free society, if it is to occur at all, must come from within. This view greatly underestimates the power of the free world to help bring democracy to countries that have never known it. Worse, the failure to exercise that power undermines the cause of freedom.

The Skeptics Abound

Days after the war in Iraq began in 2003, President Bush declared that it would end only when a free society would be established there.

> Our entire coalition has a job to do and it will not end with the liberation of Iraq. We will help the Iraqi people to find the benefits and assume the duties of self-government. The form of those institutions will arise from Iraq's own culture and choices.... [Iraqis] deserve better than a life spent bowing before a dictator. The people of Iraq deserve to stand as free men and free women—the citizens of a free country.[1]

Initially, Bush's professed commitment to seeing a free society emerge in Iraq might have been dismissed as little more than the flowery rhetoric that often accompanies war. However, when the U.S. president continued to reiterate his commitment to this goal in the face of unremitting attacks on coalition forces in Iraq and mounting casualties, it was clear that his earlier promises were more than lip service. In April 2004, after two particularly bloody weeks for U.S. forces in Iraq, he went so far as to call the policy of building a free Iraq "an historic opportunity to change the world."[2]

While Bush was insisting his administration would stay the course, confidence in the ability of America, or anyone else for that matter, to help build a free Iraq was waning by the day. Fouad Ajami, a keen observer of the Middle East, noted the changing mood in an opinion column in the *New York Times* entitled "Iraq May Survive but the Dream Is Dead":

> If some of the war's planners thought that Iraq would be an ideal base for American primacy in the Persian Gulf, a beacon from which to spread democracy and reason throughout the Arab world, that notion has clearly been set aside.... No foreign sword, however swift and mighty could cut through the Gordian knot of a tangled Arab history.[3]

Another *New York Times* columnist dismissed the idea of building a democratic Iraq as a "childish fantasy."[4] A senator from Kansas was even more blunt: "Liberty cannot be laid down like so much Astroturf."[5] As the editorials in prominent conservative magazines questioning the wisdom of Bush's Wilsonian notion of implanting democracy can attest, even many of those who had initially backed the goal of a free Iraq were clearly having second thoughts.

As long as the establishment of a democratic society in Iraq appears remote, the skeptics will have the upper hand. Nevertheless, the challenge should be put in perspective. Whatever the chances of democracy taking root in Iraq over the next few years, most people would probably admit that they are better than the chances of democracy taking hold in Syria or Saudi Arabia. The toppling of Saddam, coupled with America's determination to see a free society emerge in Iraq, would seem to offer Iraqis more hope than their Arab neighbors of undergoing a democratic transformation.

Compared to those Arab states, however, the prospects that North Korea or China can be transformed into democracies any time soon are even more remote. Some argue that free trade and sound diplomacy will eventually make both China and North Korea look no different than their democratic brethren in Taiwan and South Korea. But even the most ardent advocates of engagement will see a free China or a free North Korea as perhaps decades away; a military confrontation with those countries—as is not the case with Syria or Saudi Arabia—would come with an extremely high price tag.

Yet those convinced that the free world is powerless to help democracy take root in countries like Saudi Arabia, Syria, North Korea, and China would do well to remember that a generation ago, policymakers felt even more impotent with respect to the Soviet Union. Indeed, hardly anyone believed that the West could help trigger a democratic transformation inside the USSR.

THE SOVIET JUGGERNAUT

In the 1970s, America appeared to be reeling from crisis to crisis. The cumulative effects of the Arab oil embargo, defeat in Vietnam, the Watergate scandal, sky-high inflation, and double-digit unemployment prompted some to speak at the end of the decade of a "crisis of confidence." In contrast, the Soviet Union, a rapidly expanding military and industrial power that was inspiring the spread of collectivist ideologies across the world, seemed stronger and more confident than ever.

In those years, the idea that U.S. policy could help fundamentally transform the world behind the Iron Curtain was regarded as absolutely ridiculous. To policymakers on both the Left and Right, the Soviet Union might be resisted or accommodated from without, but it could definitely not be changed from within. Doves and hawks in the United States frequently waged pitched battles over the best nuclear strategy to deter a Soviet attack, the appropriate foreign policy to thwart Soviet expansionism, and a host of other Cold War–related issues. But these policy disagreements hid a larger consensus: Containment, in stronger or weaker form, was the only option.

It was not that people were oblivious to how the Soviet regime treated its own citizens. The invasion of Czechoslovakia in 1968 left only the most delusional in the West clinging to a vision of a post-Stalinist paradise in the USSR. Still, with the Soviet Union widely perceived as a strong, stable, and durable superpower, hardly anyone believed that America had the power to end Soviet tyranny. Pressing for democratic change might have sounded nice in principle, but in practice it was considered a toothless proposition. Even among those advocating a highly confrontational policy toward the USSR, one would have been hard pressed to find more than a handful of people who seriously thought that the internal structure of the Soviet totalitarian state could be changed.

And so, by the early 1970s, having witnessed the enormous increase in Soviet strength over the first two decades of the Cold War and fearful of the existential dangers of continued confrontation, most "prudent" statesmen supported efforts to reach an accommodation with the Soviets. The foremost champion of détente was Henry Kissinger, who would rise to global prominence as President Nixon's national security adviser and would later serve as secretary of state in both the Nixon and Ford administrations.

A devoted pupil of the realist school of foreign policy, Kissinger immediately went to work doing what realists do: deemphasizing the ideological and moral dimension of foreign policy. Kissinger thought that by framing the conflict between the superpowers as a zero-sum moral struggle between communism and capitalism or between freedom and tyranny, America's ideological foreign policy was precluding the possibility of achieving a long-term balance-of-power equilibrium between the sides. To Kissinger, who saw the USSR less as a totalitarian state with unbridled ambition and more as a great power with traditional expansionist aims, such an equilibrium was well within the grasp of American statecraft. Kissinger believed that by breaking free of the ideological straitjacket that had restricted U.S. diplomacy in the past, he could succeed in forging a "structure of peace" with the Soviets that would preserve order and stability around the world and advance American interests.

> Our objective must be twofold: We must prevent the Soviet Union from translating its military strength into political advantage, and for that we have to be strong and determined. And, at the same time, we must move

beyond a policy of constant confrontation toward the construction of a more stable relationship between the superpowers. Our purpose is to avoid, if we can, a situation where a succession of crises slides us into a world conflagration.... Frankly we do not believe there is any reasonable alternative.[6]

Kissinger found a willing partner in the USSR. The conferences, summits, and agreements that followed in short order promised hope of a new era of superpower relations. That at least is what the advocates of détente believed. But what they did not understand back then, and what their intellectual heirs still do not understand today, is that the positive response of a fear society to outside efforts of "engagement" is not a mark of peaceful intentions but merely a different tactic in an ongoing strategy of survival.

HOW FEAR SOCIETIES AVOID COLLAPSE

We have seen that the percentage of doublethinkers in a fear society increases over time. This growing disaffection forces the ruling regime to devote more and more resources to maintaining control over its own people. But why can't a fear society control its people indefinitely? A year before Amalrik published his book, Andrei Sakharov provided the answer. In an essay addressed to the Soviet leadership in 1968—an essay that would turn the most revered and decorated citizen of the country into a persona non grata of the regime literally overnight—Sakharov warned that a society that restricts intellectual freedom and prevents the free exchange of ideas would be unable to compete with societies that unleash the creative potential of their peoples. He described the fifty-year competition between the Soviet Union and the United States as a race between two cross-country skiers over deep snow. The United States had once been far ahead, Sakharov explained, and for many years the Soviets were believed to be closing the gap. Sakharov claimed, however, that the pace of Soviet "progress" was an illusion. The Soviets only appeared to be gaining ground because they were importing Western technology and science, which allowed them to ski with considerably less effort over the smooth tracks made by the United States. By leading the world in the cutting-edge fields of tomorrow, America's free society was traversing the deep snow. The USSR's lack of freedom was consigning the superpower to the role of follower, able to use the hard work of others to move forward, but incapable of charging ahead on its own.

To today's reader, Sakharov's words look rather measured. In this first essay, the man who would become the country's foremost dissident did not launch an intellectual assault against communist ideals nor did he dismiss the possibility of reforming the extant system. Rather, he was arguing for a socialism that was more free, more efficient, more human. But coming from the person who stood atop the pyramid of Soviet scientific achievement, the essay was a devastating blow. How could it not be for a regime whose lifeblood was conflict with the West and the inexorable victory of communism over Western capitalism—a victory which was then claimed to be only a decade away? At a time when leaders in the West were convincing themselves that the immense power of the USSR made reaching an accommodation with the superpower the only prudent course of action, Sakharov was saying that the Soviet emperor had no clothes: In a technological race with a free society, the Soviet's fear society could never win.

The weakness that Sakharov and Amalrik had exposed is true of all fear societies. A regime based on fear *must* maintain increasingly tight control over its population to remain in power, and such control *inevitably* triggers a process of decay. Outward signs of this decay may take some time to emerge. In fact, if a fear society is blessed with abundant natural resources, the society may prosper even when the process of internal dissolution is well under way. This is what occurred during the middle decades of the twentieth century in the Soviet Union. Rich reserves of coal, oil, iron, aluminum, diamonds, and many other commodities provided the means to sustain the regime's total control over its own people. Moreover, in an age of industrialization and mass production, methods perfected elsewhere could be put to use in the Soviet's command-and-control economy. But in an information age, when technological innovation was becoming increasingly dependent on the free flow of ideas, the Soviet's sclerotic fear society was destined to fall further and further behind the West.

In Saudi Arabia, where a degenerating fear society has been hidden for decades beneath a sea of oil, a similar breakdown is setting in. The hundreds of billions of petrodollars that have poured into the country have built cities, paved roads, and created enormous wealth and power for the regime. But as populations explode and oil revenues dwindle, the inability of the Saudi's fear society to generate growth from within will become more and more apparent. The Saudis control their fear society through a number of institutions, including those that support a global Islamist network. As these institutions come under increasing strain, Saudi Arabia and the regime that rules it will face the same bitter fate that awaits all fear societies: stagnation, regression, and eventually collapse. This process is inexorable. The only way to slow it down is to seek help from the outside. If it is unable to generate enough energy from within to provide the means to indefinitely control its people, a fear society must parasitically feed off the resources of others to recharge its depleting batteries.

This is precisely what the Soviets expected from détente. Through trade and economic benefits, as well as technological and scientific know-how, the Soviets hoped détente would bridge what was by then a widening gap with the West without forcing the regime to relax its grip over its subjects. Equally important, by restricting potential sources of competition with the West, détente would allow the Soviets to avoid a fight they were ill-equipped to win. By making it possible for scientific and technological progress to exist simultaneously with tyranny, détente would allow it to avoid crumbling from within.

FRIEND AND FOE

Overt cooperation with the West would, however, pose a new danger to the Soviets. How could the communist regime give up the ideological enemy that had served so well since the Bolshevik revolution in 1919 to stabilize its rule? Here too, the Soviets were confronting a problem faced by all fear societies. On the one hand, they need a lifeline from the outside, which necessitates cooperation with other states. On the other hand, maintaining a fear society almost always demands external enemies.

Smaller fear societies can easily resolve this dilemma by turning to larger ones for support. The tyrannical regime in North Korea has maintained power for decades because the Soviet Union or China has provided it with the resources necessary to sustain a repressive rule over the North Korean people, while South Korea and Japan have served as the external enemies that justify that repression. Other satellites of the Soviet Union, such as Cuba and Hungary, survived during the Cold War by playing a similar game. They were bankrolled by Moscow and used America as an ideological foil.

Smaller fear societies can also turn to larger free societies for support. The Cold War made this strategy possible for several dictators across the world, who used their opposition to communism to win support in the West. Here, the roles may have been reversed, with Washington underwriting the regime and Moscow serving as Public Enemy Number One, but the principle was the same: Plug into an outside source of power and mobilize people against an external enemy.

The problem for the Soviet Union was that it was at the top of the fear society food chain. There was no larger totalitarian sponsor who could bail them out and foot the bills. The only place they could turn for help was to the West— the very same West they had demonized for generations. In effect, the Soviets faced a seemingly irresolvable dilemma: The West would have to serve as *both* a friend and an enemy.

The process of détente built the new friendship; meanwhile the totalitarian regime maintained the old enemy. The Soviets seized the opportunity offered by détente to extract a range of concessions, including technology transfers, favorable arms control agreements, and preferential trading terms. At the same time, the regime stabilized its power at home by preaching hatred of the West to its own people and keeping "world revolution" alive across the globe. While Nixon and Kissinger were hailing the successes of détente and the "moderation" of Soviet foreign policy it had induced, the Soviets were turning the screws on their own people and fomenting wars in the Middle East, the Horn of Africa, and Central America. That the West would allow itself to be fooled by such duplicity only shows how powerful are its illusions that trade and contacts bring people closer together and always spur positive change. The dizzying momentum of high-level negotiations, elaborate summits, and detailed agreements blinded the free world to what was really happening.

But we dissidents did not lose our bearings. We saw détente as a foolish and misguided policy and counseled a different course. The Soviet's fear society was dependent on the West. *Why not use that dependency as leverage to force the regime to make a real choice?* Why not make clear to the Soviet leadership that the West could be a friend or a foe, but not both? If the Soviets wanted trade benefits, technology transfers, and scientific cooperation, they would have to reform a fear society that was mobilized for perpetual war against the West. If they wanted to keep that fear society intact, they would have to sacrifice Western largesse and face the consequences of renewed competition and confrontation. Whatever the choice, the days of the Soviet's fear society would be numbered.

Our conviction that a determined West could help transform the Soviet Union from within was not shared by most democratic leaders, who could not look beyond the facade of Soviet power to see a totalitarian society that was on its deathbed.

Fortunately, there were other leaders who understood the power of democratic ideals to change the world. They took steps to pry open the repressive Soviet society by forging a link between the foreign policy of the United States and the Soviet regime's respect for the rights of its own citizens. It was their faith in freedom that helped the West win the Cold War and helped the people of the USSR win our freedom.

SOVIET JEWS AWAKEN

The struggle to free Soviet Jewry, which began some years before the debate over détente, played a critical role in reversing the policy of détente and triggering a new approach toward the USSR. For the over two million Jews behind the Iron Curtain, 1967 was a watershed year. In the days leading up to the Six Day War, anti-Zionist propaganda within the Soviet Union, always present to some degree, reached a fever pitch. Meetings of workers were organized throughout the country to publicly condemn Zionism and Israel, and the official media vociferously denounced the Jewish state. As might be expected, anti-Semitism rose dramatically in a climate where attacks against Jews were justified as legitimate attacks against "Zionists."

Although most Soviet Jews were totally assimilated without the slightest ties to Israel, they were nonetheless suspected of being Zionist loyalists who were supporting the hostile forces of "imperialist aggression" against the Soviet Union's Arab allies. Whether they liked it or not, Soviet Jews with little or no connection to their religion or their people suddenly found their own self-respect tied to the fate of a tiny Middle Eastern nation thousands of miles away struggling for its existence. And the more we Jews were treated as if that distant conflict was our war, the more many of us began to internalize the idea that we and the Jewish state shared a common destiny.

With Arab leaders promising to "throw all the Jews into the sea," a besieged Israel won a lightning victory over the Soviet-armed militaries of Egypt, Syria, and Jordan. In less than a week, Israel had captured the Sinai Desert, the Golan Heights, the West Bank, and the Gaza Strip. Most important of all, Israel had reunited its ancient capital of Jerusalem. When it became clear that yesterday's underdogs, the small weak state that its enemies boasted would soon be wiped off the map, had won a miraculous victory over Soviet-trained forces, the connection we Soviet Jews felt with Israel only intensified. As we began to see ourselves in a new light, so too did non-Jews. Before the war, Jews were the object of ridicule and contempt in the USSR; now we had earned a grudging respect. Even the anti-Semitic jokes reflected the change in attitude: Jews went from being branded greedy cowards to being vilified as bullies with too much *chutzpah*.

Fortified by the sense of interconnection with the Jewish state and a growing ethnic pride, many Jews began seriously to consider emigrating to Israel despite the dangers involved in applying for an exit visa. Citizens of the USSR had no right to leave the country, and merely expressing a desire to leave was almost unheard of in a society where all dissent was banned. The innocent step of asking to leave the Soviet Union was a clear sign that doublethinkers—which almost all Soviet Jews were—had crossed the line and become dissenters. Such an act of open defiance, particularly on a wide scale, could never be permitted, so a number of steps were taken by the regime to prevent it. First, the only emigration that was allowed was for "family reunification." In fact, one could not even apply for an exit visa under this strictly regulated provision without having an official "invitation" from a relative abroad. Second, those who did apply were threatened, interrogated, stripped of their jobs, and occasionally thrown in prison. Third, the regime ensured that the "turncoats" and their families would be treated thereafter as social outcasts.

Notwithstanding these perils, the number of Jews applying to emigrate to Israel in the wake of the Six Day War began to rise dramatically. This was the result of both a strong identification with Israel and the support of Jews in the West, who quickly rallied to the side of their brethren trapped behind the Iron Curtain and who proved remarkably effective at mobilizing international pressure against the regime in Moscow. Jews inside the Soviet Union knew that the growing activism on their behalf in the free world would make it far more difficult for a regime bent on wooing the West to punish those who had applied to leave.

By the early 1970s, the number of Soviet Jews asking for invitations was in the tens of thousands. The Soviet leadership, suddenly faced with a serious challenge to their authority, took steps to stop the Jewish exodus. Since the regime did not want to endanger détente by shutting the gates completely, it embarked on a two-pronged strategy. First, it allowed a few thousand Jews to leave, but in parallel, it organized public trials against "Zionists" and persecuted "refuseniks," the name given to Jews who were denied an exit visa. The plan was to send a clear message to all Soviet Jews that the consequences for most of those who would apply to leave would be disastrous.

The strategy failed. Instead of deterring Soviet Jews, the high-profile trials convinced them how pervasive the desire to leave had become. Moreover, the trials showcased their plight, galvanizing world Jewry still further and increasing pressure on the regime to open the gates. The Soviet regime next tried to curb emigration by imposing a hefty education tax on those leaving the USSR. The tax was roughly five to ten times the average annual wage, a sum few citizens in the land of "each according to his needs" could afford. Claiming it was merely a reimbursement for the cost of government-funded higher education, the Soviets thought they had found a "legitimate" way to limit emigration to a trickle.

This served to mobilize Jewish groups outside the USSR even more. These groups raised awareness of what was happening, and teachers, scientists, intellectuals, politicians, and other groups organized protests to pressure the Soviets to reverse their policy. Naturally, they also appealed to the Nixon administration for help. But Kissinger remained convinced that quiet diplomacy had succeeded in steadily improving the emigration practices of the Soviets and that détente was the best way to address the current problem. The administration issued a few public statements expressing its disappointment with Soviet policy, and quietly worked behind the scenes.

THE JACKSON AMENDMENT

Henry "Scoop" Jackson proved far more proactive. Jackson, a Democratic senator from Washington elected to Congress in 1940, was a staunch opponent of détente. Rejecting the premise that a totalitarian USSR was a permanent fixture on the international stage, Jackson believed that the Soviet economy could not withstand the sustained pressures of competition. He viewed the Soviet regime's embrace of détente as a change in tactics meant to avoid competition with the West rather than as a commitment to peaceful coexistence. The senator was fond of comparing the Soviet's behavior in the international arena to that of a burglar who goes down a hotel corridor, trying all the doors, until he finds one that's unlocked.

In addition to his opposition to détente, Jackson was also a firm advocate for the advance of human rights around the world. Unlike some who champion human rights simply because it is "the right thing to do," Jackson believed that promoting human rights was also in the *strategic interest* of the United States, a conviction that greatly enhanced his ability to persuade politicians of all ideological stripes to support his policies. Like Sakharov, who had always said that the international community should never trust a state more than that state trusts its own people, Jackson saw the Soviet's nondemocratic structure as the key to understanding its international behavior. As one of Jackson's close aides observed,

> a government's treatment of its own citizens, especially the government of a powerful nation, is an indication of its intentions to the rest of the world. Thus in the Senator's view, human rights and international law—usually viewed as humanitarian, or at best, political, concerns— were *strategically* significant. In this, he and Andrei Sakharov found themselves soul mates.[7]

Fortunately for those struggling to free Soviet Jewry, Jackson was also the rare breed of politician whose lofty ideals were matched by the skills of a master tactician. He combined those strengths to marshal an amendment through the Senate that linked certain American trade benefits for a non-market country to the willingness of that country to uphold freedom of emigration. Even his critics would admit that Jackson had devised an ingenious way to place the Soviet Jewry issue on the public agenda and at the same time to undermine détente. The Jackson-Vanik amendment (Congressman Charles Vanik had sponsored the amendment's passage in the House) would effectively pull the rug from under a Nixon administration determined to offer the Soviets preferable trading terms as part of their grand strategy of détente. Kissinger saw these benefits as an incentive for the Soviets to moderate their *international* policies, which suited the duplicitous leadership in Moscow just fine. But by making these trade benefits conditional on the totalitarian regime undergoing *internal* reform, Jackson was in Moscow's eyes attaching a stick to the end of a carrot.

Few people understood the extent of the challenge that freedom of emigration would pose to a totalitarian state like the USSR. Kissinger fought the Jackson amendment because he was concerned it would torpedo détente, not because he thought for a moment that it endangered the Soviet regime. For their part, most of the amendment's supporters, including some Jewish organizations in the United States, as well as the Israeli Liaison Office, a government body charged with helping get Jews out of the Soviet Union, were also unaware of its potential repercussions.

For years, The Liaison Office, which played an essential behind-the-scenes role in the effort to free Soviet Jewry, had tried to "narrow" the struggle. The premise of the organization was that as long as the struggle did not become a threat to the Soviet regime—say, by making broader calls for democracy and human rights within the USSR, or by arguing that Jews should be allowed to leave for countries other than Israel—there would be a better chance to get the Jews out. That is why they were furious about my work with the broader dissident movement, even to the point of threatening my wife with "disowning" my cause.

I often thought that The Liaison Office believed it had an unwritten agreement with the Soviet leadership that if the Jews didn't make too much noise, the regime would eventually agree to allow them to leave. For some Jewish leaders who shared this misguided belief, the Jackson amendment was actually too far-reaching. They tried to convince Senator Jackson to restrict the amendment by having it apply to only those peoples who had nation-states outside of the Soviet Union to which to emigrate. This was a nuanced way of having it apply de facto to a limited number of nationalities, a proposal which the senator rightly dismissed out of hand. In general, however, the consensus view of the Jewish establishment of the time was that the Jackson amendment would put pressure on the Soviets but would not be perceived by the regime as a threat to its stability.

The perceived "narrowness" of the Jackson amendment also drew the ire of many dissidents, including Alexander Solzhenitsyn. As fervent an opponent of détente as Jackson, Solzhenitsyn nevertheless was bitter that people were wasting so much time and resources on a tangential issue like freedom of emigration. He lamented that a West that for decades ignored the horrors of the Soviet regime, and whose leaders were partners in "signing treaties, giving loans, shaking 'honest' hands" and even "boasting about these achievement to their parliamentarians,"[8] could now mobilize for what was in his mind largely a sideshow. As Solzhenitsyn saw it, the real battle was toppling the Soviet totalitarian system and restoring freedom of thought, speech, and religion. He feared that with so much attention focused on the Jackson amendment, pressure on the USSR would dissipate once the problem of Soviet Jewry was resolved.

> Thank God [the West] got it, but will this understanding last long? The moment the Jewish emigration problem will be solved, [the West] will again be deaf and blind to all the different problems of the Russian and communist society and it will stop understanding anything.[9]

There were other dissidents, however, who saw the question of freedom of emigration as a far broader issue. Andrei Sakharov was one of them. When I asked him why he so fervently supported the Jackson amendment, which would primarily help Jews, Sakharov answered that in a closed society, freedom of emigration lowers the degree of control a regime can exercise over its subjects. When people have a right to leave a country, Sakharov explained, they are less afraid and more independent. And if they are less afraid and more independent, they are more willing to stand up for the rights that everyone is being denied.

Sakharov was absolutely right. Those who saw freedom of emigration as a narrow issue simply did not realize how dangerous it was for the USSR. By allowing this freedom, the regime would lose a measure of control over its population and undermine the entire structure of its totalitarian society. This is precisely why the regime had tried to stop Jewish emigration *before* the Jackson amendment, and why it decided to allow more than 30,000 Jews to emigrate in both 1972 and 1973, far more than the number that had emigrated the previous year, in an attempt to convince the West that the amendment was superfluous. That Kissinger and others credit this spike in Jewish emigration to the positive atmosphere created by the policy of détente shows that they misunderstood what was really happening.

Those who do not understand the nature of a fear society can easily misinterpret its behavior. Even with the benefit of hindsight, Kissinger, one of the sharpest diplomatic minds of the last half century, does not seem to recognize that Soviet leaders were deathly afraid of emigration. For example, here is Kissinger's reading of the thinking behind what he calls the "curious decision" to impose the exit tax in 1972.

[P]ossibly it was an attempt to burnish the Soviet position in the Arab world, the precariousness of which had most recently been demonstrated by the expulsion of combat troops from Egypt. Or else the tax may have been designed to generate foreign exchange in the expectation that it would be paid for by American supporters of increased emigration.[10]

By attributing the Soviet decision to geopolitics or a desire for hard currency, Kissinger misses the point. It is true that geopolitical or other reasons might explain why Soviet leaders would sometimes *permit* emigration. For example, when there was a possibility of a renewed détente in 1979—in the summer of that year the Salt II agreements were signed by Carter and Brezhnev—the Soviets allowed a large group of Jews to leave the country in order to decrease tensions with the West and aid the agreements' ratification in the Senate. Similarly, throughout the 1970s and 1980s, the Soviets used high-profile dissidents and Jewish "refuseniks" as bargaining chips that could be traded at a premium to the West. But the reason why the Soviets would want to *ban* emigration should have been obvious. Freedom of emigration was a lethal threat: The regime understood that when escape is an option, the fear that was used to stabilize its rule would not be nearly as effective.

What Kissinger failed to understand about the Soviets was eventually confirmed by the Soviets themselves. In his memoirs five years after the USSR had collapsed, Anatoly Dobrynin, the veteran Soviet ambassador who had served for two decades in Washington and who nurtured the policy of détente, admitted that the real motivation behind opposition to the Jackson amendment "was not often heard."[11]

In the closed society of the Soviet Union, the Kremlin was afraid of emigration in general (irrespective of nationality or religion) lest an escape hatch from the happy land of socialism seem to offer a degree of liberalization that might destabilize the domestic situation.[12]

In addition to being an effective weapon against a fear society in principle, the Jackson amendment proved particularly effective in practice because it focused on an imminently tangible issue. The Soviets would have loved to engage in esoteric and abstract debates with the West about the nature of human rights. Freedom of emigration, however, brought everything down to earth. For starters, the extent of the demand to emigrate was measurable. The number of people who had expressed a desire to leave the USSR and who had been sent invitations from "relatives" abroad could be counted. Second, the question of whether the Soviets were respecting those demands was easily verifiable. Whereas the regime might be able to deceive the West on other human rights issues, it could never distort the number of people who were actually being allowed to leave. By focusing on such a concrete issue, Jackson gave the Soviets little room to maneuver.

In the end, the regime chose to forsake the economic benefits in order to maintain control over their population. When the gates closed on Soviet Jewry (from 35,000 in 1973, emigration dropped to 20,000 in 1974 and to just a few thousand in the years that followed), Kissinger pointed to it as proof that Jackson's confrontational approach was ill-advised. It had, Kissinger claimed, "hurt our relations with the Soviet Union, hurt us economically and—most tragically of all—hurt the people it was supposed to help."[13] But those of us in whose name Kissinger was criticizing Jackson saw things differently. We refuseniks knew that the Soviets had no intention of allowing masses of Jews to leave, and we saw the amendment as putting our plight on the international agenda. Moreover, with pressure building from the West, we were convinced that the regime could not act toward us with impunity and that this forced restraint would embolden more and more Soviet Jews to join our struggle.

The full impact of the Jackson amendment became clear to me during my own trial for anti-Soviet activities and for the far more serious charge of high treason, punishable by death. Prior to the trial, I was given the opportunity to review the fifty-one volumes of evidence the government had gathered against me. It was not by accident that any time in which I expressed support for the Jackson amendment—whether in documents I signed or sent abroad, in meetings I attended with Western diplomats or politicians, or in statements I made to foreign journalists, it was presented as evidence of high treason. Scattered inside those volumes were all the names of my fellow "accomplices": Jewish activists, Jewish tourists from abroad, diplomats, journalists, and Western politicians whom I had met. There was one name mentioned, however, not once, not dozens, but hundreds of times, the name of the man who was singled out as the head of this plot, as my closest and most important comrade in crime. It was the name of a man whom I had never met or even spoken to on the telephone, but who symbolized for me all those in the free world who had supported the struggle for Soviet Jewry, the very best that was in the West. It was the name of Senator Henry Jackson.

The debate triggered by Senator Jackson would last for years and involve four successive U.S. administrations, the Soviet regime, dissidents, human rights advocates in the West, Jewish organizations, industrialists, trade unionists, and, it seemed, just about everybody else. The debate over the Jackson amendment had clearly become a debate over the wisdom of détente itself.

In October 1972, after Jackson introduced his amendment, the *New York Times* editorialized that "[g]ood relations between Washington and Moscow are so central to world peace that the political—as well as economic—arguments for expanded trade relationships are incontrovertible," explaining that "we do not believe it is productive to try to enforce political changes in the Soviet (or any other) system through the unilateral use of economic pressure. The results are likely to be the opposite of those intended."[14]

In July 1973, Senator J. W. Fulbright, chairman of the Foreign Relations Committee, assailed Jackson's parliamentary maneuver as "a renewal of the Cold War."

> Learning to live together in peace is the most important issue for the Soviet Union and the United States, too important to be compromised by meddling—even ideal-

istic meddling—in each other's affairs.... It is simply not within the legitimate range of our foreign policy to instruct the Russians in how to treat their own people, any more than it is Mr. Brezhnev's business to lecture us about race relations or such matters as the Indian protest at Wounded Knee.[15]

Not only did Jackson's critics dismiss the idea that his amendment would help induce change within the Soviet system, they also argued that if there were any hope for a reformed Soviet Union in the future, it would come as a result of détente. Here is how a *New York Times* editorial put it in mid-1974.

The President and Mr. Kissinger have been right to point out that America cannot expect their government to bring about the transformation of the Soviet system into a democracy as the price for détente and trade. The hope must be that liberalization will follow détente: it is more likely to be prevented than accelerated by excessive outside pressure.[16]

In contrast, we dissidents were convinced that détente had given the Soviets the chance to have it both ways, gaining benefits from the West and also controlling their own people.

Thanks to the Jackson amendment, the sands in the hourglass of the Soviet's fear society were running out. The regime was again facing a lose-lose proposition. With each additional emigrant allowed to leave, the level of fear inside the Soviet Union fell. At the same time, every obstacle that the authorities placed in the path of free emigration was reducing the likelihood of an enervated fear society winning the fruits of cooperation with the West. The Soviet Union was finally being unmasked before the eyes of the entire free world. They could continue to violate the rights of their own people, but it now would come with an expensive price tag.

The notion that human rights should be part of international relations has long been part of the democratic imagination. But before the Jackson amendment, real linkage was nonexistent. Still, even the strongest supporters of the Jackson amendment could not anticipate the impact that linkage would have on the course of the Cold War. In linking American trade policy to freedom of emigration, the amendment made improving human rights in the Soviet Union a *condition* of its relations with the United States. In doing so, it gave powerful legitimacy to the connection between human rights and international relations, setting the stage for the dramatic events that would begin to unfold a few months later at Helsinki.

THE HELSINKI AGREEMENTS

In 1975, the thirty-five-nation Conference on European Security and Cooperation, comprised of most of the European states, the United States, Canada, and the Soviet Union, announced that an agreement had been reached that would be signed at an upcoming summit in Helsinki. Coming after nearly three years of meetings, the sudden breakthrough surprised many. But there was no doubt that Soviet leaders wanted to restore the atmosphere of détente that the Jackson amendment had successfully swept away.

The Soviets had much to gain from what would later become known as the Helsinki Agreements. They had exercised de-facto control over Eastern Europe since World War II. Now, the West was finally ready to give formal recognition to this "sphere of influence," confirming the USSR's status as a superpower and conferring upon it the international legitimacy it had craved for decades. Ironically, the country that had long predicted the inevitable demise of the capitalist West had always sought the approval of its ideological adversary. That the agreement also established principles for economic and cultural cooperation only sweetened the pot for the leaders in Moscow.

The deal, however, also included a third "basket." The West demanded that the Soviets, as well as their puppet regimes in Eastern Europe, uphold the basic human rights of their own peoples. Faced with the prospect of legitimizing the USSR's geopolitical position and enhanced economic cooperation, the Soviet leadership reluctantly agreed to the provision. In their view, they were getting concrete recognition of territorial borders and economic benefits in return for a non-binding commitment on an abstract issue. Given their history of failing to abide by agreements, they surely believed they were hoodwinking the West with an empty promise. Those in the Kremlin would realize only years later that the regime had in fact signed its own death warrant at Helsinki.

The huge impact these agreements would have on East-West relations was certainly not obvious from the outset. The *New York Times*, for instance, downplayed the significance of the Helsinki summit, editorializing that "[n]ever have so many struggled for so long over so little."[17] For dissidents inside the USSR, the human rights provisions in the agreements seemed no more enforceable than the Universal Declaration of Human Rights that had been signed by all the members of the United Nations in 1948. The non-binding Helsinki accord was a far cry from the Jackson amendment's clear standards for compliance and clear penalties for noncompliance. In fact, many dissidents feared Helsinki would turn into a betrayal on a par with Yalta, the World War II conference in 1945 in which Stalin agreed to hold free elections in the Eastern European countries that had come under his thumb. Here too, dissidents were concerned that the West would once again look the other way as the Soviets ran roughshod over human rights.

Within a short amount of time, however, I began to think that the Helsinki Agreements presented dissidents with a rare opportunity. A couple of weeks after they were signed, I met with a visiting delegation of American congressmen headed by a representative from Illinois, Sidney Yates. One of the major achievements of the movement to free Soviet Jewry was getting Western politicians on official visits to the USSR to meet with refuseniks. Only a year before, such meetings had been taboo. Then Senator

Edward Kennedy boldly decided to see a handful of refuseniks in a midnight meeting that was kept secret from the KGB until the very last moment. In these encounters with political figures from abroad, refuseniks got to brief politicians on the latest news about our movement, such as how many people had been denied visas and who had been arrested. These meetings were an important reminder to Soviet officials that the refuseniks had powerful friends in the West.

Though the meeting with Congressman Yates and his delegation was one of many I attended with legislators from abroad, to this day it sticks out in my mind for three reasons. First, that meeting was one of two I had with American politicians that would later be included in the charges of high treason against me. Second, Millicent Fenwick, a participant in the meeting,[18] would go on to establish the committee in Washington that monitored compliance with the Helsinki accords. Third, and most important, that meeting was the first time I had heard someone mention "the spirit of Helsinki"—a spirit Congressman Yates said the Soviets were breaking by continuing human rights violations as if nothing had changed.

In the weeks that followed, more and more of those I met from the West would refer to the "spirit of Helsinki." Still, I and many other dissidents took such statements with a grain of salt. Those who spoke of the human rights clauses of Helsinki were well intentioned but at bottom, they appeared powerless to enforce them.

Meanwhile, dissidents were beginning to think of other

ways to mobilize public opinion in the West. The Communist parties in France and Italy, by far the biggest in the free world, piqued my interest when their leaders started cautiously criticizing the Soviet Union's human rights record. Why not, I thought, take advantage of the new readiness of the so-called Eurocommunists to confront the Kremlin?

A few weeks in advance of the conference of Communist parties from around the world that took place every five years in Moscow, I decided to send a letter to the European communist leaders commending their willingness to speak out. But if they really wanted to know the truth, I wrote, they should meet with some refuseniks when they arrived in Moscow and hear firsthand about our problems. I suggested that we share ideas and begin a dialogue on how the human rights promises made at Helsinki could be kept. Who knows, I added, perhaps if they agreed to talk to us, the KGB might even decide not to arrest us for a change. As was true of nearly all high-profile international meetings, before the conference had met, many dissidents and activists had been rounded up and detained by the KGB to prevent embarrassing protests.

Though my request to meet with Communist leaders from the West was ignored, in the new post-Helsinki atmosphere, dissidents were not arrested during the conference. The episode convinced me that it might be possible to appeal to public opinion in the West and put more pressure on the Soviets by appealing to the "spirit of Helsinki." I was teaching English to Andrei Amalrik and Yuri Orlov at the time. Orlov was one of the finest examples of the Russian intelligentsia, a man of deep moral convictions who had risen from the humble beginnings of a family of peasants to become an outstanding scientist. Unlike many other scientists in the USSR, who had seen their intellectual pursuits as a means of escaping the world of doublethink around them, Orlov never turned his back on the truth. I told my famous pupils that a dialogue with politicians, media organizations, and human rights organizations in the West about what we expected from the agreements reached in Helsinki, might be able to create a public atmosphere in which it would be more difficult for the Soviets to trample our rights.

Amalrik drafted a letter announcing our plans and approached a number of dissidents to support the initiative. He succeeded in getting dozens to sign on, but his work was abruptly stopped when authorities gave him an exit visa and "suggested" he leave the Soviet Union immediately. When Orlov and I met to discuss how to proceed with our initiative, he surprised me with a courageous decision. He agreed with me that if the human rights commitments contained in the Helsinki Agreements became important to the free world, then the Soviets could not easily ignore them. But Orlov maintained that for the idea to work in practice there would have to be more than dialogue. "We should stop wasting time on convincing people to talk and start instead to collect and share facts about human rights abuses." He would accomplish this, he said, by establishing an organization that would collect information about such abuses, publish it, and share it with similar groups abroad who were also monitoring compliance with the Helsinki Agreements.

Orlov warned that while his strategy would be more effective it would also be far more dangerous. "For this," he said, "they can arrest us under Article 64." Every dissident knew about the infamous Article 64, which covered the charge of high treason and which could result in a death sentence. While I disagreed with his assessment of the potential severity of our punishment—I thought the regime might arrest us under Article 70 for "anti-Soviet activity"—I told him I was prepared to take the risk in any case. (Ironically, the next year, each of us was arrested under the charge that the other had predicted. I was arrested under Article 64 and he was arrested under Article 70).

Within days, eleven dissidents founded the Helsinki Group. Ludmila Alexeeva would become the real engine of the group, and Elena Bonner, the remarkable wife of Andrei Sakharov, who himself was already involved in many other human rights issues, also played a key role. Professor Vitaly Rubin, the other dissident-refusenik in the group, also joined us, until he received a visa and was replaced by another leading Jewish activist, Vladimir Slepak. The other members were Alexander Ginsburg, the two-time political prisoner and veteran fighter for prisoners' rights, Michael Bernshtam, General Peter Gregorenko, Dr. Alexander Korchuck, Malva Landa; and Anatoly Marchenko, who joined the group from exile in Siberia. Orlov, who had spearheaded the initiative, served as the group's chairman. I was its unofficial spokesman.

We published a statement announcing the formation of our group on April 12, 1976, less than nine months after the Helsinki Agreements were signed, in which we announced our intention to bring any violations of the commitments on human rights to the attention of the thirty-five governments that had signed the agreements.

We started our work right away, releasing a new document every few weeks. One document might present a detailed example of a specific violation of rights. Another might list the names of hundreds of Jews who were being denied the right to emigrate or the names of dozens of political prisoners. Another might discuss persecutions against groups such as Pentecostals, Lithuanian Catholics, and Crimean Tatars. The documents were given to the foreign press and were broadcast in Russian on the BBC, Voice of America, and Radio Liberty. The exposure created a wave of responses across the Soviet Union, and people thousands of miles from Moscow began reaching out to us to tell us their stories. We were flooded with requests for help.

As in the case of the struggle for Soviet Jewry, the work of the Helsinki Group was possible because we were not alone. In the West, other Helsinki groups began sprouting up. On the initiative of Congresswoman Fenwick, a special committee to monitor compliance with the Helsinki accords was established in the United States that consisted of senators, congressmen, and members of the Ford administration. It started conducting hearings on Capitol Hill using, among other things, the documents we were issuing from Moscow. My contacts with diplomats also began to change. Before Helsinki, the documents and letters that dissidents tried to send abroad were only accepted by diplomats in secret. But in the post-Helsinki atmosphere the American embassy openly and officially received our documents, sending them via diplomatic mail.

In making the promotion of human rights a central theme in his presidential campaign, Jimmy Carter also contributed to the momentum. Before Carter took power, I translated a letter from Sakharov applauding the president-elect for making human rights a high priority and bringing to Carter's attention the names of a number of political prisoners. The letter was smuggled out and delivered to Carter by Jewish tourists. Breaking with protocol, Carter wrote Sakharov back, expressing his commitment to putting human rights at the top of his administration's agenda.

Unfortunately, the degree of the dissidents' excitement with Carter's ascension to the presidency would be matched by the degree of our disappointment with him during his tenure. While I personally owe Carter a debt of gratitude for publicly declaring, in another break with protocol, that I was not an American spy as the Soviets had claimed, he was almost never willing to back his rhetoric on human rights with decisive action.

But the forces that had been set in motion could not be stopped. After a few months of work, we already felt we were helping to turn a non-binding agreement into the standard by which the Soviet Union was being judged by the world. That an empire should have feared such a seemingly insignificant organization might have surprised many Western policymakers who misunderstood the nature of a fear society. But the Soviet authorities were aware of the threat we posed to their inherently unstable rule.

The regime's decision to exile and arrest all the founding

members of the Helsinki Group did not solve their problem. The Kremlin soon realized that it could not take one step in the international arena without the bright spotlight of world opinion exposing its human rights policies and its treatment of political dissidents. If it wanted the legitimacy, scientific exchanges, technology transfers, and other benefits that Helsinki promised, it would have to fulfill its commitments on human rights. If it wanted to enjoy an atmosphere of cooperation with the West and be respected by public opinion in the free world, it would have to change its policies toward its own people. The third basket at the Helsinki talks could not be ignored.

What had been initially viewed derisively by many observers as an insignificant Soviet concession to respect human rights turned out to be one of the most fateful decisions of the Cold War. Approximately fifteen years after the Helsinki agreements were signed, the Berlin Wall crumbled, Eastern Europe was free, the Soviet Union collapsed, and the Cold War was over. As Amalrik had predicted, the Soviet's fear society was eventually its own undoing. That this chain of events occurred so quickly was due in no small measure to the tremendous international pressure that Helsinki brought in its wake—pressure that a leader with moral clarity and a deep faith in freedom used to break the backs of the Soviets once and for all.

REAGAN AND GORBACHEV

By the time President Reagan came to power in 1981, the decay of the fear society ruled from Moscow was rapidly advancing. Yet Reagan's contribution to its ultimate collapse was crucial. Today, it is fashionable to believe that the Soviet Union would have collapsed regardless of who sat in the White House or which policies were adopted in Washington. In this view, Reagan was simply lucky, a man in the right place at the right time who benefited from an inexorable historical process. Nothing could be further from the truth. Had Reagan chosen to cooperate with the Soviet regime rather than compete with it, accommodate it rather than confront it, the hundreds of millions of people he helped free would still be living under tyranny.

When Reagan took office, and indeed throughout almost his entire presidency, few people believed that the USSR was seriously in danger of implosion. In 1984, the distinguished Harvard economist John Kenneth Galbraith noted admiringly that "for the first time in its history the Soviet leadership was able to pursue successfully a policy of guns and butter as well as growth. ... The Soviet citizen-worker, peasant, and professional—has become accustomed in the Brezhnev period to an uninterrupted upward trend in his well-being."[19] That same year, Galbraith would also claim "that the Soviet system has made great material progress in recent years" and that "the Russian system succeeds because, in contrast with the Western industrial economies, it makes full use of its manpower."[20] In 1985, Paul Samuelson, the Nobel Prize-winning economist well known to American college students for his introductory textbooks on economics, was even more lavish in his praise for the Soviet's command and control economy: "What counts is results, and there can be no doubt that the Soviet planning system has been a powerful engine for economic growth. ... The Soviet model has surely demonstrated that a command economy is capable of mobilizing resources for rapid growth."[21]

About the same time that leading economists in the West were pontificating about the strength of the Soviet system, Vladimir Balakonov saw things differently. Balakonov was an economist who had defected to the West but returned to be with his family after receiving assurances from the Soviet authorities that he would not be harmed. He was immediately put into prison, and in 1984, he was in the cell next to mine. We would communicate by either tapping on the walls in Morse code, or better yet, talking through the toilet. (After draining a toilet of water it becomes an excellent telephone to your neighbor, but also a dangerous form of communication. It is very hard to plead innocence if a guard catches you with your head in a toilet). Balakonov was absolutely convinced that the USSR was teetering on the brink of collapse: "They're lying," he used to tell me. "The Soviet economy is falling apart. Oil production is going down. The railway line through Siberia cannot be finished. If the West does not cooperate with them, everything will soon collapse." Balakonov had no access to the outside world and no special information. All he could do was read a government-controlled newspaper. Nevertheless, with a dissident's understanding of the weakness of the Soviet system, he became an expert at reading between the lines of *Pravda*. His predictions about the state of the Soviet economy, communicated to me through our toilets, would prove more accurate than the predictions of those in the West who had access to the latest statistics, the best contacts, and even satellite photographs.

Fortunately, Ronald Reagan viewed the Soviet Union as Balakonov did. Instead of lending a hand to a sick society, as advocates of détente were calling for, Reagan was determined to increase the pressure. The U.S. president instinctively understood the truth that Sakharov had once tried to convey to the Soviet leadership: A fear society is no match for a free society that can unleash the creative potential of its own people. Reagan refused to accept the permanence of the USSR, let alone the inevitability of Soviet superpower parity. He insisted that America use the advantage of a free society and free market to win the Cold War. While détente had counseled more cooperation, Reagan championed fierce competition.

A few months after he took office, Reagan made his intentions perfectly clear:

> The years ahead will be great ones for our country, for the cause of freedom and for the spread of civilization. The West won't contain Communism, it will transcend Communism. We will not bother to denounce it, we'll dismiss it as a sad, bizarre chapter in human history whose last pages are even now being written.[22]

A year later, Reagan was even more blunt when he predicted that the very Marxist system that had prophesied eventual triumph over the capitalist West was itself doomed to failure.

In an ironic sense, Karl Marx was right. We are witnessing today a great revolutionary crisis—a crisis where the demands of the economic order are colliding directly with those of the political order. But the crisis is happening not in the free, non-Marxist West, but in the home of Marxism-Leninism, the Soviet Union. What we see here is a political structure that no longer corresponds to its economic base, a society where productive forces are hampered by political ones. It is the Soviet Union that runs against the tide of history by denying freedom and human dignity to its citizens. A march of freedom and democracy will leave Marxism-Leninism on the ash-heap of history.[23]

In retrospect, Reagan's prediction seems fairly obvious and his policies altogether prudent. But they weren't viewed that way at the time. In 1982, one noted Sovietologist, writing for *Foreign Affairs* magazine, warned of the dangers of Reagan's approach.

The logic of the Reagan Administration's policy toward the Soviet Union is based on one key underlying assumption: that Western policy generally and American policy specifically has the capacity seriously to affect Soviet international behavior principally by exerting influence on *internal* Soviet developments. This assumption is simply fallacious and spawns maximalist and unrealistic objectives. (Emphasis added)[24]

Another Sovietologist described Reagan's abandonment of détente and containment in order to try to "destroy the Soviet Union as a world power and possibly even its Communist system" as a "potentially fatal form of Sovietphobia ... a pathological rather than a healthy response to the Soviet Union."[25] Fortunately, Reagan didn't pay any attention to his critics.

The U.S. president's faith in freedom's eventual triumph was matched by a deep distrust of totalitarian regimes. When he justified his decision to build an elaborate strategic missile defense system as a means of safeguarding America against the belligerent intentions of a nondemocratic regime, he was essentially telling the world what Andrei Sakharov had told me years earlier: A country that does not respect the rights of its own citizens will not respect the rights of its neighbors. Again, the critics were furious, characterizing Reagan's so-called Star Wars initiative as dangerous saber-rattling and insane profligacy. But the Soviet leadership was petrified. They had always wanted to restrict competition in high-tech weaponry and keep the arms race open in low-tech weapons where the disadvantages of its fear society would not be exposed. We used to joke in prison that the Soviets were determined to fight World War III with sticks since they had enough prisoners to cut down half the trees in Siberia. When Reagan unveiled his Star Wars initiative and refused to abandon it during arms control negotiations in Reykjavik in 1986, it was as if a Soviet pensioner on his deathbed were being challenged to run a marathon. Years later, close advisers of Gorbachev admitted that the realization that the USSR could never compete with Star Wars made them finally accept demands for internal reform. A leading Soviet economist, put it this way.

> [I]f it had not been for the Reagan defense buildup, if the United States had not demonstrated that it is willing not only to stand up for freedom but to devote consider-able sums of money to defending it, we probably would not be sitting here today having a free discussion between Russians and Americans.[26]

But Reagan's challenge to the Soviets was as much moral as it was economic, which is why the impact of his policies on the life of Soviet dissidents was no less dramatic. One day, my Soviet jailers gave me the privilege of reading the latest copy of *Pravda*. Splashed across the front page was a condemnation of President Reagan for having the temerity to call the Soviet Union an "evil empire." Tapping on walls and talking through toilets, word of Reagan's "provoca-tion" quickly spread through the prison. The dissidents were ecstatic. Finally, the leader of the free world had spo-ken the truth—a truth that burned inside the heart of each and every one of us.

At the time, I never imagined that three years later, I would be in the White House telling this story to the presi-dent. When he summoned some of his staff to hear what I had said, I understood that there had been much criticism of Reagan's decision to cast the struggle between the superpowers as a battle between good and evil. Well, Reagan was right and his critics were wrong.

Those same critics used to love calling Reagan a simpleton who saw the world through a primitive ideological prism and who would convey his ideas through jokes and anecdotes. Indeed, in that first meeting with him, he told me a joke in which General Secretary Brezhnev and Premier Kosigin, his second in command, were discussing whether they should allow freedom of emigration. "Look, America's really pressuring us," Brezhnev said, "maybe we should just open up the gates." "The problem is," he continued, "we might be the only two people who wouldn't leave." To which Kosigin replied, "Speak for yourself."

Reagan's critics didn't seem to understand that the jokes and anecdotes that so endeared him to people were merely his way of expressing fundamental truths in a way that everyone could understand.

Reagan's tendency to confuse names and dates, something I too experienced first-hand, also made him the target of ridicule. In September 1987, a few months before he was to have a summit meeting with Gorbachev in Washington, I met with Reagan to ask him what he thought about the idea of holding a massive rally of hundreds of thousands of people on behalf of Soviet Jewry during the summit. Some Jewish leaders, concerned that if the rally were held Jews would be accused of undermining a renewed hope for peace between the superpowers, had expressed reservations about such a frontal challenge to the new Soviet leader.

Seeing me together for the first time with my wife, Avital,

who had fought for many years for my release, Reagan greeted us like a proud grandparent, knowing he had played an important role in securing my freedom. He told us about his commitment to Soviet Jewry. "My dear Mr. and Mrs. Shevarnadze," he said, "I just spoke with Soviet Foreign Minister Sharansky, and I said you better let those Jews go."

Not wanting to embarrass the president over his mistake, I quickly asked him about the rally, outlining the concerns raised by some of my colleagues. His response was immediate: "Do you think I am interested in a friendship with the Soviets if they continue to keep their people in prison? You do what you believe is right."

Reagan may have confused names and dates, but his moral compass was as acute as ever. Armed with moral clarity, a deep faith in freedom, and the courage to follow his convictions, he was instrumental in helping the West win the Cold War and helping hundreds of millions of people behind the Iron Curtain win their freedom.

The formula that had achieved victory was clear: Beset on the inside by dissidents demanding the regime live up to its international commitments and pressed on the outside by leaders like Reagan willing to link their foreign and defense policies to internal Soviet changes, leaders in the Kremlin eventually buckled under the strain. It would be left to Mikhail Gorbachev to preside over the USSR's collapse.

Following the deaths of three Soviet premiers in quick succession in the early 1980s, the young Gorbachev took over the reins of a country in dire straits. The information age and global marketplace were creating an entire nation of doublethinkers, as people increasingly learned about the good life beyond the Iron Curtain and the tyranny inside it. As Amalrik had predicted, the Soviet regime, forced to wage perpetual war at home and abroad to maintain stability, was devoting more and more resources to controlling its own people. As Sakharov had warned, the tight control and restrictions on freedom that were necessary to maintain a fear society were causing the Soviets to fall further and further behind in the scientific and technological race with the West. Reagan, for his part, was only accelerating the pace. Finally, the Jackson amendment, Helsinki Agreements, and Reagan administration had combined to create an environment in which policy toward the Soviet Union was being linked to *internal* Soviet reforms. With the batteries of the Soviet's fear society depleting, the demands for energy growing, and external sources of power cut off, the USSR was nearing its end.

Gorbachev believed he had two options: Do nothing and watch the Soviets fall further behind the West and lose further control over its own people, or decrease the level of fear a few notches, renew cooperation with the West, consolidate control at home, and protect the regime's status abroad. He chose the latter option. In a speech in 1985 in which he explained the need for his glasnost policy, he warned that without serious reforms, the Soviet Union would not be able to compete with the West.

Fifteen years after Sakharov's open essay to the Soviet leadership, Gorbachev was effectively making the same argument. The Soviet emperor himself was admitting he had no clothes.

Though Gorbachev understood the importance of freedom in developing advanced science, technology, and a modern economy, he failed to recognize the power freedom exercised on the human spirit. He did not realize, as Sakharov had, that by lowering the level of fear in Soviet society, people would become more independent and more willing to use their new freedoms to stand up to the regime.

While Gorbachev was certainly no Stalin and even no Brezhnev, he was also no democrat. Gorbachev was not a champion of freedom. He tried to tinker with communism in the hopes of saving it. When freedom was spreading in the Soviet Union, he tried to deny independence to the Baltic republics. While he permitted more dissent in the Communist Party, he tried to maintain the one-party system. My last conversation with Sakharov was in December 1989, a few days before he passed away. He told me that he would unfortunately not be able to make his first visit to Israel—the Weizman Scientific Institute had invited him—as he had planned. "I have to remain in Moscow because there will be a tough battle with Gorbachev in the Soviet parliament. He is trying to maintain the one-party system and defeating him is crucial to the future of democracy in the country."

Sakharov did not win this particular battle. In the heated debate in the parliament, Gorbachev and others who supported his One-Party approach attacked Sakharov and tried to silence him. The pressure of this confrontation took its toll on Sakharov. He returned home and suffered a heart attack.

In a few months, the spirit of Sakharov would win the war. The demands for freedom could not be silenced. Gorbachev's half-hearted reforms merely encouraged demands for more. To the Soviets, Gorbachev was not seen as graciously expanding their liberties. Rather, he was making them understand how little freedom they had, and how much more they wanted. The Kremlin had unwittingly released the spark of freedom that would burn down an empire.

When freedom's skeptics argue today that freedom cannot be "imposed" from the outside, or that the free world has no role to play in spreading democracy around the world, I cannot but be amazed. Less than one generation has passed since the West found the Achilles heel of the Soviet Union by pursing an activist policy that *linked* the rights of the Soviet people to the USSR's international standing. The same formula will work again today. The nations of the free world can promote democracy by linking their foreign policies toward nondemocratic regimes to how those regimes treat their subjects. Those regimes are much more dependent on the West than the Soviets ever were, giving the West far more leverage to demand change.

The problem, as I would soon find out, was not that the West lacked the power to spread freedom around the world, but that it lacked the will. This was perhaps most evident with regard to the opportunity to build a democratic future for the Palestinians in the West Bank and the Gaza Strip. The Palestinians were so dependent on the outside world that it is hard to imagine a case when the West had greater leverage to insist on the creation of a free society. That is what makes the failure to do so all the more tragic.

CHAPTER 5

From Helsinki to Oslo

A CURSORY GLANCE at the map of Europe shows the capitals of Finland and Norway only a few hundred miles apart. Yet despite their proximity, the accords reached at Helsinki and Oslo represent decidedly different approaches to international relations. In both of these Scandinavian cities, parties ostensibly seeking an end to a decades-old conflict entered into negotiations that culminated in an historic agreement. But unfortunately for the prospects of genuine Arab-Israeli reconciliation, the similarities end there. The process started at Helsinki helped end the Cold War and liberate hundreds of millions of people. The process started at Oslo unleashed an unprecedented campaign of terror and left millions of Palestinians living under a tyrant.

The differences between the two approaches should have been obvious from the start. Whereas the Helsinki agreements forged a direct link between human rights and East-West relations, the Oslo accords failed to establish any connection between human rights and the Israeli-Palestinian peace process. Worse, as would later become clear in word and deed, Oslo's architects actually believed that such a link would be detrimental to the interests of both parties. Considering the Arab regimes' abysmal record of respecting the rights of their own people, it was no surprise that representatives of the Palestinian Liberation Organization (PLO) wanted to avoid any mention of human rights. But that Israeli negotiators would delude themselves into believing that such an omission actually served Israel's interests is a sad testament to how little we learn from history.

For most Middle East policymakers, the end of the Cold War became noteworthy primarily for the collapse of the Arab countries' Soviet sponsor and for the possibility of rapid geopolitical change, both of which intoxicated the minds of those seeking a miraculous end to the Arab-Israeli conflict and the creation of a "New Middle East" overnight. Conveniently forgotten was the real lesson of the Cold War: Namely, that the environment that precipitated this historic collapse was cultivated by both the courage of dissidents like Sakharov and Orlov, who challenged the Soviet authorities to free their own people, and the bold policies of Western leaders such as Jackson and Reagan, who turned the process of liberalization and reform inside the Soviet Union into an important element of superpower relations.

To be sure, no Arab figure of Sakharov's stature has yet emerged in the Middle East to give voice to the struggle for human rights. But Israel and other democratic governments have also not carried their share of the burden. When the peace process began, the free world had a remarkable opportunity to use its influence to help the emerging Palestinian society evolve into a democratic state that could serve as the linchpin of a wider Arab-Israeli peace. Instead it did precisely the opposite, spending the better part of a decade building and supporting a corrupt dictatorship.

Sadly, the one democratic country in a region rife with belligerent, authoritarian states refused to believe—and still refuses to believe—in the universal power of its own ideals. Skeptical of their country's ability to promote change in the Arab states and tired of diplomatic deadlock, Israeli policymakers initiated a peace process at Oslo but left the real key to Middle East peace—establishing a direct link between the liberalization of Arab regimes and the peace process—gathering dust in Helsinki.

THE MARCH OF FOLLY

In 1993, the world, the people of Israel, its parliament, and virtually its entire government, were shocked to discover that secret talks in Oslo between representatives of Israel and the Tunis-based PLO had led to the formulation of a Declaration of Principles between the two sides. Israel had spent three decades fighting the PLO within its own borders and trying to expel the organization from its bases in neighboring states. Now it was treating the PLO to a triumphant return to Gaza and the West Bank.

The PLO was formed in 1964. This was *three years before* the Six Day War, during which Israel captured the West Bank from Jordan and the Gaza Strip from Egypt. Obviously, then, the reason for the establishment of the PLO was not to "liberate" these territories from Israeli rule. Rather, it was to destroy the state of Israel and, as its leader frequently boasted, "push all the Jews into the sea." The PLO's founding charter openly called for "the liquidation of the Zionist presence" and asserted that "armed struggle is the only way to liberate Palestine."

To advance its goals, the PLO perpetrated countless acts of terrorism and hoped to trigger a wider Arab war against Israel that would annihilate the Jewish state. When a surprise attack launched by Egypt and Syria on Yom Kippur day in 1973 was successfully repelled by Israel, it became clear to the PLO that the Arab states did not possess sufficient military power to destroy Israel. Deciding that its goal could only be advanced piecemeal, the organization changed tactics. In 1974, its governing council approved its so-called "phased plan," according to which the PLO would take hold of any territory relinquished by Israel—as a result of diplomatic pressure, terrorism, or a combination of both—and use it as a launching pad for the next round of fighting. One senior PLO member explained the strategy:

According to the Phased Plan, we will establish a Palestinian state on any part of Palestine that the enemy will retreat from. The Palestinian state will be a stage in our prolonged struggle for the liberation of Palestine on all of its territory. We cannot achieve the strategic goal of a Palestinian state in all of Palestine without first establishing a Palestinian state [on part of it].[1]

While the PLO claimed to be the legitimate representative of the Palestinian people, the State of Israel refused to recognize it as such or negotiate with it. After a number of Israelis started meeting openly with the PLO in the 1970s and 1980s, the Israeli Parliament passed a law in 1986 prohibiting such meetings unless explicitly authorized by the government. In the early 1990s, the governments of both Yitzhak Shamir and Yitzhak Rabin rejected negotiations with the PLO in favor of talks with the local Palestinian leadership.

Thus, the announcement in September 1993 that Rabin's Labor government had reached an agreement with the PLO came as a complete surprise. The Clinton administration, also unaware of the clandestine talks in Oslo, was thrilled: Both Democratic and Republican administrations had long supported efforts by Israelis and Palestinians to reach a compromise. President Clinton, correctly seeing the breakthrough as a golden diplomatic opportunity that was happening on his watch, quickly arranged a signing ceremony in Washington. PLO Chairman Yasser Arafat and Prime Minister Yitzhak Rabin shook hands on the White House lawn before a stunned and jubilant world.

The Oslo agreement was fairly straightforward: Israel

committed itself to transferring territory to the PLO, which would take responsibility for governing the Palestinian population in the areas under its control. In the first stage, the PLO would be placed in charge of the Gaza Strip and the West Bank city of Jericho. The PLO was allowed to establish a 9,000-man police force, whose weapons would be supplied by Israel. All issues related to the settlements, Jerusalem, refugees, and borders were to be deferred to final status talks.

The PLO's two core commitments were that it would permanently abandon the goal of destroying Israel and that it would fight terrorism. The former would require changing those clauses in the PLO charter that called for the annihilation of the Jewish state, ending all incitement against Israel, and educating the Palestinian public for peace. The latter would entail using the newly equipped police force to crack down on fundamentalist terror groups, disarming, arresting and in some cases extraditing terrorists, as well as cooperating with the Israeli security services to prevent terror attacks.

Israel immediately split into pro-Oslo and anti-Oslo camps. As a nonpolitical observer in 1993, it seemed to me that most Israelis had made up their minds about the accords not after a careful review of their contents, but based on a priori assumptions. On the Left were many who would seemingly support any agreement so long as the "peace process" appeared to be moving forward. On the Right were many who opposed any territorial compromise with the PLO, regardless of the where, when, and how.

But at the beginning of the peace process, the pro-Oslo forces clearly had the upper hand. As is always true in Israel, the moment peace seems within reach, the public quickly becomes euphoric. A hopeful atmosphere could be felt everywhere, in the streets, in markets, in schools, in songs, in art, and of course, in the media.

Unfortunately, in this new atmosphere, expressing reservations about Oslo was seen as tantamount to rejecting peace itself. For me, this proved particularly confining. Believing that our Jewish, democratic state should try to guarantee its security without controlling the lives of another people, I counted myself among those who were prepared for territorial compromise with the Palestinians. At the same time, I was gravely concerned that a number of flawed assumptions underlying the Oslo process would preclude any possibility of an historic reconciliation.

First, the premise of Oslo, as Shimon Peres had declared on numerous occasions, was that the abyss we faced with the Palestinians would have to be traversed in one giant leap of faith. According to this view, the mutual recognition called for in the accord would trigger an irreversible political and economic chain reaction that would rapidly transform our relationship with the Palestinians and quickly usher in a "New Middle East." While any agreement with the Palestinians would have necessitated crossing a psychological Rubicon, it seemed to me that the way to overcome our mutual distrust was by seeing concrete changes in the present, not by simply forgetting the past.

Second, the Rabin-Peres administration blatantly ignored

the issue of Palestinian compliance. In a sense, this logically flowed from the first assumption. If a leap of faith were all that was needed to bridge the gap between Israelis and Palestinians, then compliance with the minutiae of detailed agreements would naturally become irrelevant. Rather than hold the Palestinians accountable and establish a quid pro quo that could build mutual trust, Palestinian violations of the accords were swept under the rug in the name of keeping the peace process "on track."

Third, the architects of Oslo made no effort to reach a broad national consensus within Israel. No matter how large or vocal the opposition, its concerns were disdainfully ignored by Rabin and Peres, a mistake that Ehud Barak would later repeat. As terrorism reached unprecedented levels, these governments decided to continue the peace process, blindly pressing forward while the nation was splitting at the seams. In fact, one early stage of the Oslo agreements was passed in the Knesset by only two votes after two members of the opposition abandoned their party and traded their support for positions in the government.

But the assumption underlying the Oslo process that troubled me the most was the belief held by the Israeli government that the undemocratic nature of Arafat's regime would serve the interests of peace and security. That Israel's government had enlisted a man in the fight against Palestinian terrorism who had spent much of his life ordering the killing of innocents was bad enough. But that it believed that the fewer constraints placed on Arafat's rule, the better off Israel would be, was to me the height of madness. Not only would Arafat do our job for us, the reasoning went, but he would do it better.

OUR DICTATOR

Only a few days after the Oslo process had officially begun, Prime Minister Rabin coined the phrase that chillingly summed up the government's entire approach. Arafat would deal with terrorists, Rabin assured his countrymen, "without a Supreme Court, without B'tselem [a human rights organization] and without all kinds of bleeding heart liberals."[2] The undemocratic nature of Arafat's regime, far from being an obstacle to peace, was considered a crucial asset in the fight against terror.

When I read Rabin's remarks I was deeply troubled. Rabin was essentially arguing that a fear society among the Palestinians would serve peace and security and that the regime governing that society would be a reliable ally. Of course this was not the first time a democratic leader had made that argument. The tendency to see nondemocratic regimes as anchors of stability and security has colored Western strategic thinking for decades. Instead of pressuring Arab tyrants to free their own peoples and recognizing that their oppressive rule breeds fundamentalism, violence, and terrorism, the West has long believed that nondemocratic rule in the Middle East has prevented the region from descending into chaos. Yet while America and the West have sponsored tyrants from a comfortable distance, Israel was creating one in its own backyard.

I decided to write an article expressing my concerns about where the Oslo peace process was heading:

> The [Palestinian] society that will emerge from fighting without a Supreme Court, B'tselem and bleeding heart liberals will inevitably be based on fear, and on unlimited totalitarian authority.... [T]otalitarian regimes cannot maintain stability without an enemy. Once they finish off their internal rivals, they inevitably look for outside enemies.[3]

My criticism of Oslo was not an assault on the idea of peace with the Palestinians. On the contrary, I was convinced that the same formula that had successfully worked to end the Cold War and transform the Soviet Union—linking Western policy to the expansion of human rights and democracy—could work to build a genuine and lasting peace between Israelis and Palestinians.

> [I]f we really want to give the rosy picture of peace a chance, we must try to ensure the building of real democratic institutions in the fledgling Palestinian society, no matter how tempting a "solution" without them may be.... Palestinian autonomy can become a unique test case for the determined introduction of democracy in the Arab world. Indeed, those who are responsible for the agreement and believe most in the potential of a peace here have the most at stake in exporting democracy to the emerging Palestinian society. In the coming

transitional period, Palestinians will be totally dependent on the West and Israel, politically and economically. Making political concessions and generous financial donations without "interfering in domestic affairs" almost dooms the process. On the other hand, rigidly linking the concessions and assistance to human rights policy nurtures the chance for real peace.[4]

But the same arguments that I had heard a generation before about the incompatibility of Russians with democracy, and that had been said two generations earlier about the Germans and Japanese, were now being said about the Palestinians. On both the Left and the Right, the response to my argument about the need to build Palestinian democracy was the same: "Come on, Natan, this is the Middle East we're talking about."

Buttressing this view was an assumption that Israel had no role to play in promoting democracy among the Palestinians in any case. As Benjamin Ben-Eliezer, a senior Labor Minister, put it soon after the Oslo accords were signed: "Promoting democracy in the Middle East involves the sensitivities of time-honored cultural traditions and a multitude of different populations. As a result, those of us in democratic societies must adopt the roles of passive spectators and must patiently wait on the sidelines."[5] Shimon Peres, Israel's foreign minister, felt much the same: "I do not believe that democracy can be imposed artificially on another society."[6] When nothing would have enhanced Israel's security more than promoting a Palestinian society founded on democratic principles and institutions, Israel's leaders instead decided to usher in a peace process predicated on Palestinian tyranny. Worst of all, they were proud of it.

The Rabin-Peres government rolled out the red carpet for Arafat and his cronies. It placed the newly formed Palestinian Authority (PA) in charge of Gaza and Jericho and later transferred to its control four other West Bank cities. The 9,000-man strong PA security force would eventually swell to over 40,000 men, making it the largest per capita "police force" in the world. Israel's government implored foreign countries to shower the PA with aid and assisted Arafat in establishing a chain of monopolies over staple goods provided to and by the Palestinians. Without having faced an election, Arafat was given legitimacy, territory, money, and, most important, control over the lives of two million Palestinians.

What was obvious from the beginning was that all the power given to Arafat was not being used to improve the lives of the Palestinians but rather to strengthen his own rule. To me, this was the only possible outcome that could come from building a dictatorship. The problem was not Arafat's personality, problematic though it may be, but that the fate of the "leader" of the Palestinians was not linked to the fate of the Palestinians themselves. None of the benefits given to Arafat and the PA were made conditional on *how* they ruled. A Palestinian regime almost entirely dependent on the support of the free world was not being asked, much less forced, to build an open, democratic Palestinian society or to use its power to tangibly improve the lives of the Palestinians.

Instead, strengthening Arafat became one of the primary objectives of the peace process. The rationale was that, unlike the Hamas and Islamic Jihad terror organizations that openly called for the destruction of Israel, Arafat and his PA were forces of "moderation," interlocutors with whom an historic compromise could be reached. And in contrast to the local Palestinian leadership, the Arafat-led PLO would have enough power to crack down on Islamic terrorism.

While the world had vilified Israel for its violations of Palestinian rights, Arafat was free to treat his Palestinian subjects as he pleased. When he shut down an independent Palestinian newspaper, and threatened the lives of Palestinian human rights activists, there was barely a hint of protest. When he rigged an electoral system to ensure that his loyalists would dominate the vote, no government withheld recognition, and Shimon Peres, Israel's prime minister at the time, praised the Palestinian elections as "more democratic than those in Egypt or Syria."[7] When Arafat set up special security courts that made a mockery of due process, democratic leaders applauded him, believing the courts would help fight terror. Naïve intellectuals like Feuchtwanger had been duped about Stalin's justice system in the 1930s, but these leaders were fully aware that they were praising an exercise in tyranny.

In fact, fighting terrorism was the only demand that was ever publicly made of Arafat. But when terror attacks did not stop, however, Israel's government, determined not to stop the peace process, turned the other cheek. Democratic leaders around the world, for their part, condemned the terror attacks, but were just as likely to blame Israel for provoking the aggression against it as to cast aspersions on Arafat's commitment to the peace process. Between the signing of the Oslo accords in 1993 and the defeat of the Labor government in the elections of 1996, over 200 Israelis were killed in terror attacks, many more than had been killed in terror attacks during any similar period in the history of the state. Despite Rabin's promises to abort the peace process if the guns Israel supplied to the Palestinians were ever turned against the Jewish state, as well as mounting evidence that the PA was complicit in the terror attacks, the Oslo process continued. Rabin repeatedly declared that he would "continue the peace process as if there were no terrorism and fight terrorism as if there were no peace process."

Israel's government had trapped itself into believing that there was no alternative to Arafat's authoritarian rule. Arafat, the thinking went, was the only one who could fight terrorism and confront the "enemies of peace." It made no difference how Arafat ruled as long as he was providing Israel with security. And when he failed to do that, the only conclusion drawn was that he was too weak and would therefore have to be strengthened even further with more concessions, more legitimacy, and more money. Only then, Israelis were told by their government, would he be strong enough to stand up to the terrorists and make peace.

When American Jewish leaders expressed their concerns

about Palestinian noncompliance with the Oslo accords, Yossi Beilin, one of the prime architects of the peace process, told them it was "none of their business."[8] Uri Savir, another of Oslo's leading lights, told a pro-Israel lobby that anyone who opposed American aid to the PLO could not be called a friend of Israel.

Official attitudes toward the organization Peace Watch also revealed the mindset of those leading the peace process. Like the Helsinki Group established two decades earlier to monitor compliance with the Helsinki Agreements, Peace Watch, an organization of which I was also a founding member, was established to monitor compliance with the Oslo accords. Comprised of Israelis of all ideological stripes, from Left-wing kibbutz leaders to Right-wing settlers, Peace Watch was launched precisely because there was wide concern that as a result of the euphoric atmosphere in Israel, the Palestinians would not have to abide by their commitments. Peace Watch published papers on whether the Palestinian Authority was fighting terrorism, stopping incitement, educating for coexistence, or fulfilling the other commitments it had made. The government of Israel, determined to strengthen Arafat at all costs, not only ignored the work of Peace Watch, but it also instructed its embassies to do the same. When some questioned why Israel was not using information that could be very helpful in exerting diplomatic pressure on the Palestinian Authority to comply with its agreements, Israeli officials scoffed that it was the government's role to determine whether the Palestinians were fulfilling their commitments.

Throughout the peace process, a constant refrain of the proponents of Oslo was that "there was no alternative to Arafat." The idea that a free society could be a viable alternative was dismissed out of hand. Here is how Beilin, expressing a sentiment that was often heard in the "peace camp," put it:

I don't believe that we are going to have a democratic Middle East and you know what? I'm not sure whether all of us would applaud a democratic Middle East because we know what would happen. We know what happened in Algeria. All of us applauded the democratization and all of us also applauded the army which put an end to it and rightly so. We are all afraid of the situation. The situation where democracy is being exploited by the most reactionary and cynical forces.[9]

But what Beilin and others did not recognize were the immense dangers that a fear society would inevitably pose to Israel. Playing the double game that the Soviet regime had once perfected, Arafat's PA hid its true face by talking peace in Western capitals while at the same time inciting Palestinians back in the territories. As Arafat was signing agreements and accepting the Nobel Peace Prize, his PA-controlled media was inculcating a generation of Palestinians to hate the Jewish state, and his PA-run schools were educating Palestinian children from textbooks that had literally wiped Israel off the map.

The architects of Oslo believed that if Arafat were brought

from Tunis to the territories and given enough power to govern the Palestinians, he would have an interest in building a country, improving the conditions of his people, and fighting a terrorism that could undermine both the peace process and his leadership. But this naïve view completely ignored the crucial difference between democracies and dictatorship. Arafat had no incentive to build a country for the Palestinians or improve their lives because he was not made dependent on them. Moreover, even if he was no longer committed to the phased plan—which was a highly dubious assumption—he had no incentive to fight terrorism because he needed the Jewish state as an external enemy.

I knew enough about fear societies to realize that such a regime would inevitably threaten Israel. I thought that we should link the legitimacy, money, and concessions we and the rest of the world were giving Arafat to his regime's willingness to build a free society in the areas that had been put under its control. In my view, the PA had to be given the same choice that had once faced the Soviets: Build a free society for your people and be embraced by the world, or build a fear society and be rejected by it.

Nothing of the sort had happened. On the contrary, the PA was encouraged to build a fear society. While Arafat was turning the screws on his own people, he became the most frequent foreign visitor to the White House and the recipient of billions of dollars of foreign aid. Almost no effort was made to strengthen an independent Palestinian civil society or to invest directly in the Palestinian people. The most egregious example of strengthening Arafat instead of his people was the 1995 Paris Agreement in which Israel agreed to transfer 20 percent of Palestinian value added tax (VAT) receipts directly into Arafat's private account in a Tel Aviv bank. Arafat could do entirely as he pleased with the hundreds of millions of dollars that poured into this slush fund. For the peace process to work, I believed that the idea of strengthening Arafat had to be replaced with the idea of making him dependent on his own people. But nothing, it seemed, would shatter the illusion that only "a strong leader can make a strong peace." Nothing, that is, until the spring of 1996, when a wave of suicide bombings and the celebrations on the Palestinian streets that followed them swept Oslo's champions from power.

NETANYAHU COMES TO POWER

In May 1996, Likud leader Benjamin Netanyahu, promising to restore reciprocity to the peace process, was elected prime minister. "Bibi" Netanyahu, as he is usually called, had pledged in the campaign to continue with Oslo, but only if both sides fulfilled their commitments.

The name Netanyahu had a special meaning for me ever since the raid on Entebbe in 1976. In that raid, Israel rescued hostages on an Air France plane that had been hijacked by terrorists and flown to Uganda. The only Israeli soldier who was killed during the daring raid thousands of miles from Israel was the commander of the operation, Yoni Netanyahu, Bibi's older brother. When I was arrested, a picture of Yoni, cut out from the newspaper, was hanging on my wall. Each time I heard an airplane flying in the skies over my prison camp, it reminded me of Entebbe and lifted my spirits: I knew I was not alone. One day a plane would come to my rescue and bring me to Israel.

As ambassador to the United Nations, Benjamin Netanyahu had given my wife good political advice when she was campaigning for my release. After I left prison, when I was continuing the struggle to free Soviet Jewry, he also gave me sound advice. The fact that I was being helped by Yoni's brother was a very satisfying feeling. I will never forget our first meeting in 1986 when the bright and charismatic Netanyahu, with whom I would develop a good relationship, told me that in ten years he would be prime minister. Ten years later, he was.

My party, Yisrael Ba'aliyah, competed for the first time in the 1996 elections that brought Netanyahu to power. After the fall of the Iron Curtain, hundreds of thousands of Jewish immigrants from the Soviet Union moved to Israel. By 1995, disappointed with the political establishment's neglect of absorption issues, I and some other immigrant leaders formed a political party that would help immigrants from within the Knesset. We won seven of the 120 seats in parliament, and we eventually became a coalition partner in Netanyahu's government.

Our party was primarily founded to address absorption-related issues and would devote most of its energies to these topics, but we could not avoid taking a stand on the issue that topped the public agenda. Our platform explicitly stated our support for reciprocity, noting that "full compliance with all previous agreements must be a necessary condition for advancement in the peace process with our neighbors."[10] In the two years that had passed since the Oslo accords were signed, Israel had fulfilled its commitments and the Palestinians had not. We had transferred territory and sovereignty to the PA. The PA had not changed the PLO charter, confiscated illegal weapons, or locked up terrorists. Worse, instead of preparing the Palestinians to live in peace with Israel, the PA did precisely the opposite. I believed that Israel had to stand firm in the face of Palestinian noncompliance and not continue the peace process if violations continued.

Though other party platforms included similar statements on the need for reciprocity, ours was unique in linking Israeli concessions with the degree of democratization in the society of our negotiating partner.

> The character of the relations with our neighbors and the willingness for a territorial compromise will depend on the degree of progressive democratization of the sides represented by our negotiating partners, particularly in the area of human rights.[11]

During the negotiations over our entry into Netanyahu's government, we asked that the connection between democracy and peace be included in the government's guidelines. The team negotiating on behalf of Netanyahu and his Likud party almost laughed us out of the room. "You deal with the absorption of immigrants," they said. "Let us deal with the peace process."

The first test of the new government came in Hebron, which was the last of the six West Bank cities that was to have been transferred to the PA. It was also the only one in which Jews lived. After a wave of suicide bombings in early 1996, Shimon Peres realized that Hebron could not be transferred to the PA as scheduled and decided to postpone the handover until after the Israeli elections. Peres lost those elections to Netanyahu by fewer than 30,000 votes. With Bibi now in charge, the question was whether the new government would go through with the postponed withdrawal. New governments are obviously bound by the agreements signed by previous governments, but Netanyahu had also run on a platform of reciprocity. Given the Palestinian violations of the agreements, it was not clear what he would do.

The government came under enormous pressure both inside and outside of Israel. Because the idea that a "moderate" Arafat should be given as much power as possible had become so firmly entrenched, the government's policy of reciprocity was easier to explain in theory than to implement in practice. Even though Netanyahu had won a democratic election by insisting on Palestinian compliance, the expectation in most diplomatic quarters was that if Israel wanted Arafat to start fulfilling his commitments, its "hardline" government would have to show that it too was committed to the peace process.

In the wake of the terror attacks, months were spent trying to guarantee the security of Hebron's residents. Hebron is the site of the Tomb of the Patriarchs and Matriarchs of the Jewish people, Abraham, Isaac, Jacob, Sara, Rebekah, and Leah. [12] Adding to the immense significance of Hebron to the Jewish people is the fact that it was also the first capital city of ancient Israel, before King David moved the capital to Jerusalem. Until 1929, Jews had lived in Hebron for three millennia. In that year, part of the Jewish community in Hebron was massacred in an Arab pogrom, and the rest fled in the wake of the slaughter. After Israel captured the West Bank city in 1967, a small number of Jews was determined to resettle there. Today 400 people live next to the Tomb of the Patriarchs and Matriarchs, and approximately 7,000 live in the nearby community of Kiryat Arba.

The vote to leave Hebron finally came in December. I decided to visit Hebron the morning before the government meeting. I intended to vote in favor of the withdrawal, but an overwhelming feeling of responsibility was pressing down on me. I wanted to see for myself what would happen to the Jewish residents of Hebron if the army redeployed and handed control over most of the city to the PA. Jews from the community explained to me the risks they would face should the handover be approved. Potentially hostile Palestinians would be only a few meters from their windows. The pleading look in their eyes sent a clear message: "Please don't betray us."

Prior to making a decision on Hebron, Netanyahu obtained written assurances that were aimed at redefining the rules of the game for the peace process. A letter from U.S. Secretary of State Warren Christopher, as well as a "Note for the Record," made clear that America backed our government's position that Israel alone would determine the extent of each further "redeployment" before a final status accord would be reached. The Palestinians claimed that the interim Oslo stages entitled them to nearly all the territories,[13] and Netanyahu wanted this issue clarified before he made any concessions. No less important, the "Note for the Record" made the principle of reciprocity explicit, stipulating that the PA would have to dismantle the terrorist infrastructure, confiscate illegal weapons, end incitement, and perform the various other commitments it had agreed to at Oslo in order for the peace process to continue.

My vote in favor of the Hebron redeployment is the only vote I have cast as a minister in the Israeli government that I regret. In retrospect, our government should have been less concerned with showing that we were ready to continue the peace process, less confident of American guarantees, and more insistent that the Palestinians take steps to comply with signed agreements before we moved forward. As it turned out, our government was given little diplomatic credit for the redeployment, promises of Palestinian reciprocity never materialized, and the idea of "strengthening Arafat" gained even wider currency. The risks that Israel took did not increase our security, improve our diplomatic position, or enhance the prospects for peace. Above all, the redeployment hindered our army's ability to defend the Jewish community in Hebron, leading to lethal results four years later when the community became a prime target of Palestinian terrorists.

A Look at Wye

The negotiations over Hebron convinced me that Arafat's greatest asset was the ubiquitous conception shared by many Israelis and nearly all the international community that he had to be as strong as possible for the peace process to succeed. Even interim agreements that could have served to move the peace process in the right direction were sabotaged by the constant fear of "weakening" the Palestinian leader. I witnessed this firsthand during the negotiations over the Wye agreement, in which I took part along with Prime Minister Netanyahu, then Foreign Minister Ariel Sharon, and Defense Minister Yitzhak Mordechai. Those negotiations were an attempt to reach an agreement over the second phase of Israel's redeployment in the territories. Netanyahu's government was willing to transfer additional territory in the West Bank to Palestinian control, but it was determined to both formally and practically restore reciprocity to the peace process. From now on, we said, both sides would have to keep their commitments.

I didn't realize it at the time, but Netanyahu's decision to include me in the Israeli delegation to Wye was quite extraordinary. Although I was part of his inner cabinet, there was no obvious reason for Bibi to invite me to participate in the talks. I was neither a senior minister nor a member of his Likud party. In fact, Netanyahu's decision was criticized by other coalition parties, who also wanted representatives at the talks.

But Bibi knew I had been a consistent champion of the principle of reciprocity and that I would defend it in the negotiations. As for my ideas of the importance of building a free society among the Palestinians, Netanyahu, who spent many years in the United States, was sympathetic in principle,[14] even if somewhat skeptical in practice.

With its beautiful grounds, placid river, gorgeous sunsets, the Wye Plantation in Virginia was an ideal place for peace negotiations. The atmosphere was meticulously designed to break the tensions between the sides. The media were kept at a safe distance and participants could only be accompanied by a single aide. The relatively small delegations preserved a more informal and laid-back environment. The main transportation was motorized carts, which I shared a number of times with Palestinians, some of whom spoke fluent Russian from their days "studying" in the former Soviet Union.

But in spite of the attempts to create a tranquil setting, the meetings and talks were full of tension. Every discussion seemed to turn into a game of brinkmanship. There were different teams working on all sorts of topics: the extent of the redeployment, the size of the Palestinian police force, the confiscation of weapons, the punishment and extradition of Palestinian terrorists, the fate of Palestinians in our own prisons, the establishment of a seaport and airport in Gaza, and many other matters. Regardless of the issue at stake, we would soon discover that the biggest problem in trying to restore reciprocity was that Arafat had convinced the Americans that he was too weak to fulfill any of our demands.

The negotiations at Wye were the first time I met Arafat. The Israeli delegation had many meetings with the PA leader that week, but our first encounter with him was for me the most revealing. In that initial meeting, we began by discussing what was thought to be one of the simplest issues. Thousands of cars were then being stolen from Israelis and smuggled into the Palestinian Authority, where they would be stripped and sold for parts. Car theft had become a national epidemic. Insurance rates were skyrocketing, and the Israeli police seemed powerless to address the issue since within minutes the cars were already driven to Palestinian controlled areas into which they could not enter. For its part, the PA was doing nothing to stop the thefts. In a few cases, however, when high profile Israelis who had their cars stolen had called their "friends" in the PA for help, the cars were suddenly "found."

During the meeting at Wye, we asked the Palestinians why they were not using their massive police force to stop the thefts. Predictably, they said that to address the issue they needed to be stronger, which would require more concessions from Israel.

Arafat sat silently, his eyes darting back and forth and his lower lip trembling. He was not involved in the conversation at all. "Is this the man that is running the Palestinian Authority?" I thought to myself. He seemed hardly capable of running anything.

Suddenly, Arafat jerked to attention and blurted out,

"It's the settlers. It's the settlers who are stealing the cars, not our people." Arafat's remark was so absurd and childish that it was difficult for me not to burst out laughing. But the Palestinians were not amused. Suddenly, Arafat's ridiculous outburst changed the dynamic of the discussion. The Palestinian delegation immediately went from being on the defensive to hurling charges at Israel. The Americans, obviously embarrassed by Arafat's outrageous assertion, chose not to confront Arafat at such an early stage of negotiations and over such a secondary issue.

After Arafat's remark, it became clear to me that though he may have looked as if he were detached from reality, he was in fact totally in charge. Like a virtuoso conductor, with one word, one gesture, or even one look, his whole orchestra would change its tune.

On the third day, the Americans presented a take-it-or-leave-it proposition. When Netanyahu and the rest of our team looked it over, we were shocked at how one-sided it was. All of Arafat's previous commitments, which he had reneged on and which we now wanted fulfilled, were turned into yet another round of lip service. We all agreed that if we planned on restoring reciprocity, the American proposal was totally unacceptable. Bibi asked me to inform the Americans of our position and members of the delegation started packing their bags. I called Dennis Ross. "We understand that this is a take-it-or-leave-it proposal. Well, we cannot take it, so we're leaving." A new set of efforts began to restore the talks. Eventually, the suitcases were unpacked and the negotiations resumed.

The Americans wanted to keep a feeling that a breakthrough could happen at any moment in the hopes that this would enable the sides to reach an agreement. The following morning, the person in charge of logistics came to tell us that we all had to dress formally and wear ties, since a signing ceremony might be held later that day. I had not worn a tie for a decade and considered it part of my newly found freedom. I asked the logistics person if Arafat would also be asked to wear a tie. "I don't think so," he answered. "So we'll offset each other," I told him. "Here at least we will have real reciprocity."

For me, the highlight at Wye came on the Saturday before official talks began. Neither Sharon nor Mordechai had yet arrived for the negotiations when Clinton paid a courtesy visit on Netanyahu and me. Netanyahu graciously gave me the opportunity to share my views with the president, a rare privilege because Bill Clinton is one of the best listeners I have ever met. He was entirely engaged in our conversation, sympathetic, understanding, and extremely sharp. During our hour-long conversation, I had enough time to describe my entire conception of what had gone wrong with the peace process and what would set it right.

I outlined my whole theory on the differences between democracies and dictatorships and explained why I believed that the essential flaw in Oslo was the erroneous assumption that a dictator would be interested in delivering peace and prosperity to his people. Israel, I said, had made a historic transformation. In the wake of the Oslo agreements, the mainstream Israeli body politic had abandoned an old and cherished ideology: the belief in a Greater Land of Israel. The reality of Oslo and the acceptance of Palestinian national rights that it called for were incompatible with the vision of settling the entire land from the Jordan to the Mediterranean.

Rather than impede this transformation, Netanyahu effectively completed it. With only half of the public feeling itself part of the peace process, a fundamental shift in Israeli attitudes would have remained in doubt. The critical moment came when Netanyahu, the so-called "Right-wing" prime minister, led an overwhelming majority of Knesset members to agree to transfer parts of Hebron to PA control, a move which marked a sea change in Israeli attitudes only one year after the country had experienced one of the most traumatic and tragic events of its short history, the political assassination of Yitzhak Rabin.

The Palestinians, I said to President Clinton, had not undergone a similar transformation. All the power that was given to Arafat was not being used to build bridges between our two societies but to strengthen the Palestinians' animosity toward Israel. This, I said, had to change. Given a territorial base, international recognition, and a presidential pulpit, Arafat should use his power to convince opinionmakers, journalists, teachers, and other influential Palestinians to end the decades-long struggle against the existence of Israel.

I asked the president to ignore what Arafat was telling him or telling English-speaking journalists and look instead at what he was saying in Arabic to his own people, what he was broadcasting on television, and what he was teaching in his schools. Arafat speeches in Arabic were laced with calls for a holy war to liberate Palestine and Jerusalem. The media and schools under his control were preaching hatred toward Israel and Jews. How could it be, I asked the president, that five years after a new era was to have begun, and after we had made many concessions to Arafat, Palestinian hatred toward Israel was greater than when the peace process began? The answer, I argued, was that Arafat was acting just like any dictator by maintaining his power using external enemies. Because of the nature of the Palestinian regime and its dependence on Israel, Arafat needed Israel as both a partner and an enemy. Just as the Communist leaders in the USSR once saw the United States, Arafat saw Israel as a partner who could provide external resources and an enemy who could provide internal stability.

I repeated the case for linking concessions to the Palestinian leadership to their creating a more democratic, open, and transparent society. For example, I said, Arafat could begin by changing the PLO Charter, not in a petty, semantic fashion that had no meaning, but in a way that sent a clear message to every Palestinian that the PA had stopped seeking the destruction of Israel and wanted to live in peace with it. In doing so, he would be following in the footsteps of Anwar Sadat, who boldly and unequivocally told Egyptians that there would be "no more wars" with Israel.

Changing the charter would not immediately transform the Palestinians into a democracy living in peace with Israel. But because the architects of Oslo had conspicuously avoided imposing liberalizing commitments on the Palestinian side, the charter was one of the few tools Israel had at its disposal to induce change within Palestinian society. That change should be followed, I said, by a concerted and systematic effort by the PA to promote peace among Palestinians.

That conversation with the president was the first time since the peace process began that I felt that the importance of change *within* Palestinian society was finally understood, and by no less than the leader of the free world, the man who was devoting so much time and energy to helping Israelis and Palestinians achieve peace.

The next day, the Israeli delegation had lunch with Clinton, Vice President Al Gore, Secretary of State Madeleine Albright, National Security Adviser Sandy Berger, Ambassador to Israel Martin Indyk, and America's special envoy to the Middle East, Dennis Ross. Clinton said he had spoken with Arafat and told him that he agreed with me that the most important thing was the message Arafat was conveying to his own people. He told him that publicly changing the charter offered the opportunity to send a clear message to his people. Predictably, Arafat and his advisers warned the president that "changing the charter would weaken them and bring Hamas to power."

At our lunch, Clinton came up with a proposal to break the impasse. What do you think, Clinton asked the Israeli delegation, about the idea of my going to Gaza to publicly support Arafat and make it easier for him to change the charter? The reaction of the Israeli delegation was mixed. It was clear that such a visit would give Arafat enormous legitimacy. On the other hand, if the visit would represent a turning point for Arafat, an end to his speaking out of both sides of his mouth, and the beginning of him conveying a clear and unequivocal message of peace, we thought it might be worth the price.

After much prodding, Arafat and his entourage finally consented to change the charter if Clinton came to Gaza. No sooner had everyone agreed than a senior American administration official chased me down a corridor, frantically insisting that Israel had "put a gun to Arafat's head." There was no way, he said, that Arafat could fulfill this promise without endangering his own life. Amazingly, the official then told me he was going to try to convince Arafat not to go through with it.

I realized then that if this official believed that "strengthening" Arafat precluded the Palestinian leader from making even this minimal effort to promote peace and reconciliation, we could not hope to convince America to press Arafat to keep any of his commitments in the future. My fears that the desire to strengthen Arafat was endangering Israel's future were compounded by my concerns about the effect this thinking was having on our most important ally. Not only did it preclude any hope of America supporting efforts to link the peace process to the opening of Palestinian society, but it was also placing us in a diplomatic quagmire in which pressure would be borne only by Israel, the side that could "afford" to compromise.

Given such a mindset, it was only natural that the United States bent over backwards to accommodate Arafat when it finally came time for him to change the charter. Not only did the president reward Arafat with a trip to Gaza—the first visit by any head of state to PA-controlled territory—but the administration also spared no effort to appease the Palestinians. It was a fiasco: American officials made statements that drew a dangerous moral equivalency between the families of those who perpetrated terror and those who were its victims.[15] Arafat's speech declaring the change of the charter was as vague as possible, and the "vote" was an orchestrated raising of hands that collapsed into applause for the "Great Leader and Teacher." The whole thing was a charade.

A day in which Arafat should have sent a historic message to Palestinians to accept the legitimacy of the Jewish state and to start down the road of reconciliation was used instead to strengthen the despot's moral authority and the Palestinians sense of victimization. He was allowed to continue his game of sending a double message, one in Arabic to his own people and the other in English to the rest of the world. For all of President Clinton's understanding and sympathy, he did not make a serious effort to change the rules of the Oslo game. The key to peace still meant keeping Arafat strong and keeping the peace process moving "forward" no matter what.

AMERICA'S SILENCE

Before the farce in Gaza, the peace process was rocked by another crisis that also had its seeds at Wye. There, Arafat had demanded that Israel release 750 Palestinians whom the PA deemed "political prisoners." They had been convicted of "nationalistic" crimes against the State of Israel as opposed to car theft, burglary, rape, and other offenses. The problem was that filling such a high quota of prisoners would have required Israel to release prisoners with "blood on their hands," a phrase Israel used to describe those convicted of crimes that resulted in fatalities. Israel had only 200 prisoners without blood on their hands who fit the Palestinian definition of "political prisoners." Moreover, those of us at Wye had no intention of agreeing to the release of murderers.

When the Americans realized that Netanyahu would not budge on this issue, they asked the Israeli side for a favor to break the impasse. Since the Palestinians did not want it publicly known that they had agreed to compromise on the prisoner issue, the official agreement would say that 750 prisoners would be released. In practice, however, we would not have to release prisoners with blood on their hands. Netanyahu agreed to the proposal only after America committed itself to vouch for the oral understanding.

Immediately after we returned to Israel, the Palestinians reneged on the deal and publicly claimed that Israel had agreed to release 750 prisoners, *including* those with blood on their hands. The pressure for Israel to immediately fulfill its "obligations" began to grow. We expected America to keep its word and reject the false claims that were being made by the PA. But America stayed silent. Netanyahu called Dennis Ross to voice Israel's disappointment and had me speak to him as well. I told Dennis that after years of noncompliance with agreements, Arafat did not believe he had to abide by any of his commitments. "If after the great efforts that were made at Wye to restore reciprocity America will now allow Arafat to renege on his promises, then there will be no hope that the peace process can succeed," I said. "We must freeze everything, until the matter is resolved."

Dennis listened patiently and said he agreed with many of my points but that I also had to understand Arafat's problematic situation and how much pressure he was under, particularly from the families of the prisoners. The important thing, Dennis said, was to make sure that the peace process could move forward.

It was a message I had heard many times from my friend Dennis Ross. Dennis is a first-rate diplomat, with a terrific memory for detail, an easy manner, and a knack for building and rebuilding bridges between negotiating partners. His commitment to peace is also matched by a strong Jewish identity. On a number of Friday evenings, when he couldn't meet with Israeli government officials who do not conduct official business on the Jewish Sabbath, and before he could meet with Arafat, who preferred meetings very late at night, he was a dinner guest in my home. It was a chance to have nonofficial discussions about many things, including the peace process. I would usually tell Dennis why I felt Palestinian compliance was so important to the building of trust on both sides. He was genuinely sympathetic with my point of view, even about the importance of Palestinian democracy and the PA's respect for human rights, but he would also argue how important it was to "strengthen" Arafat's hand.[16]

Israel's government had gone to great lengths at Wye to accommodate Arafat in an effort to forge an agreement that would restore reciprocity to the peace process. But even though Arafat was blatantly breaking his word in front of the Americans, the Clinton administration was reluctant to hold him accountable. While this reluctance was present from the beginning of Oslo, America's attitude toward Arafat was especially disturbing since only a few days earlier the Wye agreement had been signed on the basis of America's explicit promise to back Israel on the prisoner issue.

Though America kept silent, Netanyahu went ahead with a vote on the first stage of Wye. I warned about the dangers of fulfilling our commitments when America's silence was helping Arafat avoid compliance. If we wanted to restore reciprocity, I argued, we would have to stand our ground. That is why, to the dismay of Netanyahu, who must have felt that I was being ungrateful after having taken me to Wye, I abstained. The first batch of 250 prisoners were released. When it became clear that many of those released were common criminals—contrary to the Palestinian public's expectations but in accordance with the Wye agreement—strikes were called in Israel's prisons, riots broke out in the territories and almost all the international community said that Israel had reneged on its commitments. Netanyahu, burned by the Americans, decided to freeze the process. By the time the Americans finally did side with Israel by confirming publicly that we were telling the truth about the prisoner issue, the damage was already done.

When Clinton came to Israel for his Gaza trip a few days later and met with the four ministers who participated at Wye, I told him that I was extremely disappointed. "There was an agreement," I said, "which America had promised to guarantee." I continued, "If America had stood by Israel two weeks ago and not worried about weakening Arafat, then the violence that took place would have been avoided."

The prisoner episode illustrated the problems that plagued Netanyahu's government from the beginning. During Bibi's tenure, a clear effort was made to replace Oslo's blind leap of faith with a more sober approach that stressed reciprocity and compliance with agreements. But only a firm Israeli stance coupled with unequivocal American backing could have made the policy a success. In the end, the combination of a bitterly polarized Israeli public and an international community, including the United States, determined not to weaken Arafat ultimately undermined the policy.

As for the issue that concerned me the most, almost nothing was done to promote change within Palestinian society. I had proposed that a committee be formed to address the problem of Palestinian incitement, but once it was established, it almost never met. The government, focused on terrorism, weapons, and prisoners, simply didn't make incitement a real priority. Money continued to be transferred to Arafat's private slush fund despite repeated protests in the cabinet that it be stopped. As minister of trade and industry, I could not overcome Arafat's determination to maintain the fear society he had created. Arafat rejected countless projects Israel proposed that would have bettered the lot of his own people because they would have served to decrease tensions between Israelis and Palestinians and release his hold on Palestinian economic life. For a long time, he successfully blocked efforts to help the Palestinian Authority establish an industrial park in Gaza that would have encouraged investment in Palestinian areas, created tens of thousands of jobs, and alleviated poverty.

Similarly, Arafat rejected my proposal to create joint ventures in the West Bank in existing industrial zones that would have fostered cooperation between Jews and Arabs and generously redistributed municipal tax revenues to depressed Palestinian areas. He was not interested in creating jobs for his people or improving the conditions in which they lived. Hiding behind the rhetoric of resisting occupation, Arafat simply opposed the development of a Palestinian society that would not be fully under his control and that would move toward genuine reconciliation with Israel. But his rhetoric worked. No one was willing to support efforts to force Arafat to improve the lives of his own people because the peace process continued to operate under the dangerous assumption that strengthening Arafat was the key to peace.

BARAK JUMPS INTO THE ABYSS

In May 1999, Ehud Barak won a landslide victory over Netanyahu. Barak was the former chief of staff of the Israeli Defense Forces and had once served as the commander of Sayeret Matkal, the country's most famous elite military unit (Bibi had been a member of the same unit). Barak seemed to bring a general's penchant for quick and decisive operations to the political arena. He saw the arduous efforts of the Netanyahu government to restore reciprocity as needless haggling over insignificant issues that only bogged down the peace process and prevented the sides from resolving the conflict. That is why he refused even to put the word "reciprocity" into his government's guidelines. To Barak, reciprocity had become "a symbol of our looking for excuses not to move forward." Instead the new guidelines specified that the commitments of Israelis and Palestinians would be fulfilled "in parallel," a vague diplomatic formulation that effectively threw the quid pro quo approach of the previous administration out the window.

Barak, however, was no champion of Oslo. He clearly did not trust Arafat and had courageously bucked his own Labor party by abstaining on a key peace-process vote as a minister in Yitzhak Rabin's government. His criticism of Oslo was that it was forcing Israel to relinquish all its assets without receiving a final peace agreement in return.

My party planned to join Barak's government and advance the absorption-related issues on our agenda. On questions of security, Barak had put most people at ease that the days of terror would not return. Most new immigrants saw Barak as he had portrayed himself during an intensive campaign in Israel's Russian-speaking media, as the country's most decorated soldier, a warrior who would never compromise their security.

During coalition negotiations, our party again brought up the question of Palestinian democracy and human rights. Barak's representatives were even more dumbfounded than Bibi's representatives had been three years earlier. After serving as a member of Netanyahu's government, most Israelis had pigeonholed me as a "Right-wing" minister, a label which suggested to many on the Left that I was not overly concerned about Palestinian rights.

Barak, the "Left-wing" prime minister, refused to put the democracy issue into the new government's guidelines. In truth, nothing could be further from the mind of Barak or his Labor party colleagues than Palestinian democracy. Yossi Beilin, appointed minister of justice in the new government, expressed what seemed to be the dominant view of nearly all the self-described "peace camp" in Israel when he said that "if we wait until [the Palestinians] become democratic, then peace will wait for our great-grandchildren, not ourselves. ... My first priority is to make peace with the Palestinians. I do not believe that it is up to me to educate them." 17

With potential negotiations with Syria on the horizon, my party did insist that a letter be attached to the coalition agreement stipulating that Yisrael Ba'aliyah's Knesset members believed that the extent of Israel's concessions to Syria should be equal to the degree of openness, transparency, and democracy within Syria. To my knowledge, this is the only coalition agreement in Israel's history that linked democracy among our neighbors with peace.

In my meetings with Barak, he told me that he was determined to jump to final status talks immediately and to resolve all outstanding issues in one fell swoop. He intended, he said, to use previous Israeli commitments to entice the Palestinians to enter into final status negotiations. To Barak, the prolonged stages of Oslo that were supposed to develop mutual trust had proven to be a failure and were likely to trigger confrontation in the future. The Palestinians, Barak argued, believed that Oslo entitled them to nearly all the territory before final status talks were completed, something Israel could not accept. Barak was confident that he would greatly improve Israel's negotiating positions: "We will explain to the world that even 50 percent of the West Bank is an enormous concession, and we will start negotiations from there."

The prime minister was particularly keen on reaching an agreement before President Clinton left office. According to Barak's calculations, a deal would have to be signed by August 2000, when a new presidential candidate was scheduled to be chosen at the Democratic National Convention, and the "window of opportunity" would close. I told Barak that by restricting himself to finishing the negotiations at a predetermined time, he was giving the Palestinians a huge advantage. But Barak was determined to achieve peace as quickly as possible.

In order not to interfere with his plans to wrap everything up by the following summer, Prime Minister Barak preferred to ignore all the Palestinian commitments that had been made since Oslo began. He continued fulfilling Israel's responsibilities under the Wye agreement, and even made additional gestures such as releasing prisoners with "blood on their hands" without demanding anything in return. I repeatedly asked that the government prepare a report on Palestinian compliance with previous agreements, but it was never put on the agenda. I voted in the government against all of Barak's concessions, protesting each time that the Palestinians were being allowed once again to avoid complying with their commitments. When Barak decided to transfer areas on the outskirts of Jerusalem's Old City to the Palestinians as a down payment that would encourage them to enter final-status negotiations, I stressed this point in an op-ed in the *New York Times*:

> [I]f the Palestinian Authority can get a toehold into the eastern part of Jerusalem without extraditing a terrorist or changing a textbook, why should it ever agree to the painful compromises that are the only way to bring real reconciliation?[18]

I also began voicing my concerns that Barak's hurried attempts to reach an agreement and keep to his self-imposed timetable were giving Arafat the ability to extract more and more concessions before serious negotiations had even started. A paradoxical situation had emerged. When Barak initially formed his government, my fear was that he would be too generous during final-status negotiations. Now I was afraid that Barak would be too generous *prior* to negotiations taking place, since he was making concessions just to start the talks. According to reports that began to circulate, the same man who had told me he would convince the world of the generosity of an offer of 50 percent of the territories was already proposing Israel give up 70 percent, 80 percent, even 90 percent of the territories. Since no official talks had begun, these were becoming Israel's opening positions in final-status negotiations.

My fears deepened in May 2000 when I found out that back-channel negotiations with the Palestinians were being conducted in Stockholm. According to the information I received, Barak had made outlandish concessions to the Palestinians, including giving up over 90 percent of the territories and half of Jerusalem. Not only had the prime minister vitiated the principle of reciprocity and agreed to concessions that were not supported by Israel's government or people, but he had also continued to erode Israel's negotiating positions without receiving anything in return.

Troubled by what I had heard, I went to speak to Barak, who denied everything. After receiving the same information a few days later from a different source, I wrote an open letter to the prime minister expressing my concerns:

In the last few days, disturbing news has reached me regarding agreements that you made or that were made in your name within the framework of negotiations with representatives of the Palestinian Authority. It pains me that you do not tend to share the developments in the negotiations with the members of the government or at least the members of the security cabinet and the heads of the parties that are coalition partners. So I am forced to learn about these developments from personal friends. . . . From the agreement being developed a dangerous reality is being created according to which Israel relinquishes, in advance, all of its assets without insisting on the settling of the final status of Jerusalem, the refugees and the borders. [19]

At the next cabinet meeting, I told Barak how I regretted never having developed the skills of a spy despite serving in prison for nine years on false charges of espionage on behalf of the United States. "I never thought that I would one day need those skills as a minister in my own government to build an international network to find out what my own prime minister is proposing to the Palestinians."

On the eve of Barak's visit to Camp David to conclude a peace deal with the Palestinians, I brought my letter of resignation to the prime minister. He argued that there was no reason for me to leave the government and even proposed that I join him at Camp David. "Look, Natan," he said, "it is true that I am prepared to make large concessions in return for a final peace agreement. But one of two things will happen. If Arafat agrees, then you and I will have a problem, but Israel will have peace. And if he says no, all of Israel will be united and the world will be with us." I told Barak that there was no chance he would bring peace and that his willingness to make such concessions after years of noncompliance would only further convince the Palestinians of our weakness.

At the time, I was fiercely criticized by many on the Left, both inside and outside Israel, who argued that by leaving Barak's government on the eve of an historic agreement, I was "betraying peace" and the struggle for human rights. The *New York Times* correspondent in Israel noted that "doves in Israel long ago stopped expressing their disappointment that Sharansky, a former human-rights champion, ended up taking a hard line on peace and joining the nationalist camp." But as I argued in a column explaining my decision to resign, peace and human rights were certainly on my mind.

> The same human rights principles that once guided me in the Soviet Union remain the cornerstone of my approach to the peace process. I am willing to transfer territory not because I think the Jewish people have less of a claim to Judea and Samaria than do the Palestinians, but because the principle of individual autonomy remains sacred to me—I do not want to rule another people. At the same time, I refuse to ignore the Palestinian Authority's violations of human rights because I

remain convinced that a neighbor who tramples on the rights of its own people will eventually threaten the security of my people.... A genuinely "new" Middle East need not be a fantasy. But it will not be brought about by merely ceding lands to Arab dictators and by subsidizing regimes that undermine the rights of their own people. The only way to create real Arab-Israeli reconciliation is to press the Arab world to respect human rights. Israel must link its concessions to the degree of openness, transparency, and liberalization of its neighbors. For their part, Western leaders must not think the Arabs any less deserving of the freedom and rights that their own citizens enjoy—both for their sake and for ours.[20]

Barak called me at home from Camp David. "Natan," he said, "I was sitting alone in my room reflecting on the historic decisions I will have to make and I thought of you sitting in solitary confinement in prison. I thought you of all people could understand the weight I feel on my shoulders, the enormous sense of responsibility I bear." By then, I knew that anything I would say about Palestinian compliance, much less Palestinian democratization, would be completely ignored. But I figured since Barak seemed so interested in making history, I might remind him of the history of his own people.

"I just heard," I told the prime minister, "that Arafat said that since Jerusalem belongs to all Muslims, he will not agree to make any compromises on Jerusalem without first consulting the leaders of Egypt, Saudi Arabia, and Pakistan. Yet you have decided to divide Jerusalem without the support of your own government, let alone the Jewish world."

"Ehud," I continued, "I do not know if you are aware of it, but according to the Jewish calendar, we are now in the middle of the three-week period in which we mourn the destruction of our ancient Temple. During these three weeks, religious Jews do not even sign a contract to buy or sell an apartment. But you, the prime minister of the State of Israel, are prepared to sign an agreement to divide Jerusalem. If you go ahead with your plan, you will be remembered in history as the first Jewish leader who voluntarily agreed to give up Jerusalem."

Ehud Barak did not give up Jerusalem. Yasser Arafat wouldn't let him. The head of the PA turned Barak's offer down and started a war instead. The tremendous international support that Barak had assumed his far-reaching offer would bring Israel never materialized. The desire to strengthen Arafat was so powerful, the belief that he was the key to peace so pervasive, that diplomats the world over both excused the actions of a tyrant who had unleashed an unprecedented wave of terrorism and blamed Israel for provoking the terror launched against it.

One thing that can be said of Barak is that he did not waver from his all-or-nothing strategy. In sticking to this approach, he exposed the true face of Arafat to Israelis before we made any more concessions to him. Had Barak responded to the intifada by forming a national unity government and forcefully responding to Palestinian aggression, he would have united the country and perhaps would still be prime minister today. But instead, Barak poured fuel on the fire by responding to Palestinian terror by offering even more concessions. Supported by less than one-quarter of his parliament, Barak recklessly continued negotiating an agreement that would not only determine the permanent borders of Israel, but also affect the identity of the Jewish people for many generations to come. Moreover, despite what he may have believed, and probably still believes, Barak's concessions, which he was never authorized to make in the first place, have still not been taken off the table. In the minds of much of the world, they have become the starting point for negotiations in the future.

Supporters of the peace process, both inside and outside of Israel, expressed their shock at the violence that greeted Barak's unprecedented generosity. They simply could not understand how Palestinian hatred toward Israel could have turned so virulent. The animalistic mutilation of Israeli soldiers, the feverish incitement in the Palestinian media, the calls to martydom that rang from Palestinian schools and mosques, and the chants of "Death to the Jews" that echoed throughout the Arab world raised the eyebrows of even the most ardent supporters of compromise.

But those dreaming of a quick solution to the conflict should not have been surprised. For seven years, Arafat was doing what all dictators do, using his power not to promote peace and better the lot of the Palestinians but rather to turn the Palestinians into a battering ram against the Jewish state. Money allocated to improve the Palestinian living standards was diverted to support a vast network of terror. Hundreds of millions of dollars earmarked for social and economic development were instead used to buy weapons to attack Israel. Broadcasting stations meant to promote democracy and freedom were used to foment incitement and justify terror. Schools meant to educate the next generation of Palestinians for peace with Israel have only inculcated hatred for Jews and their state. By allowing, and often encouraging, Arafat to create a fear society, a peace process that should have been steadily reducing a century-old animus had instead exacerbated it.

CHAPTER 6

The Battle for Moral Clarity

ON SEPTEMBER 28, 2000, a day when Israelis were celebrating the Jewish New Year, the second "intifada" began.
Unlike the first intifada thirteen years before, this was no
spontaneous uprising. The pretext for the violence was the
visit two days earlier of then opposition leader Ariel Sharon
to the Temple Mount, the site of the ancient Jewish Temple,
the holiest place for the Jewish people and the site of the
world-famous Al-Aqsa Mosque. Absurdly, many people
around the world called Sharon's visit a "provocation." In
fact, not only was it coordinated with the appropriate
Moslem religious authorities in advance, but Israeli ministers and members of Knesset often went to the Temple
Mount without incident and continue to go there today. I

myself was there recently as part of my duties as minister of Jerusalem affairs.

The calculated campaign of terror was designed to gain through violence what could not be achieved through diplomacy. Prime Minister Barak had agreed to offer Arafat everything the PA leader was believed in the "West" to have wanted: a Palestinian State in the West Bank and Gaza, a capital in Jerusalem, even a formula for resolving the Palestinian refugee issue. But Barak demanded one thing in return: that Arafat end the conflict, something the Palestinian dictator had no intention of doing. For six years, Arafat built a society based on fear, maintaining his repressive rule by mobilizing his people for war against the Jewish state. He was not about to give up the enemy that stabilized his control over the Palestinians or end the conflict that was his lifeblood.

Barak's offer temporarily wrong-footed Arafat: By refusing it, he became the obstacle to peace. To turn the diplomatic tables on Israel, Arafat waged war. That Arafat would seriously think he could force Israel, with its vastly superior army and in an ostensibly strong diplomatic position, into making concessions may seem hard to believe. But Arafat knew he had an ace up his sleeve: the lack of moral clarity in the free world, which allowed Arafat to be seen as a victim of Israel's superior military capability. Ironically, by conferring legitimacy on him, and by calling on others to do the same, Israeli governments, including those in which I served, had contributed to this lack of moral clarity.

In a world that did not recognize the moral difference between free and fear societies and in a world that expected democracies at war to act like democracies at peace, Arafat had a huge advantage. In this moral confusion, he could turn the aggressor into a victim and a state defending itself according to the highest human rights standards into an international pariah. The wall-to-wall support that Israel should have received from the democratic world in repelling the unprecedented terrorist war Arafat launched never materialized. And with moral clarity in short supply, the boundaries of legitimate criticism of the State of Israel became blurred, helping trigger a new wave of anti-Semitism the likes of which the free world had not seen for sixty years.

For the last decade, many in the free world were convincing themselves that the rise of anti-Semitism in the Middle East was an unfortunate but passing episode on the way to peace. Now, it appears as though the peace process was a passing episode on the way to a revived anti-Semitism.

THE HUMAN RIGHTS CONFUSION

One way to see today's lack of moral clarity is to take note of the confusion that continues to surround the question of human rights. Rather than serve as a sacred principle that leaves little room for doubt, human rights have always been mired in controversy. When the Universal Declaration of Human Rights was drafted at the United Nations in 1948, it was adopted without dissent, but with abstentions by Soviet bloc nations, South Africa, and Saudi Arabia.[1] As is true of any attempt to bridge the unbridgeable moral gap between dictatorship and democracy, the declaration stood for everything, and hence, for nothing.

This was good news for the Soviet Union, which always tried to undermine efforts to bring moral clarity to the issue of human rights. As Western leaders justly denounced the human rights record of the communist superpower, Soviet leaders consistently attacked liberal democracies in the language of human rights by wrapping them in the mantle of "social justice"—a social justice that was being used by those same regimes to justify the murder of tens of millions of their own subjects.

Still, for those who were not totally blinded by the egalitarian newspeak of tyrants like Stalin, Mao, and Pol Pot, the Cold War offered something of an antidote to the obfuscation of human rights issues. By splitting the world into two, the struggle between the totalitarian East and the democratic West helped clarify the conflict—at least for those willing to open their eyes—as a battle between good and evil, right and wrong.

For dissidents within the former Soviet Union, these moral lines were practically self-evident. Unlike philosophers and rights activists in the West, we dissidents did not feel the need to split hairs over the precise nature of human rights.

We knew that to determine whether or not human rights were being generally upheld in a particular country, we only had to ask a few simple questions:

Could people in that country speak their minds?
Could they publish their opinions?
Could they practice their faith?
Could they learn the history and culture of their people?

We understood that for those living in a fear society, the answer to most of our questions, if not all of them, was no. The structural elements that enable democratic societies to respect human rights—independent courts, the rule of law, a free press, a freely elected government, meaningful opposition parties, not to mention human rights organizations— were all glaringly absent in fear societies. While these structures are not always sufficient to ensure the protection of human rights, our experience had convinced us that without them, human rights would inevitably be crushed. Every political prisoner in the Gulag recognized the moral chasm that separated free societies and fear societies. We recognized that a free society did not guarantee the protection of human rights, but we knew that a fear society guaranteed their violation.

Yet the connection between democracy and human rights that seemed so clear to us dissidents was often ignored in the West. The blindness to this connection by many of those whom we saw as natural allies in the human rights struggle was a source of constant disappointment for those fighting for freedom within the Soviet Union. We dissidents could ready ourselves psychologically for a life of risk, arrest, and imprisonment. But we could never fully prepare ourselves for the disappointment that came from seeing the free world abandon its own values. And nowhere was this disappointment more bitterly experienced than from the confines of a prison cell.

An example was the trip of the world-famous evangelical preacher, Billy Graham, to the Soviet Union in 1984. For many years before and since, Graham and his followers have been a driving force for moral clarity in world affairs. But on this particular trip, Graham helped the cause of moral equivalence. When he arrived in the Baltic Republics, a region with a large number of Protestants, Graham was permitted to deliver his riveting sermons in packed stadiums. In an interview following one of those sermons, he was asked to describe freedom of religion within the Soviet Union. After remarking that he had been free to preach wherever he wanted, Graham observed that challenges relating to religious freedoms were not particular to the USSR. "You have some problems with religion," he told the Soviet journalist, and "the United States has problems with religion." Both countries, Graham said, could do better.

Sitting in my prison cell, I read about Graham's visit in *Pravda*, the government-controlled newspaper we were permitted to read. *Pravda*'s editors naturally gave pride of place to the American preacher's comments about freedom of religion inside the Soviet Union. I was dumbfounded. How could Graham possibly place religious freedom in a free society like the United States on a par with religious freedom in a fear society like the Soviet Union? Did the heated debates in America over the separation of church and state blind Graham to the fact that individuals in the USSR were completely denied the right to practice their faith? Did Graham not understand that he was giving legitimacy to a system that sought to eradicate religion completely?

Though Graham was free to preach to tens of thousands of people, my own cellmate, Vladimir Poresh, who was Greek Orthodox, was given a seven-year sentence for teaching Christian "propaganda" to fewer than ten people. Our fellow prisoners included many of Graham's fellow Pentecostals, who were first exiled to Siberia and later persecuted for trying to teach religion to their own children.

When I mentioned Graham's remarks to Poresh, it reminded Poresh of his own trial. During his pre-trial interrogation, his Bible was taken away from him. The authorities gave it back to him the day before the trial and then used his possession of it as "proof" that freedom of religion was protected in the USSR. Of course, immediately after the trial the Bible was taken from him again. Ironically, when Graham was praising religious freedom in the USSR, Poresh was on a hunger strike. Why? To get back the Bible our jailers had once again taken from him.

At least Graham later regretted his remarks. But the same cannot be said about the many peace activists in the early 1980s who showed a similar lapse of moral clarity. In response to the Soviet buildup of intermediate range nuclear missiles, President Reagan and Western European leaders were determined to deploy Pershing nuclear missiles in Europe to deter any possible Soviet attack on the Continent. Millions of people took to the streets in Western European capitals protesting that the real aggressors were the warmongering American president and his European allies, not the Soviets. The leaders of the anti-nuclear rallies pointed to the "peace activists" from the USSR who were denouncing Western aggression and marching alongside them as proof that the Soviets wanted peace. But those who were marching in Europe were a handpicked delegation sent by the Soviet regime to increase pressure on Western governments to reverse their position and remove the Pershings. Meanwhile, the real peace activists in the USSR, those who had demanded that the Soviets disarm, were languishing in prison with me.

While Graham and the peace activists certainly did not intend to crush the spirits of dissidents inside the USSR, that was the effect of their actions. I am sure Iranians fighting for their freedom felt a similar dejection when an official in the American State Department recently referred to their country as a democracy.

THE MORAL MUDDLE IN ISRAEL

When I arrived in Israel in 1986, I was inundated with hundreds of telegrams from across the world. One stuck out in particular, as it was sent from three PLO activists in Europe. At that time, contact with the PLO was against Israeli law. The telegram read: "You fought for human rights in the Soviet Union and we are fighting for human rights in Palestine. Your struggle is our struggle."

At first, I was amused. The idea that anyone could seriously claim the PLO and I were engaged in the same "struggle" seemed absolutely preposterous. I assumed that everyone could instantly recognize this fact by asking themselves the same simple questions we dissidents asked ourselves in the Soviet Union.

> Could Palestinians subject to Israeli rule speak their minds?
> Could they publish their opinions?
> Could they practice their faith?
> Could they learn their own history and culture?

Since the answer to all these questions was yes, I was quite certain that the two "struggles" were worlds apart. But there was also another important difference. Champions of human rights would *never* deliberately kill civilians to advance their agendas, nor support any movement or person who did. In fact, the dissidents I knew did not resort to *any* form of violence whatsoever, knowing that this would only cede the moral high ground that was so essential to our struggle. For the PLO, however, terrorism was a calling card. They murdered Olympic athletes, executed kindergarten schoolchildren, hijacked airliners, set off bombs in public places, and committed a host of other acts of terror.

Despite these obvious differences, I soon realized that the notion that our two struggles were the same was a widespread delusion. In my first few days in Israel, I spoke to many foreign journalists who invariably got around to asking the same question: "Will you now continue your human rights activism by fighting for Palestinian human rights?" To these journalists, my struggle and the Palestinian struggle were one and the same.

Unlike the PLO, who were simply using the human rights issue to batter the Jewish state, many of the journalists who asked me this question had a genuine regard for human rights. They were concerned with the miserable conditions in which many Palestinians lived and felt that the world had an obligation to improve them. On this point, I wholeheartedly agreed with them.

By the time I arrived in Israel, two generations of Palestinians had already been raised in squalid refugee camps, pawns in the Arab world's struggle against the Jewish state. Hundreds of thousands became innocent bystanders caught in the middle of a war that Palestinian terrorists and the Arab states were waging against Israel. The roadblocks, closures, curfews, and other measures Israel was forced to take to defend its citizens often left Palestinians unable to get to their jobs or visit their families.

Yet despite my sympathy with this suffering and my desire to see it redressed, I could never understand how anyone could equate Israel's free society with a fear society. In the Soviet Union, a true fear society, there was no dissent, no free speech, no free press, no freedom of religion, no independent courts, and no human rights organizations. Indeed, the members of the Helsinki Group had been arrested merely for *reporting* human rights abuses. For

Palestinians under Israeli rule, the situation was vastly different. They could speak freely, publish their ideas, practice their faith, appeal to independent courts, and contact human rights organizations.

When a human rights organization I deeply respected also chose to ignore the important moral distinction between free and fear societies, I realized the full extent of the problem. Amnesty International, an organization dedicated to fighting human rights abuses around the world, is well known for its support of prisoners of conscience and the right of dissent. I felt a strong personal connection to Amnesty International: Several of my friends were sentenced to prison for collecting information on its behalf, and I myself had been a beneficiary of their indefatigable efforts to raise awareness about political dissidents and to fight for their release. I thought of Amnesty as an organization with which I could completely identify.

Soon after I arrived in Israel, I met with Amnesty officials. It felt like a reunion of old comrades. I gave them information on other prisoners and the conditions of the camps in which I had stayed. They gave me a copy of their annual human rights report and told me about their ongoing campaigns for dissidents around the world. I was honored when they asked me to speak at a meeting later that year in London.

But when I began to flip through the pages of the annual report I immediately noticed that something was terribly wrong. There were pages and pages of material about human rights abuses in my new country, Israel, and very little on the nondemocratic states that surrounded us. It appeared as though Israel was a bigger violator of human rights than Saudi Arabia, a country where there was no freedom of speech, no freedom of the press, and no freedom of religion. In fact, the impression one got from the report was that Israel was one of the worst human rights abusers in the world, if not the worst. When I was given the opportunity to speak to Amnesty supporters in London later that year, I decided to address the matter head on.

I pointed out that precisely because Israel is an open society where the press is free to criticize the government and where human rights organizations are free to issue damning reports, it is much easier to garner information on human rights abuses in Israel than in closed societies. While I told the audience that I did not believe human rights abuses in Israel should ever be glossed over or hidden from the public eye, I offered what I thought was a constructive suggestion. Why not divide the report into three sections, one for totalitarian regimes, one for authoritarian regimes, and one for democracies? Without those categories, Amnesty was creating a dangerous moral equivalence between countries where human rights are sometimes abused and countries where they are *always* abused.

The reply of Amnesty officials following my speech was extremely disappointing. "We are not going to label countries," they told me. "We will simply show the picture as it is." Nearly twenty years later, Amnesty has not changed its policy. It continues to proudly state that it "does not support or oppose any political system" because it is "concerned solely with the impartial protection of human rights."[2] But how can a human rights organization be impartial about political systems that are *inherently* hostile to human rights? No doubt, its dedicated activists believe that this impartiality between fear and free societies does not undermine the cause of human rights. But it does.

HOW FREE SOCIETIES RESPOND TO HUMAN RIGHTS VIOLATIONS

In the post 9/11 world, many democratic governments now have a better appreciation of how difficult it can be to find the appropriate balance between providing maximum security to your citizens and protecting human rights. In debating issues like the Patriot Act or the rights granted to prisoners at Guantanamo Bay, Americans are confronting a dilemma that Israel has faced since the day it was established.

Human rights violations can and do take place in democratic societies. But one of the things that sets democracies apart from fear societies is the way they *respond* to those violations. A fear society does not openly debate human rights issues. Its people do not protest. Its regime does not investigate. Its press does not expose. Its courts do not protect. In contrast, democratic societies are always engaged in self-examination.

For example, look at how the United States dealt with the abuse and humiliation of Iraqi prisoners by American soldiers in Abu Ghraib prison. Even before the abuse became publicly known, the army had suspended those involved and was conducting a full investigation. And as soon as the disturbing pictures of the abuse were published, America's democracy was shocked into action. The Congress, determined to find the culprits, immediately convened public hearings, and demanded a full account of what led to the abuse. Politicians and opinion makers insisted that the people responsible for the abuse be held accountable, including those at the very top of the chain of command. The media mulled over the details, pursuing every allegation, tracking down every lead. The American people openly discussed what the abuse said about their own country's values, its image in the world, and how that image would affect the broader War on Terror. The U.S. president, for his part, apologized to the families of the victims and said that those responsible would be punished.

But let's not forget that the treatment of prisoners at Abu Ghraib under Saddam was far worse than anything America was accused of. Yet were pictures distributed of Saddam's soldiers murdering, raping, and torturing Iraqis? If they had been distributed, would Iraq's parliament have conducted public hearings? Would the Iraqi media have reported it? Would anyone have publicly called for the resignation of Saddam's defense minister, let alone Saddam himself? Would Saddam have denounced the brutality and apologized to the victims and their families?

Far from showing that all societies are the same, the human rights abuses that sometimes occur in democracies often help illustrate the tremendous moral divide that separates free and fear societies. While I have not always agreed with the decisions made by my government on issues related to human rights, my experience has made me confident that these issues are thoroughly discussed and debated and that the need to protect human rights is never ignored. I suspect that in most other free societies the situation is much the same. Every democratic state will choose its own balance between protecting security and protecting human rights, but concern for human rights will always be part of the decisionmaking process. The free world is not perfect, but the way it responds to its imperfections is only further proof that human rights can only be protected in democratic societies.

A DEMOCRACY AT WAR

The failure to acknowledge the moral difference between free and fear societies with respect to human rights is a problem for all democracies. But for a democracy at war, such as Israel, this lack of moral clarity proves particularly debilitating. The same disregard for context that leads an organization or an individual to place fear societies and free societies on the same moral footing will also result in the condemnation of a free society that is merely defending itself. Indeed, by detaching the concept of human rights from the concept of a free society, human rights can be turned into a weapon against those countries that cherish them most.

When I arrived in Israel, the biggest human rights issue was Israel's policy of administrative detention, under which prisoners are held without an open trial for up to six months and are unable to see the evidence against them. (According to Israeli law, before an administrative detention can be enforced a judge must authorize it based on his review of the evidence.) I was often asked my opinion on the issue. On the face of it, the policy seemed unwarranted. But I knew that human rights could never be judged in a vacuum. In a fear society, the entire *system* was a violation of human rights. In a free society, however, there are certain circumstances in which some rights may have to yield to defend other rights.

Being new to the country and having already seen how politicized the human rights struggle in Israel had become, I wanted to study the issue before expressing any view. At the time, the Palestinian population in the West Bank and Gaza was subject to Israeli rule, and almost all of the administrative detentions applied to Palestinians who lived in those areas. I asked for a meeting with the chief coordinator of the territories to discuss the issue. He informed me that there were about a dozen cases of administrative detention (this was, of course, before the first intifada began, after which the number ballooned to a few hundred). He maintained that each detainee constituted a serious security threat and that due to the classified nature of the cases he could not go into too much detail.

But he did give me a brief overview of one of the cases. He told me about the case of a Palestinian journalist who was allegedly serving as a courier for the PLO, passing along information to those who were charged with carrying out terror attacks. He was caught when, unbeknownst to him, he supplied information to an informant. The informant brought the journalist to the attention of his Israeli handlers. The Israeli security services feared that if they allowed the defendant or his lawyer to see all the evidence, the informant would be killed, and the identities of many other informants would be exposed. Israel's informant network, he argued, had been critical in preventing terror attacks in the past and would be critical to the future. He warned, therefore, that taking the person out of administrative detention and granting an open trial (rather than having only an Israeli judge review the evidence) would cause great damage to Israel's security and endanger the lives of many of its citizens.

While there could be disagreement over whether any specific case warranted administrative detention, I acknowledged that in principle there *could* be circumstances when this policy *might* be acceptable. But for some people, administrative detentions are *never* acceptable. By taking such a position, these people surely feel that they are protecting human rights. They are not. By indiscriminately condemning a free society that upholds human rights but which is sometimes forced to encroach on certain freedoms to save lives, they do not advance the cause of human rights. Protecting the right to life, the most precious human right of all and the right that makes the exercise of all other rights possible, is the highest obligation of any government. Of course, it can be very tempting to use a security argument to justify abuse. It is much easier to hold someone in administrative detention than to hold a trial. That is why it is so important to limit administrative detentions as much as possible and why democracies must be constantly on alert for abuses. As a minister, I was among those who were constantly insisting that the criteria for applying administrative detention should be as narrow as possible. I also did not hesitate to ask security officials to justify their detention of a number of prisoners. But to argue that in principle, administrative detentions are *never* justified, that I was not prepared to do.

Those fighting for human rights who do not distinguish between free and fear societies will be shorn of a moral compass. Sadly, by detaching moral concepts from the context that give them meaning, human rights activists are just as likely to find themselves championing a genuine human rights cause as unwittingly defending dictatorial regimes. Thus, it is no wonder that there is little appreciation for the challenge Israel faces as a democracy trying to maximize the security of its citizens and at the same time protect the human rights of Palestinians.

THE TERROR BEGINS

Given this moral confusion, it was not surprising that when the Palestinian intifada began, a dangerous moral equivalence was introduced. In an effort to be "evenhanded," statesmen, politicians, diplomats, and journalists would often refer to the "extremists on both sides" who were trying to undermine peace efforts. One would think that they were referring to two groups of fanatics, each dedicated to killing innocent people. But no: The extremists on the Palestinian side were terror organizations like Hamas and Islamic Jihad that were wholeheartedly opposed to any compromise; and on the Israeli side were those Jews who were unwilling to transfer any territory to the Palestinians under any circumstances. Is there really not a moral difference between the two?

Leaving aside the difference in the goals of the two sides, the difference in the *means* employed to advance those goals should preclude any comparison. The Palestinian extremists use terrorism and the blackmail that accompanies it to achieve their objectives. They systematically blow up buses, discos, cafes, and pizza shops, murdering and maiming scores of innocent people. In contrast, the so-called Jewish extremists try to advance their Greater Land of Israel agenda by convincing a majority of their fellow citizens of the justice of their positions. They are not murderers. The phrase "extremists on both sides" in fact describes two completely different phenomena. In the Palestinian case, it refers to terrorists. In the Israeli case, it refers to people who are part of a democratic process and respect democratic laws, but who hold views that are not considered mainstream.

Another obvious moral difference between Israel's free

society and the Palestinian's fear society is how each treats the real extremists. The Palestinian Authority turns them into martyrs, naming public squares and soccer teams after suicide bombers, encouraging hundreds of thousands to join funeral processions for mass murderers and trying to indoctrinate a generation of Palestinians to emulate their actions.

The response of both the government of Israel and the people of Israel to the handful of real extremists that we do have in our society is very different. The horrible attack of Baruch Goldstein, a Jew who massacred Palestinians worshipping in a Hebron mosque, is considered by almost all Israelis as a mark of shame on the country.

Another phrase that is often mistakenly applied to the conflict, the "cycle of violence," is no less morally obfuscating. There is no moral equivalence between Palestinian terror attacks and Israeli counterterror operations. The Palestinian terrorists are *deliberately* targeting civilians. Israeli military operations do sometimes *unintentionally* harm innocent civilians, but Israel never targets civilians. It targets terrorists. Israeli counterterror strikes are meant to save innocent life and Palestinian terror attacks are meant to take it. Indeed, whereas the more innocent Palestinian lives are lost in an Israeli military operation, the more the Israeli government considers the operation a failure, the more a Palestinian terror attack claims innocent Jewish lives, the more the terrorists consider that attack a success. To see the behavior of both sides as equally reproachable requires a complete moral blindness.

Ironically, if there is a "cycle of violence," its origins lie in Israel's policy of trying to ease the suffering of the Palestinians. After the terror attacks started in September 2000, Israel was forced to adopt a series of measures to thwart them, including imposing closures and curfews on parts of the territories, establishing checkpoints, and setting up roadblocks. While these measures helped reduce the security threats to Israel, they also made life extremely harsh for Palestinians. With Palestinians not able to work in Israel, there was massive unemployment and widespread poverty. Freedom of movement within Palestinian areas was severely restricted. Some children could not get to their schools, and the transfer of goods to and from the territories ground to a snail's pace.

Still, from the beginning of the intifada, the question of how to improve conditions for the Palestinians was discussed in the Israeli government at least as much as how to fight Palestinian terror. Again and again, the government would authorize a relaxation of the military's hold on the territories and allow Palestinian workers to enter Israel. But with Israel's guard lowered, the terrorists would invariably use the opportunity to perpetrate new attacks, sometimes within hours of restrictions being removed, forcing us to adopt the harsh security measures once again.

Here, too, moral clarity was abandoned. When Israel's free society was defending itself against an unprecedented campaign of terror, most of the international community was calling for an end to the "cycle of violence" and a return to the negotiating table. When the Palestinian terrorists struck, international condemnation of the attacks did not lead to a newfound appreciation for Israel's need to maintain the closures, checkpoints, and roadblocks that improved its security. On the contrary, Israel was condemned for imposing "collective punishment" on the Palestinian population. When Israel chose to target individual terrorists with precision air strikes, its actions were condemned as illegal extrajudicial assassinations. It seemed as though in the eyes of many, the Jews had a right to defend themselves in theory but could not exercise that right in practice.

After much hesitation, two years ago, Israel decided to build a security fence in the West Bank. After the initial assault on the Palestinian's terrorist infrastructure, our government understood that there were three options to maintain an acceptable level of security for our citizens. The first was to wage a total war against Palestinian terror using weapons that would claim many innocent Palestinian lives. The second was to keep our reserves constantly mobilized to defend the country. The third option was to build the security fence.

Had the Palestinian Authority become a partner in fighting terror, as it was obliged to do under all the agreements that it signed, none of these options would have become necessary. But lacking a trustworthy partner, Israel had to choose. The first option was unacceptable to us because of the price it would exact from Palestinian civilians. The second was unacceptable because of the price it would exact from Israelis. The fence was the most just and least harmful choice.

To date, no anti-terror measure that Israel is prepared to use has proven more effective against suicide bombers than the security fence. Of the hundreds of suicide bombers who have targeted Israel over the last few years, only one came from Gaza,[3] where hostility toward the Jewish state is at least as high as it is in the West Bank. Why? Because there is a fence around Gaza.

In places where the West Bank fence has been completed, suicide bombers have been stopped. Yet despite the fact that it saved lives, in mid-2004, the fence was declared illegal by the UN appointed International Court of Justice (ICJ) at the Hague on the grounds that it encroached on Palestinian lands and harmed Palestinians. The first part of the claim was demonstrably false, since the West Bank is disputed territory whose final status, according to U.N. resolutions, must be determined through negotiations between Israelis and Palestinians. As for the second, some Palestinians were indeed harmed by the fence—property was confiscated along the proscribed route, some farmers were separated from their lands, and a few villages were even split in two. But the harm caused by the fence to Palestinian life cannot be judged in a vacuum. In the last four years, Palestinian terrorists have savagely murdered 1,000 of Israel's citizens. The fence is stopping these murders. To address the issue of the fence while ignoring Palestinian terrorism makes a mockery of human rights. But that is precisely what the International Court did, mentioning the word "terrorism" only twice in its sixty-page decision, both times in citing Israel's position on the fence.

In contrast, Israel's Supreme Court, in its own 2004 ruling on the fence, sought to balance Israel's security needs against the need to prevent unnecessary harm to Palestinians. The Israeli Supreme Court has proven itself over the years fully capable of making these types of judgments. In fact, it is the only Supreme Court in the world that makes decisions during the course of a battle, deciding what methods can and cannot be used by the army, and thereby immediately changing the nature of military operations. As to the fence, the Israeli Supreme Court ruled that in places where harm to the Palestinians' quality of life was unjustified, the fence must be moved.

The difference between the two rulings was to be expected. One cannot expect moral clarity from a court which is appointed by a United Nations that is an amalgam of both democratic and nondemocratic regimes. Passing judgment on a free society defending itself from terror is something the UN appointed court is ill-equipped to do.

JENIN: THE BIG LIE

Two years before the ICJ's decision on the fence, the moral confusion of the international community reached a nadir during the battle of Jenin. On the evening of March 29, 2002, in the dining hall of the Park Hotel in Israel's coastal city of Netanya, scores of Israelis were celebrating the traditional Passover Seder with their families, recounting the Jews' exodus from ancient Egypt that marked their journey from slavery to freedom. A suicide bomber walked into the middle of the dining hall and blew himself up, killing 29 Israelis and wounding dozens more. The attack brought the Israeli death toll during that month to 130, by far the most lethal month of terror since the violence began.

The next day, I was called to an urgent government meeting that started at 9 p.m. and ended at 7 a.m. the following day. Members of Prime Minister Sharon's national unity government, then in power for little more than a year, agreed that a change of policy was needed. Instead of merely trying to use checkpoints and roadblocks to intercept suicide bombers heading toward our cities, we would have to enter the Palestinian-controlled population centers from where the bombers were being dispatched. We authorized Operation Defensive Shield, sending our forces into Ramallah, Nablus, Jenin, and other cities and towns in the West Bank in order to destroy as much of the terrorist infrastructure as possible.

Jenin would be the most dangerous military operation of all. Fully 25 percent of the bombing and shooting attacks against Israel had been carried out by terrorists from Jenin. In the center of the city of 45,000 people is a refugee camp. More suicide bombers had been dispatched from this relatively small refugee camp in the previous two years than from any other place in the world. Even Palestinian Authority forces, who themselves were no strangers to terrorism, were afraid to enter the camp during the eight years in which it was under their control. The camp was considered a stronghold of Hamas, one of the world's most ruthless terrorist organizations. Our troops knew that a bomb could be hidden underneath any car and that a terrorist could be waiting behind any door. We also realized that just as the terrorists deliberately target civilians, they also intentionally use them as human shields. This exacted a heavy price on much of the Palestinian population who lived in fear of Israeli reprisals for terror attacks, because not even Israel's precision strikes were perfect. In the Jenin refugee camp, the terrorists had holed up in an area where nearly 1,000 Palestinian civilians were living.

Israel's government had to decide what action to take. There were many precedents of other countries conducting military operations in densely populated areas to which we could turn for guidance. Syria's regime, facing resistance from Muslim fundamentalists in 1982, leveled the town of Hama, killing 20,000 people. Russia, confronting a similar situation in Chechnya, flattened Grozny with heavy armaments and killed hundreds of civilians.

For Israel, such indiscriminate action was unacceptable. Still, recent history showed that democratic governments had gone to great lengths to minimize risk to their own soldiers, even if it meant greatly increasing the chances of civilians being harmed. For example, after Serbian forces expelled Kosovars in 1999, NATO pilots bombed Serbia's infrastructure while safely flying at very high altitudes, an operation that lowered the risk to themselves but resulted in over 500 Serbian civilian deaths. Only a few months before the operation in Jenin, American and British pilots in Afghanistan were doing much the same and achieved similar results at a high cost in civilian life.

In Jenin, Israel's government decided to pursue a course that placed much greater risks on Israel's soldiers but that greatly reduced the dangers to Palestinian civilians. We announced over loudspeakers our intention to clear out the terrorist infrastructure in the camp and warned everyone to leave. Then, instead of bombing from the air or using tanks or heavy artillery, our soldiers were sent on a harrowing mission. They painstakingly went from house to house, moving through a hornet's nest of booby traps, bombs, and armed terrorists. After thirteen Israeli soldiers were killed during one mission, we still refused to use our air force or heavy artillery. We pressed on, making tactical changes, such as using armored bulldozers to flatten houses that were being used by the terrorists for cover, that decreased the risks to our troops without increasing the dangers to innocent Palestinians.

But in an environment that lacked moral clarity, one of the finest examples in history of a democracy protecting human rights in wartime became infamous as a horrific assault on human rights. Relying on phony information produced by Palestinian sources and claiming that Israel had killed over 500 civilians,[4] leveled a hospital, deliberately shot children, and executed prisoners, almost all the foreign press harshly criticized the Israeli action. The vilification rang out across the world, but the British press was in a class all by itself. The *Independent* called the Israeli operation "a monstrous war crime."[5] A. N. Wilson, writing for the *Evening Standard*, called it a "massacre, and a cover-up of genocide."[6] The *Guardian*, not to be outdone, ran a lead editorial opining that "Jenin was every bit as repellent in its particulars, no less distressing, and every bit as man made, as the attack on New York on September 11."[7]

The truth was very different: At the end of the operation, fifty-two Palestinians lay dead, almost all of whom were armed.[8] On the Israeli side, twenty-three soldiers had been killed by Palestinian terrorists. This extremely high casualty ratio was a function of Israel's willingness to endanger the lives of its own soldiers in order to save the lives of hundreds, if not thousands, of Palestinian civilians. Indeed, Israeli soldiers died to save innocent Palestinian lives.

Working its way through the Israeli court system today is a lawsuit against the Israeli Defense Forces and the Israeli government brought by some of the families of the soldiers who died in Jenin. The petitioners contend that the government's primary obligation should have been to defend its own troops, even at the cost of more Palestinian civilian casualties. Whether Israel, unlike every other country facing similar threats, should have imposed such risks on its own citizens in order to save innocent Palestinians is certainly a matter of legitimate debate. One thing, however, is certain: The operation in Jenin was an expression of an unprecedented commitment to the human rights of a foreign civilian population during wartime. It is actions like this that allow the noted legal expert Alan Dershowitz to state confidently that "no country in history ever complied with a higher standard of human rights."

To far too many people, such a statement may seem shocking. In the last few years, Israel has been portrayed, and therefore perceived, as a brutal occupying power that represses Palestinians. The fact that this perception, often fueled by graphic television images with little context, is not true does not make it less real to the people who hold it. Nor are the realities of checkpoints, searches, and closures pleasant ones. The suffering of Palestinians is real and therefore the sympathy for suffering is also real. But moral clarity demands more than sympathy. It demands an understanding of context, of cause and effect. It demands a sense of proportion. Only then will the painful choices that Israel makes, which are nonetheless moral choices, be understood.

The New Anti-Semitism

A lack of moral clarity has also hampered Israel's fight against a wave of anti-Semitism that has spread across the world over the last few years. Whether this "new anti-Semitism" is different from its predecessors is debatable,[9] but few could argue that it is focused on the State of Israel. Everywhere one looks, the Jewish state appears to be at the center of the anti-Semitic storm.

The rise in viciously anti-Semitic content against Israel disseminated through state-run Arab media is quite staggering. Arab propagandists, journalists, and scholars now regularly employ the methods and the vocabulary used to demonize European Jews for centuries—branding Jews Christ-killers, charging them with poisoning non-Jews, fabricating blood libels, and the like. In a region where the Christian faith has few adherents, a lurid and time-worn Christian anti-Semitism boasts an enormous following.

In 2003, the Syrian authorities, following in the footsteps of the Egyptian government, produced and broadcast a rabidly anti-Semitic film during Ramadan (which would ensure the highest ratings for the twenty-nine part miniseries), in which rabbis were portrayed slashing the throats and draining the blood of non-Jewish children to use for making Passover matza, and wealthy Jews were depicted plotting a global conspiracy to dominate the world. In fact, the only difference between one of the episodes in the Syrian film and Hitler's infamous anti-Semitic film *Eternal Jew* was that the latter was in black and white. Using modern technology the original authors of the Czarist forgery, *The Protocols of the Elders of Zion,* couldn't even imagine, Arab satellite television broadcast these films to tens of millions of Muslims throughout the Middle East, and millions more in Europe.

In Europe, the connection between Israel and anti-Semitism is equally conspicuous. For one thing, the timing and nature of the attacks on European Jews, whether physical or verbal, have largely revolved around Israel. For example, the anti-Semitic wave itself, which began soon after the Palestinians launched their terrorist campaign against the Jewish state in September 2000, reached a peak in April 2002 during Operation Defensive Shield.

Though most of the physical attacks in Europe were perpetrated by Muslims, most of the verbal and cultural assaults came from European elites. Thus, the Italian newspaper *La Stampa* published a cartoon of an infant Jesus lying at the foot of an Israeli tank, pleading, "Don't tell me they want to kill me again." The frequent comparisons of Ariel Sharon to Adolf Hitler, of Israelis to Nazis, and of

Palestinians to the Jewish victims of the Holocaust were not the work of a handful of hooligans spray-painting graffiti on the wall of a synagogue but of university educators and sophisticated columnists. No less a figure than the Nobel Prize-winning author José Saramago declared ringingly of Israel's treatment of the Palestinians: "We can compare it with what happened at Auschwitz."[10]

The centrality of Israel to the revival of a more generalized anti-Semitism is also evident in the international arena. Almost a year after the current round of Palestinian violence began, and after hundreds of Israelis had already been killed, a so-called "World Conference against Racism" was held under the auspices of the United Nations in Durban, South Africa. It turned into an anti-Semitic circus, with the Jewish state being accused of everything from racism and apartheid to crimes against humanity and genocide. In this theater of the absurd, the Jews themselves were turned into perpetrators of anti-Semitism, as Israel was denounced for its "Zionist practices against Semitism"—the Semitism, that is to say, of the Palestinian Arabs.

The Israel-centered focus of this latest wave of anti-Semitism poses a unique challenge in a world lacking moral clarity. Classical anti-Semitism is easy to see. The films that show Jews draining the blood of non-Jewish children or plotting to take over the world are immediately recognizable as anti-Semitic. When I showed the clips of the Syrian anti-Semitic film to European and American leaders, they were shocked. When the French prime minister saw it, he immediately took steps to stop the film from being broadcast to French Muslims via satellite. There was no debate whether the film was a "legitimate criticism of Israel." It was seen as anti-Semitism, pure and simple.

But the new anti-Semitism is far more subtle. Whereas classical anti-Semitism is aimed at the Jewish people and Jewish religion, the new anti-Semitism is aimed at the Jewish state. Since this anti-Semitism can hide behind the veneer of legitimate criticism of Israel, it is much more difficult to expose. Making the task even harder is the fact that this hatred is often advanced in the name of values most of us would consider unimpeachable, such as human rights.

I have never believed that the Jewish state should be above criticism. Indeed, a democratic state like Israel can appreciate that criticism is not only legitimate but an essential means to effect positive change. But we must separate legitimate criticism of Israel from anti-Semitism, something we cannot do in an environment that lacks moral clarity.

After I became the minister of diaspora affairs in 2003, I thought a great deal about this problem and I tried to come up with a "test" to resolve it. I call it the 3D test, but only the name is original. The test itself merely applies the historic criteria that once identified anti-Semitism.

The first D is the test of *demonization*. Demonization has always been a primary expression of anti-Semitism. Jews were portrayed for centuries as the embodiment of all evil. They were accused, among other things, of deicide, drinking the blood of non-Jewish children, poisoning wells, and controlling the world's banks and governments. To determine whether criticism against Israel today is legitimate or whether it is anti-Semitic we must ask ourselves whether the Jewish state is being demonized. Are its actions being blown out of all sensible proportion? For example, the comparisons between Israelis and Nazis and between Palestinian refugee camps and Auschwitz—comparisons that are heard practically every day within "enlightened" quarters of Europe—can only be considered anti-Semitic. Those who live in refugee camps clearly live in miserable conditions. But even those who would wrongly blame Israel for the fact that four generations of Palestinians have lived in these camps cannot legitimately compare these camps to Auschwitz. Those who draw such analogies either do not know anything about the Holocaust or, more plausibly, are deliberately trying to paint modern-day Israel as the embodiment of evil. This criticism is excessive, grotesque.

The second D is the test of *double standards*. For thousands of years, a clear sign of anti-Semitism was treating Jews differently from other peoples, from the discriminatory laws that many nations enacted against them to the tendency to judge their behavior by a different yardstick. A different yardstick means double standards, and double standards mean anti-Semitism.

Similarly, today we must ask whether criticism of Israel is being applied selectively. It is anti-Semitism, for instance, when Israel is singled out by the United Nations for human rights abuses while the behavior of serial abusers, like China, Iran, Cuba, and Syria, is ignored. It is anti-Semitism when the only meeting ever held by signatories to the Geneva Conventions on prisoners of war in the more than half century that the convention has been in operation, and in which there have been millions of abused prisoners of war, is used to condemn Israel. Likewise, it is anti-Semitism when Israel's Magen David Adom, alone among the world's ambulance services, is denied admission to the International Red Cross.

The third D is the test of *delegitimization*. In the past, anti-Semites tried to deny the legitimacy of the Jewish religion, the Jewish people, or both. Today, they are trying to deny the legitimacy of the Jewish state. It has become acceptable in many quarters to question whether or not Israel has a right to exist. While criticism of an Israeli policy need not be anti-Semitic, the denial of Israel's right to exist is always anti-Semitic. If other peoples have a right to live securely in their homelands, then the Jewish people have a right to live securely in their homeland as well.

If we are to fight the new anti-Semitism, we must make sure that we do not blur the line between legitimate criticism of Israel and anti-Semitism. Like a pair of glasses in a 3D movie that allows us to see everything with perfect clarity, the 3D test will ensure that those lines remain clear.

Clarifying the line between good and evil, and between right and wrong, will do more than help win the fight against anti-Semitism. It is the key to overcoming so many of the challenges that now confront Israel. Without moral clarity, Israel will be lost, uncertain of the justice of its cause and unable to defend its own rights, let alone the rights of others. With moral clarity, the people of Israel will find the strength to overcome any challenge that confronts them, from waging a just war to forging a true peace.

CHAPTER 7

A Missed Opportunity

IN FEBRUARY 2001, Ariel Sharon won a landslide victory over Ehud Barak. Under Israel's direct election law, which has since been scrapped, elections were held only for prime minister and not for the Knesset. Thus, despite Sharon's unprecedented victory (he received 62 percent of the vote), he had to form a coalition with the same parliament that had been elected along with Barak in 1999. With a Likud faction of just nineteen members and a parliament evenly split between Right and Left, Sharon was determined to form a national unity government.

I had long believed that a government based on wide consensus would be better suited to address the enormous challenges confronting Israel. I had criticized both Netanyahu and Barak for failing to form national unity governments when they had the chance, and I was very pleased when Sharon decided to establish one.

I first heard the name Ariel Sharon as a young dissident. For many Soviet Jews, he was the legendary hero who had changed the course of the Yom Kippur War with his military daring, saving Israel from a potential catastrophe and wiping the smirks off the faces of gloating KGB agents back in the USSR. In those days, I never thought that one day I would be sitting next to him around an Israeli cabinet table. In Bibi's government, Sharon and I developed a sentimental bond. He sat next to me and the other minister from my new immigrant party, Yuli Edelstein. When I started conversing with Yuli in Russian during one of the first government meetings, Sharon warned us to watch what we said since he understood Russian, which he had learned as a child. We also both shared a strong attachment to Jewish issues, and I was always impressed by his strong pride in his heritage. "I am first Jewish and only then Israeli," he used to say, to the surprise of many of his Israeli-born colleagues.

Of all the ministers I have encountered over the years, Sharon is by far the most knowledgeable about Israel. When he spoke in a government meeting, you could rest assured that he had full command of the topic. Sharon is an expert on the country's geography, defense, agriculture, history, industry, and, it seems, just about everything else. Knowing Israel like the back of his hand, he can tell you the location of every village and hamlet in the country, the name of every flower in the Negev, and the products produced in every factory in the Galilee. He loved to walk around with maps and used them as a reference to explain his plans to secure Israel's future. But he himself didn't need any map. It was all in his head.

Sharon cobbled together a national unity government and made Shimon Peres his foreign minister. Almost immediately, it became clear that there would be constant tension in the government. The sea change in Israeli public opinion that had occurred in the wake of the failure of Camp David and the beginning of the intifada was not reflected in Israel's parliament, and this was especially true inside Israel's Labor party. Most of the leading Labor ministers did not change their pro-Oslo views. They remained convinced that Arafat and the PA were the only alternatives and that nothing should be done to weaken them. Rather than meet the escalation of Palestinian terror with a firm response, they counseled restraint. According to the logic of their approach, the Palestinian terror attacks coupled with Israel's muted response was gaining Israel the sympathy of the world, and this sympathy could be used to pressure Arafat into taking action against the terror organizations. A strong response, it was thought, would create international sympathy for the Palestinians and put no diplomatic pressure on the PA to crack down on terror.

On Friday night, June 1, 2001, a Hamas suicide bomber struck outside the Dolphinarium discoteque, killing twenty-one young Israelis, most of them teenagers, and injuring over 100 more. It was the worst suicide bombing since early 1996. After eight months of Palestinian terrorism, after scores of innocents had been murdered, after it should have been clear that Arafat was part of the problem, not the solution, the Dolphinarium attack was thought by many to have crossed the line—Israel would finally go to war to defend its people.

An emergency security cabinet meeting was called for the next day in Tel Aviv. Because of the gravity of the decisions being made and their potential impact on human life, the meeting was held on the Jewish Sabbath. I violated the Sabbath by driving to the meeting from my home in Jerusalem. It was only the second time since I had come to Israel that I had violated the Sabbath. The first time was in 1991 when I took part in Operation Solomon, an urgent airlift that brought thousands of Ethiopian Jews to Israel during Ethiopia's civil war.

The cabinet meeting was tense. Most of the ministers were in favor of a sustained military assault on the Palestinian terrorist infrastructure. Silvan Shalom, the finance minister at the time, argued that Arafat should be expelled from the territories. During the discussions, Peres left the room two or three times to speak to foreign leaders. When he returned the message was always the same: "The sympathy of the world is with us. Let us not squander that sympathy but use it to pressure Arafat to act against Hamas."

Shimon Peres, unlike many Israeli politicians, is constantly bringing a global view to Israel's situation. Separate issues are not important to him in and of themselves. They are only relevant as part of his wider understanding of international affairs. That is why his achievements have always been of historic proportions and why his failures have been as well.

Despite strong support inside the cabinet in favor of a large-scale military operation, Sharon took Peres's advice and Israel checked its response. The terrorism, however, only got worse. In the next few weeks, there were scores of attacks, and many more suicide bombings, including the horrific explosion in a Jerusalem pizza shop that killed fifteen and wounded 130 more.

Then came 9/11. As three thousand lay dead in New York and Washington, thousands of Palestinians were dancing in the streets, reveling in the carnage. Arafat, who had done everything to indoctrinate his people in a culture of death and hatred—against Jews, against Israel, and against America—realized the potential dangers to his rule and rushed to donate blood to the victims of 9/11.

September 11 could have been a turning point for the PA. President Bush had declared that "you are either with us or with the terrorists" and that he would "make no distinction between the terrorists and those who harbor them." Now, many thought, the PA would have to act against the terrorists or be swept away with the other enemies of the United States. But the PA did not act. In October, the Israeli minister of tourism, Rehavam Ze'evi, was murdered by the Popular Front for the Liberation of Palestine, another infamous terror group. The killers eventually took up refuge in Arafat's own headquarters in Ramallah. In December, there was another wave of suicide attacks, and in January, a ship carrying weapons and ammunition from Iran bound for Palestinian terror groups was seized by Israeli commandos in the Red Sea. The evidence clearly pointed to Arafat and the PA, but Israel continued to act with restraint.

With each attack, the tension between keeping the national unity government intact and fighting terrorism grew stronger. The country was demanding action. The leaders of the Labor party were demanding restraint. After the Passover night bombing of the Park Hotel during the bloodiest month of terrorism in Israel's history, the policy of restraint was finally abandoned. The people of Israel had simply had enough. Sharon heeded their call and launched Operation Defensive Shield. The forceful response that I and many thought had been postponed for far too long was finally set in motion, leading in short order to a dramatic decline in terrorism. Ironically, at the moment when peace seemed most remote, it would soon become a real possibility.

AN ECHO FROM WASHINGTON

On April 4, 2002, President Bush made a speech in the White House Rose Garden. If that speech is remembered at all today it is for Bush's request that Israel, which had just launched Operation Defensive Shield, "halt incursions into Palestinian-controlled areas and begin the withdrawal from those cities it has recently occupied."[1] Determined that the Israeli Defense Forces complete its anti-terror mission, Israel's government ignored the request, temporarily leading to increased tensions between Washington and Jerusalem.

As for the rest of the speech, even those who closely follow events in the Middle East will have long forgotten it, since it ostensibly broke no new ground. The president reiterated his support for a two-state solution to the conflict. Once again, he was critical of Yasser Arafat, who he said had "betrayed the hopes of the people he was supposed to lead." And the president announced his intention to send Secretary of State Colin Powell to the region, the latest in a line of emissaries that the president had sent to the region since he was sworn into office.

But I remember that speech particularly for the following lines: "[The Palestinians] deserve a government that respects human rights and a government that focuses on their needs—education and health care—rather than feeding their resentments."[2]

What must have seemed to many like an insignificant aside was a breakthrough. For years, the democratic world, including Israel, had been determined to strengthen Arafat and his Palestinian Authority, turning a blind eye to the fear society Arafat was building. Now, the U.S. president was expressing concern not only for how the Palestinians were being treated by Israel, but also for how they were being treated by their *own* government.

The president's speech energized me. I had no doubt that his historic statement would be ignored if there were no follow-up. So I decided to begin working on a diplomatic plan based on helping the Palestinians establish a free society and on linking the peace process to the expansion of freedom within that society. For six years, as a minister in three different Israeli governments, I had criticized the free world's failure to create such a linkage—in speeches, in meetings with diplomats, in op-ed pieces, and above all, inside the Cabinet. Ariel Sharon had no diplomatic plan of his own on the table so, considering what Bush had said in his speech, I thought it was high time I finally translated my ideas into a concrete plan.

About ten days after Bush's speech, while I was still working on my plan, I was interviewed by CNN.[3] At the time, Secretary Powell was visiting Israel and had met with Arafat, whom Israel was trying to isolate diplomatically. While most of the interviewer's questions centered on whether American and Israeli policy toward Arafat were at odds, I took the opportunity to compliment President Bush for saying in his speech a week earlier that the Palestinian people deserve a government that respects human rights.

That evening, I flew to Washington to speak at a massive solidarity rally for Israel. Organized in less than a week, the rally nevertheless attracted over 100,000 people from all over the United States who came to express their support for Israel's fight against terrorism. After the rally, I met with Condoleezza Rice, the president's national security adviser. She said she had watched my interview the day before and pointed out that even though the president had gotten a tremendous amount of feedback from around the world following his April 4 speech, I was the only one who had drawn attention to the president's remarks about Palestinian human rights. Rice told me she thought those remarks were extremely important and that the administration planned to develop the idea further in the weeks and months ahead.

After listening to Rice, I thought that this would be a good opportunity to discuss my plan. I knew that the idea of building a free society and the impact it could have on the region would resonate with Rice, who is an expert on the Soviet Union. Rice, an extremely sharp thinker, listened intently and expressed understanding for my overall approach. At one point, however, she mentioned that she felt the Saudis should play a role in the peace process. While my plan included a role for Jordan and Egypt, the two Arab states that had formal peace agreements with Israel, I would never have considered including the Saudis. Saudi Arabia, a fear society of the first order, not only had no peace treaty with Israel, but it was also funding terrorism against us by supporting Hamas and by giving cash payments to the families of suicide bombers. Thus, despite the overall positive impression I had from my conversation with Rice, I knew that getting the Americans to fully understand the logic of my approach would take a great deal of work. And first, I would have to convince my own prime minister of the merits of it.

A PLAN IGNORED

I returned to Israel and finished a draft proposal. It called for the establishment of an interim Palestinian Administration, which would be chosen by a coordinating body headed by the United States. The interim administration, which would not include those who were directly or indirectly responsible for terror, would be responsible for running the lives of the Palestinians in the areas under its control (only external security would remain in Israel's hands) and would work over a transition period of at least three years to develop the Palestinians' civil society and democratic institutions. Freedom of speech, freedom of the press, freedom of political, social, and religious organization would be guaranteed and educational programs encouraging terror would be replaced by programs that promote peace. Economic assistance would be made conditional on maintaining these freedoms and changing the educational programs.

The interim Palestinian administration would also work to dismantle all the refugee camps under its control and to build a normal existence for their inhabitants. Israel, Arab countries, and international organizations would support this effort. An international fund would be established to develop Palestinian economic infrastructure. After three years, free elections would be held and the government of Israel and the elected representatives of the Palestinians would negotiate a permanent peace.

When I met with the prime minister on April 24, three weeks after Bush's speech, I presented my plan to him and explained the logic behind my approach in the following letter.

Honorable Prime Minister,

The Oslo agreements were based on the belief that if we transferred to Arafat control of territories in Judea, Samaria and Gaza and control over the Palestinian population who lived there, he would turn into Israel's partner in protecting peace and security in the region. Moreover, many of Oslo's supporters saw the establishment of a dictatorial regime in the territory under Arafat's control as an advantage rather than a disadvantage. They worked under the assumption that freed from the constraints of democracy, Arafat would be better able to deal with the terrorists of Hamas and that he would, in parallel, also be dedicated to creating prosperity for his people and promoting peace. As time passed, these prophecies proved to be false because they completely ignored the basic difference between the interests of a dictator and the interests of a democratic leader . . .

[W]hen Israel and other countries in the free world were convinced that "a strong leader will bring a strong peace" and therefore saw strengthening Arafat's power as the supreme objective, Arafat invested every dollar and shekel he received in increasing hatred toward Israel and in building an infrastructure of terror to use against it. Faced with the choice of peace and prosperity or misery and terror, Arafat always chose the latter . . .

Now is the time for new leaders who, unlike Arafat, will be interested in improving the lives of their own people by, among other things, forging a peaceful relationship with Israel. Still, it is impossible to ignore the fact that after nine years of sowing hatred and encouraging terrorism against Israel, it will be very difficult to find Palestinian leaders who will dare to support such a policy openly. To allow these leaders to work openly and without fear, a transition period is needed both to enable the foundations of democratic life to be established in Palestinian society and to neutralize the effects of the hateful propaganda and terrorist acts against Israel.

In our meeting, I asked the prime minister to read over the plan carefully and explained that what I was suggesting was an entirely different approach to the peace process. I explained why I was certain that we could find a broad basis of agreement with the American administration and mentioned Bush's remark and my conversation with Condoleezza Rice as examples. As always, Sharon was charming and attentive. He told me he would look into the matter.

A few days later, my mother died at the age of 93. Her advanced years did not make the loss any less painful. She had been a voice of moral clarity throughout my life, and despite her age, confronted the KGB alongside me with remarkable determination. After my release, with the great battle against evil behind her, her fighting spirit did not diminish. She was determined to do whatever she could to help Israel's new immigrants begin their lives in their new country and would not permit me for a single moment to rest on my laurels. Time and again, she insisted that I do everything in my power to continue to fight for the principles we both believed in.

I received a warm and compassionate phone call from Sharon in which he apologized for being unable to pay his condolences. He told me he was on his way to Washington to meet with President Bush and that he intended to use some of the elements of my plan in his discussions with him.

While I do not know what was said during Sharon's meeting with Bush, I was not optimistic. The president, I was told, was going to give a major policy address on the Middle East sometime in June and what I had heard about that speech was far from encouraging. According to my information, Bush was planning to be very tough on Arafat, but still give the Palestinian leader one more chance to fight terrorism and become a peace partner. It sounded like the mistakes of Oslo were going to be repeated.

In June, I was invited to be the keynote speaker at the American Enterprise Institute's World Forum at Beaver Creek, Colorado. The World Forum, sponsored by AEI, the prestigious Washington think tank, is an annual conference that brings together leaders from government, business, and academia to discuss the most pressing issues of the day. Considering that President Bush was supposed to make his policy speech on the Middle East a few days later and that many officials in his administration were attending the conference, I decided to devote my talk to the relationship between democracy and peace.

At that time, Israel was being hit by another wave of Palestinian terrorism, and as is often the case in our small country, this wave hit close to home. Two days before my speech in Beaver Creek, a suicide bomber had murdered nineteen people riding on a bus. The bombing took place a few hundred meters from my house and just a few minutes after my eldest daughter, Rachel, had left for school. My wife ran out of the house to check on her. She was not at the bus stop. She had decided to take a car pool that morning. But a dozen other families whose daughters and sons were on their way to school would not be so fortunate. The next day, another Palestinian terror attack killed seven people and injured dozens more, including my secretary, Dina. In the car ride to Beaver Creek, I received updates about another terror attack that had killed four members of a single family. In my speech, I focused on this terrorism and what it meant for Israel and the world.

> Every day we are in the midst of a struggle for our survival, and every day there are new victims of the cruel terror. But we know very well that it is not a tribal war between Jews and Arabs in the Middle East. We are in the midst of the first world war of the twenty-first century, waged between the world of terror and the world of democracy, between those for whom human life is held in the highest value and those for whom human life is merely an instrument to reach certain political aims. The world of democracy will win this struggle. But in order for the victory to be everlasting, it is crucial, but not sufficient, to destroy terrorism. It is imperative to expand the world our enemies are trying to destroy, to export democracy.[4]

I then explained why democracy was so crucial to international stability and security, why linkage had been so successful during the Cold War, and why the free world had betrayed its democratic principles at Oslo. I outlined my plan to help the Palestinians build a free society and help Israelis and Palestinians forge a lasting peace.

The next day, I met with Vice President Cheney, who was also attending the conference. I have always had an excellent relationship with Cheney and find him to be a very thoughtful and intelligent man. Even though I had discussed the link between democracy and peace with the vice president before, our meeting, initially scheduled for thirty minutes, went on for over an hour and a half. We talked about the situation in Israel and I told him how disappointed I was to hear that President Bush was planning to give Arafat another chance. "What kind of message will it send," I asked, "if the person leading the free world in a global war on terror gives another chance to a man who has built an autonomy of terror and who is now unleashing another wave of terror attacks?" To which Cheney replied, "But I understood your government agreed with the president's approach and that it is the Palestinians who still have a problem with the speech."

Cheney's statement took me by surprise, and I thought that it was important that there should be no misunderstanding. "Look," I continued, "we have many disagreements in our government, just as you often have in yours between the State Department and the White House or between other agencies. The positions of Foreign Minister Shimon Peres, as you know, are very different from those of Prime Minister Ariel Sharon. As for what I am telling you now, I am not speaking on behalf of my government. I am simply giving you my personal opinion, which is that the president will be making a big mistake." When Cheney asked me what I thought the president should speak about instead, I returned to the important link between democracy and peace, between a free society for the Palestinians and security for Israelis, ideas for which the vice president had a great deal of sympathy. I argued that the only viable partner for Israel was a Palestinian leadership devoted to improving the lives of its own people. Cheney promised he would pass along my ideas to the president.

A SPEECH IGNORED

On June 24 the president finally delivered his much-anticipated speech. Since I was traveling back from America, I did not have a chance to watch it live, but a friend in Washington who did see it told me I would not have been disappointed. When I finally read the text of the speech, it was almost too good to be true.

President Bush turned his back on Yasser Arafat's dictatorship once and for all, calling on the Palestinians "to elect new leaders, leaders not compromised by terror."[5]

He spoke of the Palestinians' right to live in a free society and to improve their lives, telling them that they "deserve democracy and the rule of law," "an open society and a thriving economy," and "a life of hope for your children." He outlined what type of changes Palestinian leaders were expected to implement, from creating "entirely new political and economic institutions based on democracy, market economics and action against terrorism" to formulating "a new constitution which separates the powers of government" to establishing a "system of reliable justice to punish those who prey on the innocent." He pledged the full support of the United States, the international donor community, the European Union, the World Bank, and the International

Monetary Fund for reform efforts. Crucially, President Bush seemed to *link* American diplomatic and economic support to the willingness of the Palestinians to embrace change *within* their society. Not since the days of Ronald Reagan's presidency had the idea of linkage been embraced so forcefully.

> I call upon [the Palestinians] to build a practicing democracy, based on tolerance and liberty. If the Palestinian people actively pursue these goals, America and the world will actively support their efforts. . . . If [the Palestinians] energetically take the path of reform, the rewards can come quickly. If Palestinians embrace democracy, confront corruption and firmly reject terror, they can count on American support for the creation of a provisional state of Palestine.[5]

President Bush also placed the goal of helping the Palestinians build a free society into a broader context, making it clear that he believed in both the universal appeal of freedom and its power to change the world.

> If liberty can blossom in the rocky soil of the West Bank and Gaza, it will inspire millions of men and women around the globe who are equally weary of poverty and oppression, equally entitled to the benefits of democratic government. . . . Prosperity and freedom and dignity are not just American hopes, or Western hopes. They are universal, human hopes. And even in the violence and

turmoil of the Middle East, America believes those hopes have the power to transform lives and nations.

I re-read the speech, almost pinching myself. It was a beautiful expression of the principles I also believed should be the foundation of the peace process. (The parallel between the president's words and my own ideas was so strong that a *Washington Post* reporter questioned whether I had become one of Bush's speechwriters.[6]) In a decade full of speeches, meetings, summits, and agreements, these principles were ignored. Now they were being championed by the leader of the democratic world.

From my perspective, the president's speech was potentially no less dramatic than when, twenty years earlier, Ronald Reagan had called the Soviet Union an evil empire, shattering the illusions of those who believed that a fear society could be a friend and that peace could be made with tyranny. Now, Bush's speech could finally dispel the delusions of those who believed that a fear society would fight terrorism and that peace could be made with a dictator. And Bush's moral clarity could chart a bold, new course centered on the expansion of freedom and democracy among Palestinians.

For me personally, however, there was an important difference between the two speeches. Two decades earlier, I was confined to a prison cell on the border of Siberia. Reagan's words and leadership strengthened my resolve and the resolve of my fellow inmates, but there was little else we could do. But in 2002 I was an Israeli minister, making decisions along with my colleagues about the very issues Bush was addressing. Now, I was in a position to act.

My experiences over the previous decade had taught me that my fellow Israelis would be reluctant to see the wisdom of Bush's vision. Indeed, very few people in Israel thought the president had outlined a viable course to peace. To be sure, everyone realized that Bush had abandoned Arafat. But neither those on the Left nor those on the Right had much faith in the possibility of building a free society among the Palestinians. Thus, Bush's calls for reform and his championing of Palestinian democracy were greeted by the Israeli Left with disappointment and by the Israeli Right with complacency.

After nearly two years of Palestinian terrorism, the colossal failure of Oslo had still left little impression on significant portions of the Israeli Left. This group continued to believe, despite all evidence to the contrary, that strengthening Arafat and negotiating with his PA was the only hope for peace. To them, a speech that abandoned Arafat and linked American diplomacy to internal Palestinian reforms was tantamount to a nail in Oslo's coffin. Lacking faith in Palestinian democracy, most of the Israeli Left was depressed by a vision of peace that one British columnist described as "demanding that Palestine become Sweden before it can become Palestine."[7]

On the Right, many opposed Bush's support for a Palestinian state, but this support was nothing new. What was new was that the U.S. president was now making American support for a future Palestinian state conditional on Palestinian democratization and reform. Since most of the Right had little faith that the Palestinians could ever build a free society, they saw the president's speech as precluding the possibility of a Palestinian state ever emerging. In short, the Left and Right in Israel responded to the president's speech as they did precisely because neither had much faith in Palestinian democracy.

Yet regardless of what Israelis thought about the speech, because it had come from the U.S. president it could not be ignored. For years, I had turned to the *Wall Street Journal, New York Times, Washington Post,* and other papers abroad in order to espouse the principles that were now being championed from Washington. But in Israel's Hebrew-speaking media, these ideas were never given a hearing because almost no one took them seriously.

In the days after the president's speech, this began to change. I met with journalists and said the same thing I had been saying for a decade, only this time they listened. In newspaper, television, and radio interviews, instead of having to discuss the ins and outs of the latest political crisis, I had the opportunity to talk about the connection between democracy and peace and about the importance of linkage. I understood that the media's sudden interest was motivated neither by a recognition of the need to reassess the false premises of Oslo nor by a new open-mindedness. It was simply a function of the need to understand the logic behind the president's ideas. To the question, "What in the world could the president be thinking?" I was supposed to provide an answer. When I had discussed those same ideas in the past, most Israelis looked at me as if I were visiting from another planet, a cosmonaut whose quirky notions of freedom had no place in the Middle East. But now that the president had become an astronaut, I was expected to describe the view from outer space.

I saw this new willingness to listen as a rare chance to try to mobilize public support for policies that I thought were critical to Israel's future. I met with Sharon and implored him to formulate a plan based on the June 24 speech. Whether it was my plan, his plan, or someone else's plan did not matter. The important thing, I said, was to take advantage of the unique opportunity the president had given us.

I was concerned that even within the Bush administration there was not enough support for the president's ideas. If it were true, as was reported, that the speech had undergone radical revisions over the course of a few weeks, then support for Bush's new vision could evaporate just as quickly. Without follow-up, what had been a radical departure from the policies of the past could lose momentum, and conventional diplomatic thinking would return.

For the next few weeks, I tried to persuade my ministerial colleagues in Sharon's national unity government of the need to seize the moment, but I had no takers.

I tried to address this skepticism in Israel's leading Left-wing paper, *Haaretz*.

Many on the Israeli Left have largely been unmoved by Bush's bold vision. Skeptical that the Palestinians will ever be able to build a free society, they see an American policy that is linked to Palestinian democratization as hopelessly naïve.... The source of my faith is a belief that the essence of democracy has universal appeal.... While each culture is unique and may have its own ordering of values, I do not believe that any people wants to live in a society where the fear of imprisonment is omnipresent. Today, the Palestinians live with this fear and do not yet have the opportunity to speak their minds.... The reforms that are necessary will not create a liberal democracy overnight. But given a genuine chance to build a free society, I have no doubt that the Palestinians will seize it. Any attempt to leap over the "democratic obstacle" that President Bush has erected reminds me of the attempt to establish a "New Middle East" by bolstering a friendly dictator. Now, as then, the only results that are to be expected are a protracted conflict and brutal terror. Instead of again making last-ditch efforts to strengthen a dictatorial regime—either under the leadership of Arafat or someone else—the Israeli left should instead join the efforts of aiding the Palestinians in building a free society, thereby helping the two peoples create a stable peace in the region.[8]

A ROAD MAP BACK TO OSLO

President Bush's words hovered in the air for three months waiting for someone to bring them down to earth. Unfortunately, Israel did not seize the moment. In fairness, Israel's government was absorbed with the fight against an unremitting Palestinian terrorism. It was also not inactive on the diplomatic front. We continued to insist on the implementation of the Mitchell and Tenet plans and on isolating Yasser Arafat. Moreover, the cult of death and violence which the PA had propagated made the prospects of a free society emerging among the Palestinians seem even more remote to Israelis than it had in the past.

I failed to persuade my colleagues in the Israeli government to start a new diplomatic process based on President Bush's historic speech. Those who agreed with me on the need to renew diplomatic efforts remained fixated on breathing new life into Oslo, something that Prime Minister Sharon thankfully was not prepared to do. But Israel's government presented no new plan, adopted no new policies, and didn't even hold a discussion on how the principles articulated in the June 24 speech could be realized.

Into this vacuum stepped the U.S. State Department. As I have learned over the years, most officials in the State Department (although certainly not all) are deeply skeptical about democratic reform, preferring what they see as the stability of a dictator to the dangers of democracy. This attitude has reigned in the State Department for decades and has colored its thinking on policymaking across the globe. Whether they are counseling "engagement" of nondemocratic regimes or turning their back on the pro-democracy forces fighting them, State Department officials will consistently seek accommodation rather than confrontation. So when I discovered the State Department had developed a diplomatic plan based on Bush's speech, I was worried. When I found out that the plan assigned a key role to a diplomatic quartet comprised of the United States, the EU, the United Nations, and Russia, I was even more concerned. Those who were repsonsible for turning the principles Bush had outlined on June 24 into a concrete proposal were the same forces that were vociferously opposing the president's strategy to build a free Iraq—a strategy based on those same principles. Clearly, the other members of the quartet would only magnify the State Department's bias against democratic reform in favor of the "stability" of a strongman.

In October, when I read an initial draft of what had been labeled "The Road Map to Peace," my concerns proved justified. Its authors had stripped President Bush's June 24 speech of what I thought was its historic message. What was kept was the vision of two states, Israel and Palestine, living side by side. But discarded was the idea that a Palestinian state would emerge as a *result* of real democratic change within Palestinian society. To be sure, the Road Map included all the right words—reform, democracy, constitution, transparency, and so on—but the plan itself ensured that these words would be little more than lip service.

Perhaps this was most obvious with regards to the timeline and order of events in the Road Map. As I have explained, elections in a fear society can never come at the beginning of a reform process. Invariably, such elections cannot be free because they will be held in an environment of fear and intimidation. Moreover, those elected in that type of environment will have absolutely no interest in reform. That is why the plan I proposed to the prime minister six months earlier stipulated that *before* elections could be held, a transition period of "at least three years" would be required. Admittedly, this was an ambitious schedule given that Palestinian society had been systematically poisoned with hatred for the last decade. Still, I believed that the process of liberalization and democratization could begin to bear fruit by then if international support efforts were truly directed at building a free society for the Palestinians.

The Palestinians are a relatively small, educated, and entrepreneurial population with decades of exposure to Israeli democracy. A peace process dedicated to strengthening them rather than their corrupt, unaccountable rulers would succeed much faster than people thought. After a few years in which a Palestinian administration—albeit one appointed by outsiders—worked to develop the Palestinians' civil society, economy, and democratic institutions, a fear society would gradually be replaced by a free society. The Palestinians would then be able to choose their leaders in free elections. By virtue of being dependent on the people they governed, those leaders would work to improve the lives of Palestinians, and as a result would have a vested interest in peace with Israel. With these leaders, I believed, Israel could make peace.

Rather than call for elections *after* reforms were well under way, the Road Map wanted them "as early as possible." In a matter of months, new leaders were to be chosen, a Palestinian state was to be established, and final status peace talks could commence. How could anyone possibly believe, I asked myself, that a poisoned Palestinian society subject to unremitting incitement by its own media and educational system could be ready to choose a new leadership in a matter of months and be ready to peaceably join the community of nations in less than a year? How could anyone believe that such a leadership would really be dedicated to reforming Palestinian society, to improving the conditions of the Palestinians, and to making peace? The Road Map was the voice of Bush but the hands of Oslo. While its language paid homage to the June 24 speech, the plan's authors were actually searching for a new strongman who would succeed where Arafat had failed. The new Palestinian regime under an "empowered" prime minister was packaged as a government of "reform," but the timetables and snap elections gave the game away. The Road Map was effectively calling for a quick game of musical chairs among the Palestinian leadership, turning reform efforts into a farce.

This was not my only criticism. In his June 24 speech, President Bush had brought moral clarity to the peace process by making a clear distinction between a fear society and a free society, between terror states and democratic states. But one did not have to read far into the Road Map to watch this moral clarity disappear. In Phase I of the Road Map, both Israel and the Palestinian Authority were to end "official incitement" against the other. I understood why this was needed on the Palestinian side. Arafat's controlled media was calling for a million martyrs to redeem Jerusalem, and his educational system was denying Israel's right to exist. But I could not understand what official incitement Israel was supposed to stop. Clearly, this clause was put in to make the plan more "evenhanded." But by creating a moral equivalence between the sides, the Road Map was in effect whitewashing incitement against Israel.

I implored Prime Minister Sharon to reject the Road Map on the grounds that it was at odds with Bush's June 24 speech. Others inside Sharon's national unity government thought there was no reason to create tension with the Bush administration over a preliminary draft when the Road Map might die on its own. I was hoping there would be a debate in the government or the security cabinet on the issue, but there was none. When I asked why, I was told that there was no "official" Road Map to discuss, only a work in progress.

By not rejecting the plan, Israel allowed work on it to continue. By December 2002 things had grown much worse. At the end of the month, the Quartet was due to meet to formally adopt the plan. In mid-December, I was in Washington, where I met with officials in the White House and the State Department. Since our government had no official position on the Road Map—we still had not discussed it—I felt free to express my reservations to everyone I met. I explained that the plan was diametrically opposed to the principles Bush articulated in his June 24 speech and would result in failure because, like Oslo, it would preclude the possibility of building a free society among the Palestinians.

Sharon, who was well aware of the contents of the plan,

did try to influence its final wording and remove some of its more egregious clauses. But on the eve of the Road Map's formal adoption by the Quartet, I could not escape the impression that Sharon's silence, if not acquiescence, was returning Israel to the mistakes of the past. With each passing day, the Road Map was increasingly becoming the Bush administration's policy.

When Labor pulled out of the national unity government in early November, Prime Minister Sharon decided to call elections rather than form a narrow Right-wing government. The elections were scheduled for the last week in January, and the Quartet decided to postpone the presentation of the plan until after the elections.

In those elections, Sharon led the Likud party to a huge victory, winning thirty-eight seats, twice as many as the Labor party. It was Sharon's second landslide victory in two years. My party, Yisrael Ba'aliyah, was decimated at the polls, winning only two seats, after having won seven and six seats in two previous elections. Despite our poor showing, the election debacle was a bittersweet experience for me. When our party first ran in the 1996 elections, we had pointed out that since our goal was integrating the new immigrants into Israeli society, we would know we had succeeded when our party became obsolete. The more "Israeli" the new immigrants became, the less likely they would be to feel that an immigrant party was needed to help open the doors of Israeli society. Thus, though our party had lost most of its political power, we were proud that we had achieved our raison d'etre.

Sharon invited me to serve as a minister in his second government as well, with responsibility for diaspora affairs and Jerusalem. I was interested in this position because Jerusalem and Israel's relationship with diaspora Jewry were both very close to my heart. Moreover, with the battle for integration behind me, I thought I could contribute to the fight against anti-Semitism that had become an increasingly critical issue and which would fall under my new authority.

At the end of April, two months after Sharon formed a Center-Right government, the Palestinian Authority confirmed the nomination of Mahmud Abbas, also known as Abu Mazen, as prime minister, a post that had not previously existed. America had made the release of the new diplomatic plan conditional on the appointment of Abbas, one of the "reforms" that was supposed to put the peace process back on track. As promised, the Road Map was immediately released. A few days later, representatives of the Quartet met formally to endorse the plan.

At the end of May, Sharon brought the Road Map, including a fourteen-point statement clarifying Israel's reservations with the plan, to a vote of the cabinet. Some of these reservations were points Israel had failed to get incorporated into the text of the Road Map while it was being drafted. Other reservations were included to win the support or the abstention of some of the wavering ministers.

Not surprisingly, the debate in the government split almost entirely according to who supported or opposed a Palestinian state. The former voted in favor, while the latter voted against or abstained. I voted against the Road Map not because I was opposed to a Palestinian state but because of what *kind* of Palestinian state I believed it would create. I shared the concerns of some other ministers that in granting the Palestinian Authority a state even before final status talks would begin, the Road Map was rewarding Palestinian terrorism. I also agreed with them that by internationalizing the conflict, the plan was undermining Israeli sovereignty. But my chief concern, which I expressed in the government, was that the Road Map had abandoned the principles of Bush's June 24 speech. In the end, by a vote of twelve to seven, with four abstentions and fourteen reservations, the Israeli government accepted the Road Map.

A week later in Aqaba, President Bush stood between an elected Israeli prime minister and an unelected prime minister of the Palestinian Authority and proclaimed a hopeful new era. Ten years after the famous handshake on the White House lawn, it was déjà vu on the shores of the Red Sea. With Abu Mazen held up as a "moderate" leader who would fight Palestinian terrorism and make peace with Israel, it was clear to me that Oslo's false assumptions would once again guide the peace process. Like their Oslo predecessors, those supporting the Road Map did not recognize that moderation is not a function of a leader's disposition or promises, but rather a function of the nature of the society he or she governs. The Road Map had it precisely backwards. One can rely on a free society to create the moderate, but one cannot rely on a moderate to create a free society.

It is ironic that the same American administration that

was behind the principles articulated in June 2002 whole-heartedly embraced a diplomatic plan that abandoned those principles in June 2003. For me, it was as if Ronald Reagan, one year after making his evil empire speech, would have accepted a renewed détente between the superpowers.

In hindsight, the Bush administration's support for the Road Map seems even more shocking. In speech after speech on Iraq, Bush has stressed the relationship between freedom and peace and between democracy and security. In doing so, he has been a strong and steady voice of moral clarity in a world that mostly rejects these ideas. Equally important, during his presidency, America's policies have largely reflected those ideas. Yet when it came to the Israeli-Palestinian conflict, the rhetoric and the policy of his administration diverged. I am sure that President Bush does not see the Road Map as an abandonment of the principles he has consistently championed. Indeed, when he declared that "there can be no peace for either side in the Middle East unless there is freedom for both,"[9] I have no doubt that he meant it. Nevertheless, the Road Map will not bring to fruition the ideas the president articulated on June 24. It will not bring genuine freedom to the Palestinians, and therefore will not bring genuine peace.

DISENGAGING FROM DEMOCRACY

In the week following the Aqaba Summit, yet another wave of Palestinian terrorism and violence hit Israel, culminating in a suicide bombing on a Jerusalem bus that murdered 16 passengers.

The Road Map required the Palestinian Authority security forces to take "sustained, targeted, and effective operations" aimed at confronting all those engaged in terror and to ensure the "dismantlement of terrorist capabilities and infrastructure." Instead, Abu Mazen tried to negotiate a "hudna," a temporary truce in which all the terror groups would agree to halt violence. The idea of a temporary truce was certainly not new. In fact, it is exactly how many PLO leaders, including Arafat, saw Oslo from the start.

In 1994, speaking at a mosque in Johannesburg, South Africa, Arafat said that he considered the Oslo agreement like "the agreement which had been signed between our prophet Muhammed and Koraish."[10] The agreement to which Arafat was referring was a peace treaty made in the seventh century between the founder of Islam and the Arabian tribe of Koraish. Having grown much more powerful two years after making the pact, Muhammed broke his word and destroyed the Koreish, slaughtering all its male members. In effect, Arafat saw the Oslo accord as a temporary "peace" that could be broken whenever it suited him.

But Israel's government ignored this statement and many others like it, explaining that Arafat was just playing internal politics. He had to appear tough, Israelis were told, until he had grown strong enough to fight the rejectionists. The important thing was not to weaken him and to keep the peace process moving.

But Arafat has never repudiated terrorism. In trying to

bypass the Palestinian commitment to fight terrorism by getting terror groups to hold their fire until further concessions could be wrought from Israel, Abu Mazen was trying to do with the Road Map what Arafat had done with the Oslo agreement. But after a decade of incitement, support for terrorism had become so deeply woven into the fabric of Palestinian society that the idea of a temporary hudna could not keep the terrorists at bay.

Prime Minister Sharon wisely rejected a tactical ceasefire between Palestinian terror groups and demanded that the "new" Palestinian government abide by its commitment to dismantle the terrorist infrastructure. As for the other Palestinian commitments in the Road Map, they were blocked by Arafat. Arafat was supposed to be relegated to symbolic status, but he refused to give up any of his authority, keeping control over the PA's security forces and finances. With power over Palestinian guns and money, Arafat ensured that the Road Map's reforms went nowhere. By September, Abu Mazen had resigned his post.

The Israeli government's unequivocal stance on the need for Palestinian compliance no doubt contributed to solid American backing for its position. Unlike the prisoner controversy following the Wye agreement, when the Clinton administration hesitated to make good on its promise to guarantee an oral agreement, the Bush administration refused to allow the Palestinians to renege on their signed commitments. Others, however, were ready to let the Palestinians off the hook. When it became clear that the Palestinians were not prepared to fight terrorism, the "international community" grew impatient. Here too, it felt like we had returned to the days of Oslo when in spite of Palestinian noncompliance, the world pressured Israel to keep the peace process moving. Both inside and outside of Israel (and even around the cabinet table), Sharon's government was accused of not doing enough to "strengthen" Abu Mazen. In fact, some respected voices abroad began to question the wisdom of making the Palestinian commitment to fight terrorism a condition for moving forward. It would have been better, they argued, to take steps in parallel. It all sounded familiar: Demands for compliance give way to parallel steps, which eventually give way to one-sided concessions.

At the beginning of December, statesmen from around the world flew to Switzerland to attend a signing ceremony in Geneva. The Geneva Initiative, the brainchild of Yossi Beilin, a former architect of the Oslo agreement, was supposed to have resolved all outstanding issues between Israelis and Palestinians. There was only one problem. The people who signed it represented hardly anyone but themselves. Beilin was rejected by his own Labor party and failed to enter the Knesset. On the Palestinian side, the figures involved had even less public standing. However, that did not stop former and current presidents and prime ministers from attending the ceremony. When Israel's democratically elected government was trying to mobilize international support for the struggle against Palestinian terrorism, Beilin was doing his best to restore international legitimacy to a PA that was implicated in terror attacks and that was responsible for inciting the Palestinian population against

Israel. At a time when Palestinian children were strapping on suicide belts and when PA-controlled television was inciting Palestinians against the Jews and their state, Yossi Beilin assured those attending the majestic signing ceremony that "peace is right around the corner."[11]

Like the anti-war marchers in Europe in the early 1980s who were convinced that their own governments were escalating the arms race and provoking tension with a peaceful Soviet Union, Beilin told his audience in Geneva that it was Israel's government that didn't want peace. Former U.S. President Jimmy Carter showed similar moral clarity when he praised the Geneva Initiative which "the people support" and noted that the "political leaders are the obstacles to peace."[12]

A couple of weeks after the ceremony in Geneva, Prime Minister Sharon announced his intention to unilaterally disengage from the Palestinians if the PA refused to implement the Road Map. Sharon said that the purpose of his so-called disengagement plan would be to "grant Israeli citizens the maximum level of security"[13] and "minimize friction between Israelis and Palestinians." Sharon said that he did not intend "to hold Israeli society hostage in the hands of the Palestinians" and made it clear that Israel would not "wait for [the Palestinians] indefinitely."

The logic of the prime minister's approach was understandable. He assumed that there was no Palestinian peace partner and no prospects for one on the horizon. Second, based on the experience of the last ten years, Sharon was convinced that Israel would come under increasing pressure to make large concessions despite Palestinian noncompliance. Thus, Sharon thought it would be better for Israel to act unilaterally to secure its interests while it still could. Many Israelis who had lost hope that a Palestinian peace partner would emerge, and believed that Israelis and Palestinians must separate from one another, supported Sharon's ideas.

In April 2004, Sharon formally unveiled his disengagement plan. It called for the removal of all Israeli settlements and military installations in the Gaza Strip as well as the uprooting of four isolated settlements in the West Bank. President Bush, who saw the plan as an "historic opportunity" and who hoped to give Sharon as much political backing as possible, made unprecedented statements in support of Israel's traditional positions, ruling out both a "right of return" for Palestinian refugees and an Israeli return to the "indefensible borders" of 1967. In the weeks before the vote, Sharon gave ministers the opportunity to discuss his ideas and to present alternatives.

I was opposed to Sharon's disengagement plan because I did not accept the premise that there was no potential Palestinian partner and no hope for peace. Of course, the peace I envisioned was very different from what the architects of Oslo and Geneva had in mind. The peace I envisioned was one that ignored neither the nature of the society on our doorstep nor the human rights of our neighbors.

In my view, one-sided Israeli concessions would only strengthen the forces of terror and fear within Palestinian society, making it even more difficult to promote positive change and decreasing the chances of a viable partner for peace emerging in the future.

As I had done so many times over the previous decade, I tried my best to convince my fellow ministers that the road to peace is paved with freedom. But my arguments could not pierce the skepticism. "I understand that in the Soviet Union your ideas were important, but unfortunately they have no place in the Middle East," Sharon told me, as many of my colleagues nodded in agreement.

Despite the skepticism, I still have not lost my faith in an Israeli-Palestinian peace anchored in freedom. The peace I believe in is based on the belief that all peoples can build free societies. It is based on the two ideas that guided my struggle for human rights in the Soviet Union: that a fear society is inherently incapable of upholding human rights and that the most reliable measure of a state's intentions towards its neighbors is its treatment of its own citizens. And it is based on the conviction that by linking the peace process to the expansion of freedom within Palestinian society, Palestinians will be free and Israelis will be secure.

The Palestinians lived under Israeli rule for a quarter century. But after less than a decade under Arafat's regime, their hatred toward Israel is higher than at any time in the past. Why? Because a fear society has descended on the Palestinians. Until that fear society is replaced, there will be no end to Palestinian suffering, no improvement in their condition, and no chance for peace. That fear society will surely breed terrorism and poison generation after generation of Palestinians to hate Jews and the Jewish state. It matters not if Israel signs a peace treaty with such a society or seeks to disengage from it: A fear society will *always* remain a danger to Israel.

Peace and security cannot be achieved, as some believe, by simply leaving the territories. That will only bring the terror closer to our cities and our families, and create a terror state on our border that will threaten Israel and the world. The only way a Palestinian state will not endanger the Jewish state is if it is a state whose leadership is dependent on the people they govern.

For ten years, and with five different prime ministers, Israel has tried various approaches to peace with the Palestinians. Rabin and Peres sought to create a "New Middle East" with a Palestinian dictatorship. Netanyahu tried to establish reciprocity. Barak jumped to final status negotiations. Sharon embraced unilateral disengagement. During this time, most of the world and many in Israel measured progress in the peace process by the percentage of territory that was handed over, by how close the Palestinians were to establishing a state, or by how close Israel was to removing settlements. Thus, according to the world's criteria, the peace process was either speeding ahead or stuck in neutral. In contrast, I measured progress by the extent of freedom within Palestinian society. But according to my criteria, despite the efforts of Israeli governments to make peace, the peace process was going steadily in reverse because there was less freedom and more fear within Palestinian society than before Oslo began.

There is another way. History has shown us that a few years of freedom can make a world of difference. In 1944, Germany had descended into depths that are scarcely imaginable today. A few years later, West Germany, a free society once more, was building its democratic institutions and becoming a peaceful member of the free world.

The culture of death and violence that has engulfed Palestinian society can also change quickly. But the change is unlikely to happen on its own, nor will it be the product of an Israeli withdrawal or a phony peace. It will happen when the free world abandons the false assumptions that have guided diplomacy in the region for decades. It will happen when the world's democratic leaders, especially those in the United States and Israel, embrace the principles that President Bush outlined on June 24, 2002, and ensure that those principles shape their policies. Above all, it will happen only when those democratic leaders have faith that freedom has the power to change our world—even when its seeds are planted in the rocky soil of the West Bank and the Gaza strip.

Conclusion

IN JANUARY 1997, eleven years after my release from prison, I made my first trip back to Russia. Only once during that time did I have any interest in returning. That was in 1989 when Andrei Sakharov died. Sakharov had been with my family during our most difficult days, and I wanted to support his family in their hour of need. But since I was officially still considered a spy by the Soviet government, my request for a visa was denied. In the 1990s, after I was "rehabilitated" and free to travel to Russia, I declined many invitations. When I was appointed Israel's minister of trade and industry in 1996, however, I knew that I would soon be expected to go as part of my duties in the government, which included developing Israel's economic relations with Russia.

Many people on official trips to Moscow visit the Bolshoi Theater, but I had been to the Bolshoi many times during my university days at the Moscow Institute of Physics and Technology. Besides, what I really wanted to see was my other alma mater, the KGB prison at Lefortovo, in which I had spent sixteen months undergoing interrogations before my trial and sentencing. After much hesitation and delay, my Russian hosts finally agreed to make Lefortovo part of my itinerary.

After a number of meetings with Russian ministers, I arrived at the prison. Inside, I thought I was at the theater. The dark and dreary place of my memory was now filled with light and immaculately clean. I stood in the prison cell I had lived in, walked through the winding corridors I had been led down, and visited the library whose books had once transported me to a different world. I presented the warden with five copies of my prison memoir, *Fear No Evil*, and told him that I would know glasnost was complete when current inmates were permitted to read my book. (In later years, I received word that the book was a favorite among prisoners, who particularly liked my stories about Lefortovo and my advice on how to handle interrogations.)

When the official tour ended, I asked to see the punishment cells. During my nine years in prison, I had spent 405 days in such cells, and I wanted to show my wife, Avital, who agreed to accompany me on the trip, what they were like. The warden took me to a normal cell, emptied of furniture, with a guard inside. "These are the punishment cells we have today," the warden told me. "What you remember, we no longer use."

I knew he was lying. "Look," I said, "why don't we go down to the basement and I'll show you the punishment cells myself." He motioned to a guard, spoke on a walkie-talkie, and twenty minutes later, we went downstairs. When I entered the cell, I was standing in the same cold, dark, small room that I remembered. I asked to be left alone for a few minutes with Avital. "Do you recognize the cell?" I asked her. "You were always in here with me." "I know I was," she replied.

As we left the grounds of the prison, I was besieged by a throng of reporters who had been waiting outside in the snow. One of the first questions was why I had returned to Lefortovo. "Isn't it a very painful memory?" one journalist asked. "Are you some sort of masochist?"

"To the contrary," I said, "it is inspiring to be here. Twenty years ago, in this very prison, the head interrogators of the KGB, the most powerful organization of the most powerful empire in the world, told me again and again that the movement for Soviet Jewry was dead, that the dissident movement was finished. Jewish activists and dissidents inside the country, they said, had been arrested. 'Your supporters outside the country are scared and they will distance themselves from you because of the charges of espionage. You have nothing to hope for. You have nobody to rely on.'

"Twenty years later, the KGB has disappeared, the Soviet Union has disintegrated, global communism has collapsed, over one million Jews have left the big prison called the USSR, and hundreds of millions of people are free." One would think that no more proof was needed of the power of freedom to change the world.

Unfortunately, this proof has not resolved the doubts of the skeptics. Many people remain convinced that freedom is not for everyone, that its expansion is not always desirable, and that there is little that the free world can do to promote it. Just as they were wrong a generation ago about Russia, and two generations ago about Japan and Germany, the skeptics are wrong today.

The formula that triggered a democratic revolution in the Soviet Union had three components: People inside who yearned to be free, leaders outside who believed they could be, and policies that linked the free world's relations with the USSR to the Soviet regime's treatment of it own people. Whether this same formula is applied to a great power like China or a weak despotism like Zimbabwe, a secular totalitarian regime like North Korea or a religious tyranny like Iran makes no difference. It will work anywhere around the globe, including in the Arab world.

I have no doubt that the Arabs want to be free. Many ask how I can be so sure when there is no Arab Sakharov and no Arab Gandhi. I am sure because I know that the extent of dissent in a society, like so many things in life, is largely a function of price. In the 1930s, there was no Russian Sakharov because Stalin executed all voices of dissent and few in the West paid any attention. Convinced that communism was just or that Stalin was an ally or that repression was Russia's fate, the potential forces of freedom in the West either didn't know what Stalin was doing, didn't want to know, or didn't care.

In the 1970s, when dissent was punishable "only" by

prison or exile, when a spotlight was shined on how the Soviet regime treated its people and when a handful of leaders argued for a policy of linkage, a few hundred dissidents had the courage to step forward. But we were only the tip of an iceberg. Beneath the surface were hundreds of millions who wanted their freedom.

The democratic forces in the free world today are largely silent about how Arab regimes treat their own people. Most security hawks fear that "weakening" these regimes will endanger stability and the free flow of oil. For their part, most human rights liberals have not embraced the cause of human rights within the Arab world anywhere near as vigorously as they once embraced the cause of human rights within the Soviet Union. Yet despite the lack of support for Arab dissent, the Arab voice for freedom is getting louder.

In the fall of 2001, I was sitting in my office at the Housing Ministry in Jerusalem when I received a call from a Palestinian businessman in Ramallah. At that time, Israel had placed that West Bank city under siege to prevent further terror attacks. The man introduced himself as Omar Karsou and told me he was calling from a pay phone in Ramallah so that his conversation with me would not be discovered.

"I was surprised to read an article you wrote about the need for democracy for Palestinians. Do you really believe what you wrote?" he asked. "Every word," I said, "but why does it surprise you?" Karsou replied, "Because for us, you are a right-wing minister. You are supposed to be our enemy. Yet when I read your article, I agreed with every word. I too believe that the biggest problem for the Palestinians is the lack of freedom in our society. We are all suffering from dictatorship and corruption."

We wanted to meet immediately to discuss the problem, but it was almost impossible for Omar to leave a besieged Ramallah for a discreet meeting with an Israeli minister, so we agreed to meet in the future. We spoke a number of times by telephone, but met face to face only six months later in Washington. In moving his family out of Ramallah and organizing efforts to promote freedom and human rights for Palestinians, Omar became a dissident.

I am a Zionist. Omar is not. Though I am prepared to make compromises for the sake of peace, I believe in the historical right of the Jewish people to the land of Israel. Omar does not. Yet when it comes to our views on the way that Israelis and Palestinians can live in peace with one another, we see almost completely eye to eye. Both of us believe that Israel should not rule the Palestinians. Both of us believe that only by ending the Palestinians' fear society will it be possible to end Palestinian suffering. Both of us believe that the corrupt dictatorship of the Palestinian Authority is the prime source of Palestinian suffering. Both of us believe that Israel and the free world share responsibility for helping to build and maintain that corrupt dictatorship. And both of us believe that only if the Palestinians build a free society will there be peace.

Every time I listen to Omar, I am reminded of my own past. After years of hearing false arguments about how the struggle for the rights of Palestinians is the same as my struggle for rights in the Soviet Union, I have finally found someone about whom I can honestly say, "his struggle is my struggle." But there is also an important difference. When we in the Soviet Union were fighting for human rights, we knew we could be arrested and imprisoned. But we also believed that the free world would stand by our side, a belief that strengthened our resolve enormously. Omar Karsou, however, cannot rely on that solidarity. Had he stayed in Ramallah and fought for human rights, PA leaders could do to him what they wished without endangering their support in the free world. And now that he has escaped Palestinian tyranny, few are ready to help in his struggle for Palestinian freedom. Why? Because they do not want to weaken the Palestinian Authority, "the only hope for peace." At this time, most doors in the democratic world remain closed to Omar.

When I returned to Israel, I tried to convince others to support Omar's effort to strengthen democratic voices within Palestinian society. After looking into the matter, one of my colleagues told me that Omar might be a good man, but that he had absolutely no power. It reminded me of Stalin's sarcastic remark about the pope, "How many divisions does he have?" My colleague was right. Omar has no divisions. Arafat and the PA have all the power. They have a 40,000-man armed police force and control over which Palestinians will receive permits to work in Israel, which families will get food distribution from international organizations, and who benefits from the hundreds of millions of dollars of international aid that are supposed to build a better life for Palestinians. But the PA has this power only because Israel and the free world gave it to them. We helped—and continue to help—undermine efforts of people like Omar Karsou to build democracy for the Palestinians.

Omar Karsou is one of many dissidents in the Arab world fighting for more democracy in their countries. Armed with nothing more than a computer and the Internet, one can find the names of many of them:

Salaheddine Sidhoum of Algeria
Abd al-Raud al-Shayeb of Bahrain
Saad Eddin Ibrahim of Egypt
Dr. Muhamed Mugraby and Samari Trad of Lebanon
Fathi El-Jahami, Fawzi Orafia, Ashur Shamis, Abd Al-
   Qader, Al Hudheiri of Libya
Abdelaziz Mouride and Ali Lmrabert of Morocco
Bassem Eid and Issam Abu Issa of the Palestinian
   Authority
Abdullah Al-Hamad, Mohammed Said Al-Taib, Towfiq
   Al Qaseer, Najeeb Al-Khanizee, Abdul-Rahman
   Alahim, Ali Al-Deminy, and Shaikh Sulaiman Al-
   Rashoud of Saudi Arabia
Dr. Mudawi Ibrahim Adam and Saleh Mahmud Osman
   of Sudan
Aktham Naisse, Muhammed Mustafa, Sherif Ramad-
   han, Khaled Ahmad Ali, Muhammed Ghanem, and
   Mahleb Muhammed Ghanem of Syria
Zoheir Yahiaoui, and Mokhtar Yahyaoui of Tunisia
Hashem Aghajari, Ahmad Batebi and Siamak Pourzand
   of Iran

There are many, many more.

Imagine what would happen if the enormous support the free world gives to nondemocratic regimes in the region were given to the people, like these dissidents, whom those regimes repress. From the army of doublethinkers in the Middle East, hundreds and then thousands of dissidents would emerge and the end of these fear societies would draw nearer.

I am also confident that the leaders of the free world can serve as an enormous force for democratic change. In the last few years, President Bush has seemingly used every forum, every stage, and every address to assert his unequivocal belief that the region can be free. He has argued forcefully that there is an inextricable link between freedom and peace, between democracy and security. And he has made the case for helping build democracy both in terms of respecting the rights of those who are denied freedom and protecting the security interests of his own nation. On the other side of the Atlantic, British Prime Minister Tony Blair has made similar arguments, and democratic leaders elsewhere have supported efforts to build free societies in Afghanistan and Iraq.

To create a critical mass for these ideas, however, the unique partnership that once brought together the "human rights camp" and the "security hawks" must be reconstituted. In the Cold War, political leaders, religious leaders, human rights organizations, writers, and journalists transcended partisan and ideological divisions to work together to confront tyranny and support those inside the Soviet Union who were fighting for freedom. To win the battle against today's tyrants, we must once again turn political opponents into allies and unite the world's democracies in a common purpose. We must recapture moral clarity by recognizing that the great divide between the world of fear and the world of freedom is far more important than the divisions within the free world. At a time when freedom and fear are at war, we must move beyond Left and Right and begin to think again about right and wrong.

I am also confident that a policy of linkage can be pursued successfully. True, linkage without leverage is impossible, but Middle Eastern regimes are even more dependent today on the West than the USSR was in 1975. This may seem hard to believe to those who are convinced that the free world is dependent on Middle East oil. But consider that in 1978, among the top oil suppliers to the United States were Saudi Arabia, Libya, Iraq, Iran, and Nigeria. In short order, three of those states became avowed enemies of the "Great Satan." But the sky did not fall. Prices did not even rise dramatically. In fact, even with the recent spike in prices, oil today is still cheaper in real terms than it was a quarter century ago. If a country like Saudi Arabia responds to pressures to reform by choking off oil supplies, the free world will survive the blow. Saudi Arabia won't.

The Soviets used nuclear blackmail to instill fear in the West. Middle Eastern regimes use oil blackmail to instill that same fear. But to paraphrase U.S. President Franklin Delano Roosevelt, in standing against this tyranny, the only thing the democracies have to fear is fear itself. If the free world uses its enormous leverage, the Arab regimes will no longer be able to violate human rights with impunity. And the more freedom the people of the Arab world enjoy, the more secure all of us will be.

Just as Helsinki helped liberate hundreds of millions of people and defeat an evil empire that threatened the democratic world, the same approach today can transform the Middle East from a region awash in terror and tyranny into a place that provides freedom and opportunity to its own people as well as peace and security for the rest of the world.

Linkage worked after Helsinki because dissidents inside the Soviet Union and leaders outside the Soviet Union turned a nonbinding agreement into an internationally accepted measure of Soviet intentions. This must now be done in the Arab world.

The first step may already have been taken. Early in 2004, a document produced at a conference in Alexandria, Egypt, pointed to the urgent need for political, economic, and social reform in the Arab world. What makes this document potentially so significant is that the conference was attended by representatives of civil-society institutions within Arab states and that the document was written by Arabs themselves. The fact that nondemocratic Arab regimes have tried to block further action on the issues that were raised at Alexandria only proves how important this document can become.

The critical next step can be taken if the reforms called for in Alexandria are turned into a yardstick by which to chart the progress of Arab regimes, and if democratic states are prepared to link their policies toward those states to this progress. The United States, for example, might insist that if the Saudi regime wants American protection, it will have to change its draconian emigration policies and improve its record on women's rights. European states, for their part, might demand that if the Palestinian Authority wants to keep receiving financial support, it will have to prove that this money is being used to improve the lives of the Palestinian people and not to fund terrorism and corruption.

I was encouraged by a recent visit to Washington where I testified before the U.S. Commission on Security and Cooperation in Europe, a commission that was set up, like the Helsinki Group, to monitor the Helsinki accords. When I told them the names of the Arab dissidents who had been arrested in only the last few weeks, members of the commission promised that the fate of Arab dissidents would be placed on the agenda just as the fate of Soviet dissidents had been placed on the agenda a generation ago.

The lesson of Helsinki is that when demands to uphold human rights are backed by effective action, the cause of freedom and peace can be advanced. In the atmosphere created after Helsinki, the Soviets were forced to choose: Respect human rights, or give up all the benefits of cooperation with the free world. That is how the acceptance of human rights commitments, which was once seen as a hollow promise, turned out to be one of the most fateful decisions of the Cold War.

The danger today is that the commitments to spread human rights and democracy in the Middle East will remain an empty promise. In order to ensure that the free world's commitments become more than lip service, nondemocratic regimes in the region must understand that they, too, face a clear choice: If they continue to repress their people and stifle dissent, they will lose all the benefits the free world has to offer, from legitimacy and security guarantees to direct aid and trade privileges.

The free world should not wait for dictatorial regimes to consent to reform. If there are courageous leaders in the Arab world who are genuinely willing to democratize and liberalize their countries, then they should be applauded and supported. But if we condition reform on the agreement of nondemocratic leaders, it will never come. We must be prepared to move forward over their objections.

We must also not wait for the support of international organizations. Many of the countries that wield influence in these organizations are nondemocratic regimes. Surely, we cannot rely on those who deny freedom to their own people to support efforts to expand freedom around the world.

I do not believe in an end of history. The diversity of the world ensures that there will always be argument and conflict. But I do believe that there can be an end to lasting tyranny— that we can live in a world where no regime that attempts to crush dissent will be tolerated. Just as the institution of slavery has been all but wiped off the face of the earth, so too can government tyranny become a thing of the past.

To protect and promote democracy around the world, I believe that a new international institution, one in which only those governments who give their people the right to be heard and counted will themselves have a right to be heard and counted can be an enormously important force for democratic change. Such a coalition of free nations could turn a government's preservation of the right to dissent—the town square test—into the standard of international legitimacy. Countries that fail to meet this standard would not be accepted into the community of nations. They would be shunned and sanctioned, and the people they repress would be embraced and supported.

If a coalition of free nations acts in this way, then the decay of today's fear societies will be accelerated and the dangers of one man, one vote, one time, will soon disappear. Perhaps in less than a couple of generations, the world could become a community of free nations in which each country would build a democracy that suits its unique culture, history, religion, and traditions, but where no nation would be able to undermine the right to dissent that truly is God's gift to humanity.

This community of free nations will not emerge on its own. It will require both the clarity of the democratic world to see the profound moral difference between the world of freedom and the world of fear, and the courage to confront fear societies everywhere. I am convinced that a successful effort to expand freedom around the world must be inspired and led by the United States. In the twentieth century, America proved time and again that it possessed both the clarity and courage that is necessary to defeat evil. Following that example, the democracies of the world can defeat the tyranny that threatens our world today and the tyrannies that would threaten it tomorrow. To do so, we must believe not only that all *people* are created equal but also that all *peoples* are created equal.

NOTES

PREFACE

1. Yoel Marcus, "Anatol's kippah and Sharon's elbow," *Haaretz*, February 14, 1986.

INTRODUCTION

1. Schlesinger is reported to have made this statement after his return from a trip to the Soviet Union in 1982.
2. J. William Fulbright and Seth Tillman, "Our new opportunity to beat swords into plowshares," *Chicago Tribune*, April 19, 1989.
3. Ibid.
4. Kissinger himself makes this distinction between his and Jackson's approach in *Diplomacy* (New York: Simon & Schuster, 1994), p. 755.

CHAPTER 1: IS FREEDOM FOR EVERYONE?

1. President Bush's State of the Union Address, January 28, 2003.

2. Presidential address to joint session of Congress, September 20, 2001.
3. Presidential address to the nation, September 11, 2001.
4. Comments by President Bush in Indonesia, as reported in the *Washington Post*, October 22, 2003.
5. George Will, *Washington Post*, August 17, 2003.
6. Arnold Toynbee, *Foreign Affairs*, 1934, quoted in Joshua Muravchik, *Exporting Democracy* (Washington, D.C.: AEI Press, 1991), p. 72.
7. Ibid.
8. Emil Ludwig, *How to Treat the Germans* (New York: Willard Publishing Co., 1943), p. 66.
9. Waldo Frank, "Our Island Hemisphere," *Foreign Affairs*, Vol. 21, No. 3, April 1943, p. 519.
10. See Bodin, *Six Livres de la Republique, 1576*.
11. Marquis de Custine's *Russia in 1839*, edited and translated from the French by Phyllis Penn Kohler and published under the title, *Journey for Our Time* (New York: Pellegrini and Cudahi, 1951), p. 254.
12. Richard Pipes, "East Is East," *New Republic*, May 3, 1999.
13. Pipes covered many of these points in the above article.
14. David Remnick, "Can Russia Change?" *Foreign Affairs*, January 1997.
15. John Loyd, "Russia's Implausible Dictator," *New Statesmen*, February 14, 2000.
16. Muravchik, *Exporting Democracy*, p. 91.
17. See Sir George Sansom, "Liberalism in Japan," *Foreign Affairs*, April 1941.
18. Ibid.
19. Muravchik mentions this quote in "Push for More Democracy," *Washington Post*, November 15, 1994.
20. G. F. Hudson, "Why Asians Hate the West: The Third Phase in the Orient," *Commentary*, May 1952.
21. John Derbyshire, "Unpleasant Truths," *National Review Online*, August 2, 2002.
22. Speech to the National Endowment for Democracy, November 6, 2003.

23. Ibid.
24. "The Law of Man or the Law of God?" *The Economist,* September 13, 2003.
25. Ibid.
26. Bernard Lewis, "The Return of Islam," *Commentary,* January 1976. It should be noted that Lewis has not in fact dismissed the possibility of democracy emerging in the Muslim world today.
27. Ronal Inglehart and Pippa Norris, "The true clash of civilizations; conflict between democracy and Islam," *Foreign Policy,* March 1, 2003.
28. Adrian Karatnycky, *"The 2001–2002 Freedom House Survey of Freedom: The Democracy Gap,"* in Freedom House's Freedom in the World 2001–2002, p. 12.
29. UN: *Arab Human Development Report, 2002,* p. 2.
30. President Bush's State of the Union Address, January 28, 2003.

CHAPTER 2: A FREE SOCIETY AND A FEAR SOCIETY

1. Susan Azadi with Angela Ferrante, *Out of Iran: One Woman's Escape from the Ayatollahs* (London: Macdonald & Co. Ltd., 1987), pp. 131–132.
2. A letter from North Korea, from the *Chosun Journal,* www.chosunjournal.com.
3. To those who are versed in the world of the natural sciences, perhaps the following analogy could be useful to explain the phenomenon of doublethink. According to the second law of thermodynamics, entropy, which roughly speaking is the degree of disorder in a system, always increases when external influences are absent. One of the primary goals of a fear society is to keep the citizens thoughts in "order"—i.e., aligned with the regime. In conditions where there are no external influences—for example, brainwashing by the regime—the thoughts, ideas, and reactions of people, like the movement of gas molecules in a closed system, become more and more "disordered." They increasingly clash with the ideology of the

regime. External influences can reduce the extent of the clash, but they can never remove it entirely.

Additionally, the restrictions of a fear society can be compared to the borders of the system in which entropy is being measured. The smaller the size of the system in which gas molecules are moving, the more frequent the collision of those molecules with the borders of that system. Likewise, the more restrictive a fear society is, the more often the "disordered" thoughts of those living in fear collide with the red lines imposed by the regime. Or in other words, the more often the mechanism of self-censorship must be used, and the more doublethinkers there will be. Thus, we can formulate two laws about a fear society. First, the number of doublethinkers in a fear society is increasing over time. Second, the more restrictive a fear society, the faster the growth of doublethinkers within that society.

4. Leon Feuchtwanger, Moscow 1937 (Zacharov, Moscow 2001), p. 11. The translations from the Russian version are provided by the author.

5. Ibid., p. 11.

6. Ibid., p. 101.

7. Nic Robertson, "Support for Taliban Wavering," CNN, November 1, 2001.

8. Ibid.

9. Aparsim Ghosh, "Waiting to Kill Americans," Time.com, March 3, 2003.

10. Fred Hiatt, "Defectors Describe Harsh Life in North Korea," Washington Post, April 11, 1989.

11. Steve Vincent, "Baghdad, with Victims; following Sadaam Hussein's tyranny," Commentary, December 1, 2003.

12. "This World uncovers the 'gas chambers' of North Korea," BBC News, February 1, 2004.

13. PA Television Broadcast, June 9, 2002, translation provided by Palestinian Media Watch.

14. Fred Hiatt, "Defectors Describe Harsh Life in North Korea," The Washington Post, April 11, 1989.

CHAPTER 3: *Dognat Y Peregnat*

1. John Quincy Adams, Fourth of July Address, 1821.
2. Michael Mandelbaum, "Foreign Policy as Social Work," *Foreign Affairs,* January/February 1996.
3. Speech by Krauthammer to the American Enterprise Institute on February 10, 2004.
4. Paul Brooker, *Defiant Dictatorships: Communist and Middle Eastern Dictatorships in a Democratic Age* (New York: New York University Press, 1997), pp. 7–8.

CHAPTER 4: MISSION POSSIBLE

1. President Bush's speech at MacDill Air Force Base in Tampa, Florida, March 26, 2003.
2. President Bush's Address to Nation in Prime Time Press Conference, April 13, 2004.
3. Fouad Ajami, "Iraq May Survive, but the Dream Is Dead," *New York Times,* May 26, 2004.
4. Quoted in John Tierney, "The Hawks Loudly Express Their Second Thoughts," *New York Times,* May 1, 2004.
5. Quoted in George Will, "Foreign Policy requires more optimism than force," *Washington Post,* May 30, 2004.
6. Interview with Kissinger in *U.S. News and World Report,* March 15, 1976.
7. Dorothy Fosdick, ed., *Staying The Course, Henry M. Jackson and National Security* (Seattle: University of Washington Press, 1987), p. 116.
8. A. I. Solzhenitsyn, "Two Hundred Years Together" Volume II (Russki Put, Moscow 2002), p. 487. The translation from the original Russian is provided by the author.
9. Ibid. The quote in question refers to a note Solzhenitsyn wrote at the end of 1972.
10. Kissinger, *Diplomacy,* p. 753.
11. Anatoly Dobrynin, *In Confidence* (New York: Times Books, 1995), p. 268.
12. Ibid.

13. Interview with Kissinger in *U.S. News and World Report*, June 1975.

14. "The Jackson Amendment," editorial, *The New York Times*, October 6, 1972.

15. "Fulbright Assails Efforts to Link Soviet Trade Accord to Emigration Issue," *New York Times*, July 12, 1973.

16. "Trade, Détente ... and Emigration," *New York Times*, June 30, 1974.

17. "European Security and real détente," editorial, *The New York Times*, July 21, 1975.

18. Interestingly, Mrs. Fenwick sat silently in the meeting taking notes the entire time. I was embarrassed the next day when I asked Yates if she was his secretary. "That woman is no secretary," he told me. "That's Millicent Fenwick, a very capable congresswoman from New Jersey."

19. John Kenneth Galbraith, *New Yorker* magazine, 1984, cited in Dinesh D'Souza's *Ronald Reagan* (New York: Simon & Schuster, 1997).

20. Ibid.

21. Paul Samuelson and William Nordhaus, *Economics* (New York: McGraw-Hill, 1985), pp. 775–776, cited in D'Souza, *Ronald Reagan*.

22. Ronald Reagan, Commencement Address at University of Notre Dame, May 1981.

23. Ronald Reagan, Address to the British Parliament, June 1982.

24. Seweryn Bialer, professor of political science, Columbia University, *Foreign Affairs*, 1982/1983.

25. Stephen Cohen, "Sovieticus," April 9, 1983, cited in D'Souza, *Ronald Reagan*.

26. See Freerepublic.com.

CHAPTER 5: FROM HELSINKI TO OSLO

1. Abu Iyad quoted in *Al Sapir*, January 1988.

2. *Al Hamishmar*, September 3, 1993 [Hebrew].

3. Natan Sharansky, "The Kind of Neighbors We Need," *Jerusalem Report*, October 21, 1993.

4. Ibid.

5. Benjamin Ben-Eliezer, "Securing Peace: An Israeli Perspective," in Washington Institute of Near East Policy, *Gaza-Jericho and Beyond: Building Peace, Security and Prosperity in the Middle East* (Washington, D.C.: WINEP, 1993), p. 28, cited in *Electing Dictatorship: Why Palestinian Democratization Failed* (Unpublished Dissertation on file with the Author), Daniel Polisar, p. 355.

6. Peres, *Battling for Peace*, New York: Random House, 1995, p. 339.

7. Batsheva Tsur and news agencies, "Abbas: Palestinian Independence Within 3 years," *Jerusalem Post*, cited in Polisar, p. 346.

8. Aryeh Bender, "'It's None of Your Business,' Beilin scolded the Members of the Conference of Presidents," *Maariv*, March 2, 1995, p. 6, cited in Polisar, p. 331.

9. Remarks by Yossi Beilin at the Washington Institute for Near East Policy, Washington, D.C., December 6, 1996, cited in Polisar, p. 369.

10. Yisrael Ba'aliyah Party Platform 1996.

11. Ibid.

12. Rachel is the only one not buried there. Her tomb is outside of Bethlehem.

13. Arafat himself claimed in an interview with the *Washington Post*'s Lally Weymouth that the interim phases of the Oslo accord required Israel to pull out from 92 percent of the West Bank.

14. In his book, *A Place Among the Nations*, Netanyahu argued that there are two types of peace, a peace with dictators that could only be preserved by deterrence and a peace with democracies that is self-enforcing.

15. A comparison was made between the children of terrorists and the children of terror victims. A similar moral equivalency would return later in the Road Map's call for both sides to end incitement. In both cases, the Americans hoped that their "evenhanded" language would make it easier for Palestinians

to make difficult decisions. In both cases, the Palestinians did not deliver and these misguided attempts only served to undermine moral clarity.

16. After the peace process broke down, Ross would later write that the failure of the process was largely attributable to the failure to insist on Palestinian compliance.

17. Remarks by Yossi Beilin at a conference in Tel Aviv on foreign policy and human rights, November 18, 1999, cited in *Electing Dictatorship: Why Palestinian Democratization Failed*, Daniel Polisar, p. 355.

18. Natan Sharansky, "Too Eager to Close the Deal," *New York Times*, June 6, 2000.

19. Letter to the Prime Minister, May 30, 2000.

20. "No Justice, No Peace," *Wall Street Journal*, July 6, 2001.

CHAPTER 6: THE BATTLE FOR MORAL CLARITY

1. In the Soviet Union, it was impossible to get the text of the declaration.

2. The two quotes are taken from Amnesty's web site.

3. The bomber was a British citizen who got through a Gaza border crossing with his foreign passport.

4. A charge made most prominently by Saeb Erekat on CNN, June 20, 2002.

5. *Independent*, April 16, 2002.

6. A. N. Wilson, *Evening Standard*, April 15, 2002.

7. *Guardian*, April 17, 2002.

8. The casualty figures are from the U.N. investigative report into what happened at Jenin. In the U.N. report, the number of armed combatants was twenty-six. Israel's own investigation concluded that only three of the casualties were unarmed.

9. In an essay in the November 2003 issue of *Commentary*, I expound on this question.

10. Saramago's comments were made following a meeting with Arafat in 2002.

CHAPTER 7: A MISSED OPPORTUNITY

1. President's Speech, April 4, 2002.
2. Ibid.
3. Interview on CNN from April 14, 2002.
4. *Democracy for Peace*, Essential Essays, AEI 2002. The essay was a transcript of my speech at Beaver Creek on June 24, 2002.
5. This quote and those that follow refer to President Bush's speech on June 24, 2002.
6. Dana Milbank, "White House Notebook," *Washington Post*, July 2, 2002.
7. Jonathan Freedland, "George W's Bloody Folly," *Guardian*, June 26, 2002.
8. Natan Sharansky, "Palestinian Democracy: Relevant and Realistic," *Haaretz*, July 18, 2002.
9. President's speech, March 14, 2003.
10. Speech in English in Johannesburg Mosque, May 10, 1994.
11. Speech by Yossi Beilin at signing ceremony of Geneva Initiative on December, 1, 2003.
12. Speech by Jimmy Carter at signing ceremony of Geneva Initiative on December 1, 2003.
13. Prime Minister Sharon's speech at Herziliya Conference, December 18, 2003.

ACKNOWLEDGMENTS

In 1995, the two authors met in Jerusalem. They quickly realized that despite their differences in age, background, and experience, when it came to freedom, they spoke the same language. They have worked together during the past nine years on dozens of articles and essays, many of which focus on the themes developed in this book.

The ideas and principles presented in these pages are those Natan has championed and lived by for three decades. Ron's efforts are directed at deconstructing these ideas and principles in order to make them explicable to those for whom they are not self-evident. Hopefully, the sum of their efforts has proven better than its parts.

Facilitating this joint effort were many who deserve special mention. Marvin Josephson and Peter Osnos believed in this project from the very beginning. Marvin, Natan's friend and the literary agent for his prison memoir, *Fear No Evil*, maintained for years that Natan's experience after the Gulag was no less worthy of a book. Peter, the publisher of PublicAffairs and Natan's partner-in-crime in Moscow where the former was a correspondent for the *Washington Post*, was always confident that this book could and should be given a fair hearing by all sides of the political debate. He embraced the project and was a constant source of encouragement. Clive Priddle, the book's editor, used his professionalism, intelligence and good humor to force the authors to clarify their arguments and make their case as coherent and concise as possible.

Rachel Freidman, our researcher, was a rare find. She thoroughly examined the author's inquiries, pointing them in directions they had not even considered and strengthening their overall argument. Her editorial suggestions were also particularly insightful. Lidia Voronin, a former Soviet dissident and comrade-in-arms who works in Washington, helped with the research as well.

Ari Weiss, Natan's longtime friend and confidante, Roman Polanski, Natan's colleague and close adviser, and Neil Kozodoy, the editor of *Commentary* magazine and a good friend, all slogged through the entire manuscript. Their incisive comments were as unique as the people who made them. Thanks are also due to Bill Novak, Vera Golovensky, Dore Gold, and Daniel Polisar.

Above all, the authors are indebted to their families. Mayor Jay Dermer showed patience well beyond his months, keeping his sitting, crawling, and walking in his father's study to an absolute minimum and flashing his adorable dimpled smile without fail. Rhoda Pagano Dermer read the manuscript in all its stages, acting at times as a sounding board, at others as an editor and occasionally as a computer technician. Her questions, comments, and criticism were always constructive and greatly enhanced the quality of the book. No less important, she also graciously allowed the authors to use her home at all hours of the day and night, proving to be as good a hostess as she is a wife and mother.

When Natan wrote his prison memoir, Rachel was in diapers and Hanna was not yet born. With the world of fear behind him, a quiet life in Israel for his new family seemed in the offing. But it was not to be. Yet Natan has been blessed by a family who selflessly accommodates their father's public and political life and still make him feel like a stay-at-home dad.

During the writing of this book, seventeen-year-old Rachel coincidentally wrote her high school thesis comparing the political systems of ancient Athens and Rome. The fascinating discussions on democracy triggered by her thesis helped give her father a bit of historical perspective. At the same time, fifteen-year-old Hanna became a counselor in a youth movement and displayed in the months when this book was written as much tolerance, indulgence, and humor toward her father as she did toward her young scouts.

But it was Avital Sharansky who reminded Natan once again that while striving to promote freedom around the world, freedom, as well as happiness, begins first and foremost with love and support at home.

INDEX

PublicAffairs is a publishing house founded in 1997. It is a tribute to the standards, values, and flair of three persons who have served as mentors to countless reporters, writers, editors, and book people of all kinds, including me.

I.F. STONE, proprietor of *I. F. Stone's Weekly*, combined a commitment to the First Amendment with entrepreneurial zeal and reporting skill and became one of the great independent journalists in American history. At the age of eighty, Izzy published *The Trial of Socrates,* which was a national bestseller. He wrote the book after he taught himself ancient Greek.

BENJAMIN C. BRADLEE was for nearly thirty years the charismatic editorial leader of *The Washington Post.* It was Ben who gave the *Post* the range and courage to pursue such historic issues as Watergate. He supported his reporters with a tenacity that made them fearless and it is no accident that so many became authors of influential, best-selling books.

ROBERT L. BERNSTEIN, the chief executive of Random House for more than a quarter century, guided one of the nation's premier publishing houses. Bob was personally responsible for many books of political dissent and argument that challenged tyranny around the globe. He is also the founder and longtime chair of Human Rights Watch, one of the most respected human rights organizations in the world.

For fifty years, the banner of Public Affairs Press was carried by its owner Morris B. Schnapper, who published Gandhi, Nasser, Toynbee, Truman and about 1,500 other authors. In 1983, Schnapper was described by *The Washington Post* as "a redoubtable gadfly." His legacy will endure in the books to come.

Peter Osnos, *Publisher*